Ethnicity in a Technological Age

Ethnicity in a Technological Age

Edited by
Ian H. Angus

Canadian Institute of Ukrainian Studies
University of Alberta
Edmonton   1988

Publication of this book is made possible in part through financial assistance provided by Multiculturalism Canada

Canadian Cataloguing in Publication Data
Main entry under title:

Ethnicity in a technological age

A collection of essays based on a May 1986 symposium held at Peter Robinson College, Trent University, Peterborough, Ontario.
ISBN 0-920862-59-4

1. Ethnicity - Canada. 2. Multiculturalism - Canada.* I. Angus, Ian H. (Ian Henderson), 1949-   II. Canadian Institute of Ukrainian Studies.
FC104.E85 1988   305.8'00971   C88-091226-X
F1035.A1E85 1988

Cover design: Steve Tate
Cover photograph: *Fish on Friday* by Natalka Husar (1985)

Typesetting: The Typeworks, Vancouver

Printed in Canada

Distributed by University of Toronto Press
5201 Dufferin St.
Downsview, Ontario
Canada M3H 5T8

For my parents, Ross and Joan,
Scot and Cockney, immigrants,
With love and gratitude.

In using other cultures as mirrors in which we may see
our own culture we are affected by the astigma of our
own eyesight and the defects of that mirror, with the
result that we are apt to see nothing in other cultures
but the virtues of our own.
  Harold Innis

In human life there must always be a place for love of
the good and love of one's own. Love of the good is
man's highest end, but it is of the nature of things
that we come to love what is good by first meeting it
in that which is our own—this particular body, this
family, these friends, this woman, this part of the
world, this set of traditions, this country, this
civilization.
  George Grant

Earth, you nearest, allow me.
Green of the earth and civil grey:
within me, without me and moment by
moment allow me for to
be here is enough and earth you
strangest, you nearest, be home.
  Dennis Lee

CONTENTS

Introduction

The contemporary tension between universal civilization and national cultures relegates those at the margins of the world-system to a deficient "otherness." Either their difference from the imperial centre is essential, which justifies their exclusion, or it is merely contingent, in which case they can expect only assimilation. In the New World this external other is internal as well. Despite a ruling elite dependent on its imperial connections, the heterogeneity of immigrant cultures has replaced a national source of cultural values. The encounter between diverse ethnicities, native cultures and the wilderness is the *essentially plural* source of New World civilization. While this diversity of traditions has generally oscillated between the exploitation of minorities and a trivializing legitimization of ethnic cultures as consumer options, a significant tendency in Canadian thought has criticized the centralization, homogenization, and repressive universalization inherent in modern empires. One may recall the notions of oral tradition (Harold Innis) and "one's own" (George Grant) in this context. This tendency must now be extended to encounter both the persistence of ethnic allegiances and the cultural mechanisms of the technological world. While "ethnicity" is the figure for otherness in this text, it invites comparison with the other figures of race, sex, and class. Moreover, the contemporary situation demands reflection on the ground of otherness itself. Recovering and justifying the otherness denied and specularized by industrial culture is the starting-point for a uniquely Canadian contribution to the crisis and renewal of civilization.

In questioning the meaning of ethnicity in Canada and the contemporary world, one is confronted with a problem of how to begin. It is all too evident nowadays that social research often proceeds by the application of scientific theory to ever-larger domains of social life. It is impossible to find a pristine corner of human experience unaffected by the intrusions of science. With the determination of empirical regularities in behaviour, the application of techniques of social intervention by authorities to social actors serves to bring the social world increasingly under administrative control. Such productive deployment of theory extends to the management of symbolic systems as well as the obvious crudities of police science. No responsible social thinker today can avoid the question of the relation of theory to social practice. The scientific-technical model of social inquiry depends, not on the motives of individual investigators, but on the model of knowledge employed. Application of a pre-determined theoretical grid that isolates separate empirical behaviours from the complex of meaningful social experience and regularizes them with reference to significant underlying factors manipulable by social agencies can only issue in practices that normalize a subjected population. From scientific management to advertising research, the social sciences collude in the advancing ground-plan of social control. Such disembodied intelligence is thrown over its subject-matter like a net, trapping only the edible and the ungainly. The former is used to justify the enormous resources now given over to productive social knowledge. The latter is added to the techniques of police science, still waiting in the wings when the more refined methods of symbolic management fail.

A more tentative social thought must abandon itself to its object. It is in search of a theoretical elaboration, not arriving forearmed. As such, it is not trapped in its starting-point but opens to dialogue and criticism, and hopes without guarantee to reach social actors in the elaboration of their projects. It wishes to speak, but not to give orders. Such situated reflection joins particular concerns to universalizing discourses, though it terminates, not in an "instance of knowing," but in the self-reflection of the inquirer as a social being.

Beginning in abandonment to its object, situated reflection will not take just any matter to study. It presupposes a concern, a relation to the object in question, that is not itself generated by reflection, though it may be deepened, made problematical, and transformed in the process. Such social thought begins from love, which can be educated by reflection, but not generated from it. Love inheres in attachments to the particulars of the world we inhabit. We cannot be sure of sharing them, or of sharing the world. The cynical emptiness of much social science comes from a failure to share this gamble with love.

The symposium at Peter Robinson College, Trent University, in May 1986 from which these essays and discussions come, was such a gamble. Many spoke of their perplexity at being there since they were not experts in ethnic studies. Several spoke of the difficulty of writing essays, of the pain that was unearthed in bringing this matter to thought. We shared, through the love that ties each of us in his/her own way to the particularities of the world, the joy of thought which does not renounce this love, which re-connects with the diversities and risks of social life. Thus, it was a symposium, not the dry conferring with which we are all familiar. As Plato's *Symposium* is filled with speeches in praise of love, we began with praise and proceeded to inquiry. Though, to be sure, this praise was necessarily already intertwined with criticism of the official discourses of government and economy.

What was this praise? I suppose this book is the answer. In beginning, in approximation, one could say: love of diversity. We began with a suspicion that the universal mechanisms of capitalist industrial society pulverize attachments to particulars, and that the universals of philosophical discourse may be in league with these pulverizations. We wanted to rescue diversity, to recall the exploitation to which the "other" has been subjected, and to see this otherness differently. We also knew the traps of diversity. Otherness may be staged as consumer options. A ruling elite that saw itself as sharing nothing with the native people, or with those strange ethnics, may be brutal. There were more questions than answers. From these questions emerged underlying tensions which separate and yet tie together the individual contributions. It is fitting that they are now bound together. Such a questioning of love of diversity intervenes in three discourses already underway: Canadian social thought, post-modernism, and the philosophy of civilization.

Canadian social history is fundamentally marked by the fact that it is the history of a perpetual colony. As Harold Innis carefully documented, the asymmetry of staple resource extraction and importation of manufactured goods leads to an endemically unstable economy, a series of boom and bust cycles dependent on external markets. Dependency theory explains the disparity between a resource economy with underdeveloped industry and industrial consumption with up-to-date goods and information through the dynamics of the centre/periphery relationship. Thus, we are able to comprehend a form of industrial capitalism distinct from its emergence from a prior feudal system as in Europe, and from its concentration from an early independent, broad-based capitalism as in the United States. Centre/periphery dependency creates a society in deep polarity between the most modern imperial tendencies and the archaic, almost unhistorical, encounter with the wilderness at the margin.

If we extend dependency economics into political theory, the contours of a Canadian account of power and community can be discerned. Marx's account of industrial capitalism rooted inequality and exploitation in the specifically capitalist structures of industrial organization and the market. The division of labour, while extensively developed under capitalism, could be separated from its coercive and destructive side by the removal of capitalist structures. Dependency theory implies, however, that the development of industry within an imperial framework irrevocably stamps the division of labour with relations of unequal power. These relations cannot be removed from the given infrastructure of the economy even if it overcomes its capitalist form. In short, that inequality and (at least potential) exploitation are inseparable from the heritage of the imperial division of labour. The political vision that emerges from this is that of self-sufficient communities withdrawn from a crippling international division of labour. The haunting possibility of the New World is an anarchist model of self-sufficiency, rather than a Marxist model of a highly developed division of labour free (somehow) from exploitation. This implication of dependency theory only succeeds in differentiating Canada from a European model. In this respect, it is very much like the United States, where the model of self-sufficiency derives as a political vision from the early, largely independent commodity-producers.

In contrast to the American vision, however, where the model of self-sufficiency has largely collapsed with the individualism of independent commodity-producers, in Canada the focus is on the dependence of communities, since it is primarily communities, often ethnically-based, that settled the country. Thus, the political vision is oriented to the self-sufficiency of communities. Canadian conservatism and socialism share a common thread of concern with community, and with national independence. Liberals, on the other hand, have succumbed to the individualism and continentalism of "free" markets. This historic formation is now in the process of realignment, possibly with permanent implications. The Conservative Party has abandoned whatever allegiance they had to the conservative strain of community and national independence in favour of the ideology of free trade and subservience to the American empire. Liberals are sliding pragmatically toward protectionism and multiculturalism without any coherent political position to substitute for their historic one. Perhaps the door is open to the Left. A re-figuration of the socialist vision in Canada, which must come to terms with the New Democratic Party but need not be limited to it, must recover the sources in Canadian social history from which political thought emerges. The vision of self-sufficient communities can be recovered and extended by a contemporary analysis of ethnicity. Ethnicity can thus be seen as a central theme in the re-figuration of power and community in Canadian political thought.

Moreover, this re-figuration carries within itself the polarity described by dependency economics between up-to-date industrial consumption alongside the retarded development of industrial production. There is at present a world-wide discourse about post-modernism which is concerned with precisely such polarities. The information society, post-industrial society, society of the image, and so forth are seen as in tension with the earlier industrial processes that brought them about. The key figure in this discourse is about ''loss of reference'' in which social representations are seen as floating without being grounded in definitely accessible social realities. Society becomes a circulation of signs whose origins and references are arbitrary or unknowable. While it is difficult to discern how much in this discussion is diagnosis, how much advocacy, and how much over-heated enthusiasm, it is at least possible to say that the homogenizing and coercive implications of previous technological development are undergoing some sort of change. The role of images of considerable diversity in this change forces the discussion of ethnicity to consider carefully its contemporary context. If we cross Canadian political thought with this discourse, we may ask whether post-modernity is a genuine diversity or rather a universalized dependency, now without a permanent centre.

With respect to the philosophy of civilization, ethnicity may provide an entry to re-thinking the formulations of identity/difference and origin/telos on which the universal claims of civilization are based. The growth of social, state, and civilizational structures that relegate ethnic allegiances to a merely contingent status in order to justify an over-arching concept of humanity have become questionable in our time. This is so not only because the concept of humanity as a unity requires that it stand over against nature. The ecological consequences of this are becoming increasingly apparent. Another reason is that the natural substratum to be transformed by civilization has been associated with specific social groups—non-white people, women, the working class, and ethnics. It is not clear that this association is simply a mistake that can be corrected without a fundamental re-formulation of humanism. So, too, the questions of origin and identity require re-examination. The Greeks, at the origin of our civilization, imagined themselves autochthonous, as sprung from the earth. The Christian Bible divorced humans from the earth in order to grant them dominion over it, but both were sprung from the creative will of God. In short, in both civilizing myths origin was normative; it engendered telos. Identity was to be recovered, unveiled behind the forgetting inherent in temporal life. In the New World there can be no such recovery, certainly for Europeans. To the extent that we ask this question seriously, we must confront the ability of the indigenous people to live with the wild. Similarly, recovery cannot be of an origin that unites us. Our origins are plural and defined by separation. Our origin is wilderness. In this sense, the question of civilization in the New World has always been a post-modern question. Ethnicity can re-figure this question, connect it to the discourses of post-modernism and Canadian social thought, and define a new space for the critique of industrial capitalist culture.

The influence of these three discourses permeates the essays and discussions collected in this text. It is not so much "proceedings" but "inhabitings," successive dialogic encounters that seek to circumscribe a home. The tensions between them constitute ongoing questions for such a homecoming, even the doubt as to whether it is possible. 1) History is understood as received social being, as a heritage to be recovered and preserved, but as also and perhaps even simultaneously, a project, an act of the imagination, a poesis. 2) Technology is understood, in the first place, as the homogenization and marginalization of difference produced by industrial culture. But there also is the possibility that we are entering a new stage of industrialism based on consumption and information technologies that no longer requires such exclusion. Such a new stage is not necessarily entirely benign. A plurality of fragmented discourses staged as consumer options, a Disneyland of free choices, may well be the current tendency. In this case, a critical theory of society must become more radical, reach deeper into the formation of identity in order to renew itself and its relation to social practices. 3) Identity is itself caught in a tension between the necessity of the community and the possibility of existential realization. Moreover, existential realization of ethnic identity itself contains a more subtle polarity, though possibly one of infinite implication. Though we are all separated from origin, is our goal a return to a transformed home or are we now condemned to construct a beginning for ourselves? Exile or wanderer? On the one side is the great alienation story made famous by Hegel and Marx, but with roots deep in Homer and the Bible. Could there be a new attempt to connect wandering and wilderness, to found civilization on a new story in the New World? We do not yet know what this might look like. These tensions are between the essays, within the essays, perhaps necessarily enfolded within the thoughts and sentences that enable the asking of the question of this book.

These tensions are most apparent in a basic alternative, far more simple to formulate than to answer unequivocally. Are we all ethnics now? In the culture of industrial consumption, overlaid on capitalist production, has all attachment to history, to non-consumer symbolisms, to group solidarity, become marginalized? What about the history of persecution of ethnic minorities by an English-speaking ruling class? What of the fact that technology is used by some against others? What about the persistence of highly differentiated relations of power and reward in today's Canada? We have focussed here on ethnicity as the figure for diversity, cultural plurality, and power, but these issues expand to the entirety of contemporary society, including race, sex, and class. All have their minorities. An ethnic is named from the outside; stripped, excluded and exploited. The ethnic may also to some degree, perhaps to an increasing degree, refuse assimilation and demand a new order. This question will not be settled by discussions only. It is first on the political agenda in the struggle over what Canada will be. We hope that our deliberations may be of some help.

Behind this lies the question of the one and the many, but now politicized. Who has the power to name as "one"? We cannot regard our particularity as merely contingent, because it has been marginalized, excluded, and smashed. How can one pass on to the universal without somewhere to pass from? The task now is to recapture and rejustify the particular without entirely jettisoning the universal. Naming both enables and excludes. Any articulation can be revealed as a partial incarnation, which reminds us to be self-critical and not to merely elevate ourselves to the universal. This traditional reminder has not lost its pungency, but perhaps there is a new reminder. Articulation turns mere contingency into particularity—an opening to and glimpse of homecoming. Naming as enabling recovers the power of the many, the many who inhabit the one.

1. REPRESENTATIONS OF ETHNICITY

Roman Onufrijchuk

Post-modern or Perednovok: Deconstructing Ethnicity

1. Introduction

> If the eventual fusion [of cultural groups] is what we are after, then the en-
> couragement of "heritage arts" is at best a transitional stream on the way
> to the main river. Yet this is implicit in most government policy as formu-
> lated: that multiculturalism is to help immigrants integrate themselves into
> Canadian society, retaining their cultural heritage only to ease the cultural
> shock of entering this rarefied atmosphere. A disposable cocoon, as it
> were—the opposite of an inheritance.[1]
>
> Mavor Moore

Ethnicity is already a construct—an edifice. It is the product of history
and discourse. This ethnicity emerges from the official discourse of Canadian federal multicultural policy which is itself already circumscribed by
cultural policy, even if the latter represses the former. Canadian cultural
policy is itself determined by the current global cultural configuration
sometimes called post-modern. Even a rehearsed deconstructing of the
edifice must proceed within this framework.

The largest of these forms is global culture. As noted, the current configuration has been called post-modern. To this I should like to add another category that is perhaps more optimistic—*perednovok*. *Perednovok*
is a time in the spring when food stored for the winter is gone, yet the

winter wheat is only just turning the fields a promising green. In time the wheat will ripen and there will be much to eat, if one can survive the hunger till then. What is called post-modern may be a *perednovok*. Investment has been great but what remains to be seen in the nature of the harvest.

2. Two theses

I. To be an ethnic means to be in an embedded and corporeal relation to an extended and circumscribed community which experiences and seeks to express its collective history and culture, its memory and language as inheritance and project.

There is a shared history: time is neither empty nor is it homogeneous. That is to say there is a meaning within time. History appears as still unfulfilled and its telling remains incomplete. There is shared culture and there is a shared language (taken widely as a metaphor for any structured system of social meaning) which facilitates expression and, at least to some extent, the experience of reality.

Culture and history are a given as inheritance. They are handed down and received as gifts or burdens from previous generations. They are neither inventions nor are they figments of the imagination. They were real in the world and as transmitted in embodied relations they remain real. Culture and history are also a project or projects: both lay claim on the activities, choices and valuations of the present as it is attuned to the future. To be an ethnic is to be in a corporeal and an embedded relation to language and memory, culture and history and the community that these sustain and which in turn sustains them.

This experience and condition, as inheritance and project, might be called a focal concern.[2] This configuration of language, intent and memory is deeply and decisively significant. It is deep in that it cannot be easily exhausted of its meanings. It is decisively significant in that it constitutes the framework in which sense is made of the human condition. This includes the mysteries of the general and the particular such as the mystery of generations and the horizon posed by death.

Finally there is the question of circumscription. The word ethnicity implies that for a group associated around a common history and culture, their inheritance and the nature of their projects appear as a distinguishing feature differentiating this group from the larger social formation in which this group is encased. Ethnicity is an internal social distinction, somehow simultaneously exclusive and excluded. A rough genealogy of the word suggests this. It meant a group connected through kinship and distinguished from the Demos of the *polis*. With the spread of Chris-

4

tianity it came to mean heathen or those who were yet to be converted. These meanings still obtain, especially in light of multiculturalism and the ethnicity which emerges from it. Ethnicity is envisioned as a vestibule from which fully fledged individual Canadians take wing.

Thus ethnicity exists only because it is thus determined by the shared culture and history, by the shared inheritance and projects of the larger group. An ethnicity is embedded qua ethnicity by the discourse of a larger norm, a dominant discourse. It is this circumscription that generates ethnicity.

II. The official discourse of the federal multiculturalism policy produces an ethnicity. Both discourse and implementation involve four strategic manoeuvres which taken together strictly delimit the nature of the possible relationship between the inheritance and project that inform the association of groups that are termed ethnic. In short, multiculturalism produces an ethnicity which does not develop, an ethnicity trapped in a repetitive loop. Ethnicity is envisioned as a small nucleus of ever-diminishing forces, a final state from which to emerge into the limited configurations and settings of post-industrial culture.

Multiculturalism produces a specific ethnicity. Communal groups are named and policy is set in place to cater for their needs. By this means both a social category and its needs are produced. Social power inscribes its interpretation of their reality as if it were reality. Official multicultural policy and discourse seem to form the following configuration of forces and limits from which this thing called ethnicity proceeds: legitimation, appeasement, containment, and integration.[3]

a) Legitimation of the current asymmetrical distribution of social, institutional, and cultural privilege and power between the two founding or charter ethnocultural groups in Canada.

The multicultural policy was born out of the reaction by minority cultural groups in Canada to the proposal by the federal government to declare an official languages policy. The intent of this policy was appeasement of a growing cultural consciousness and political demands expressed by the Francophone majority in Quebec. In order to gain and hold the co-operation of ethnic minorities and to legitimize the proposed official languages policy, multiculturalism was introduced as a context for the specification of French and English as the languages (cultures) of Canada.

In short, the multicultural policy is to legitimize a gesture of redistribution of power and privilege made by a dominant linguistic and socio-economically powerful group to another not as powerful, yet large enough and threatening enough to warrant special attention.

5

b) Appeasement of ethnic demands for access to the prestige and power exhibited by one charter people that was now being extended to the second charter people. This appeasement operated at a socio-political level: by changing the agenda from socio-economic demands to the politics of language and culture the former, more threatening demands were sublimated and therefore appeased.[4]

The policy can be interpreted as an appeasement of the emerging and increasingly sophisticated ethnic leadership. This therefore achieved the acceptance and acquiescence by the leadership and intelligentsia of ethnic groups of the bilingualism policy enacted by the federal government. In this sense the appeasement aspect of the multicultural policy is inseparable from the legitimation aspect of the policy.

By providing a reserve of resources the federal government facilitated employment for an emerging intelligentsia within ethnic communities. This provided an opportunity to create what are called professional ethnics who differ from other kinds of cultural facilitators, art educators, and numerous arts and cultural administrators in that the culture the professional ethnics promote was already described as something separate from civilization or culture.

c) Containment of all possible cultural growth and development in the sphere of this ethnicity. This delimiting of the growth and development of the arts and art in its extended sense was achieved in two ways.

On the one hand, multiculturalism and the institutional and funding frameworks that it provided effectively differentiated between cultural production in the ethnic milieu and Canadian art and cultural production proper as these latter two are enshrined within a Canadian cultural policy. This was already based on assumptions about what culture and art are and implied that neither existed to any significant extent in the group designated as ethnic. Furthermore, this was based on the idea that ethnicity was a condition characterized by loyalty to an inheritance and not a project. Ethnic expression was thus evaluated with reference to its repetition of traditional forms and not the ability of ethnic expression to produce creative forms.

Finally, and perhaps most significantly, given that culture is intertwined with the arts, and given that a more critical and experimental aspect of ethnic expressive forms was either denied or structurally displaced into the realm of art and culture, this in turn denied or displaced any possible articulation or expression of a critical ethnicity in either imagination or realization.[5]

On the other hand, the institutional and funding apparatuses of multiculturalism tenaciously exhibited a reluctance and an unwillingness to provide sustained financial and institutional resources that would facilitate the comprehensive development of a base (both cultural and economic) that could support development of ethnic cultures and groups. This was expressed in part by the refusal of the CBC and the CRTC to embrace the proposals of the multicultural framework and provide access for various ethnic groups to the public airwaves except in the context of commercial broadcasting.

This raises an intriguing question. To what extent would Canadian culture flourish were it entirely dependent on commercial broadcasting? In the private sector state support of various kinds favours Canadian content, but it is in the public sector that significant support for Canadian cultural expression takes place. In this context, given the degree to which multiculturalism promotes or facilitates ethnocultural development, it can easily be said that the enormous subsidies to Canadian culture and the arts that are derived from the CBC were aimed at the development and further entrenchment of the Anglo- and Francophone biculturalism which is the de facto policy of the federal government. Thus, on the one hand, the policy encourages development by separating ethnic culture from culture and the arts as such while, on the other hand, it refuses to provide for meaningful assistance for ethnocultural development.

   d) Integration of particular configurations of community, language, history, culture (inheritance and project) into a synthetic, and highly suspect category: ethnicity.

Integration is indeed the grounding metaphor of the multicultural policy. The policy is supposed to facilitate the contribution by ethnic groups to overall Canadian society and culture. As I have noted above, the contribution had nothing whatever to do with any living or critical, artistic or cultural expression: contribution was limited to a repetition of celebratory forms and arts not a development of cultural forms that might come from an engagement of the traditions in their new context. It seems that a tradition that sustains no commentary, no exploration of limits and structures relative to its current positioning in the living world becomes an artifact, an exhibit, a spectacle. For there to be an engagement of the text of tradition there needs to be a community for which this text and its commentaries represent not just an inheritance but also a project. It is a question of empowerment.

Human rights are a basic concern, to be sure. The desire, policy, and practices that set out equal access to all are indeed the basis for an equitable and open society. Indeed this account of freedom remains a great legacy of the Enlightenment and western civilization—one that remains

7

just a promise for far too many of the world's population. However a question about this legacy can be inserted here. Is it integration into freedom and enrichment or alienation and deprivation?

The integration that serves as a grounding metaphor for the policy of multiculturalism has a number of manifestations. I will elaborate on three expressions of this integration: the signs of entrepreneurship, diversity-as-unity, and exotica.

Ethnicity as entrepreneurship is the first form of expression. Recent issues of *Cultures Canada*, the official publication of the office of the minister responsible for multiculturalism give admirable portrayals of the nature of ethnic integration.[6]

Ethnicity is a resource, but it is not a cultural resource but rather an economic one. "Multiculturalism Means Business" the headline proclaims. On the one hand, the ethnic is perceived as hard-working and possessing a work-ethic from which other Canadians can learn. On the other hand, the ethnic is seen as an pathway to foreign markets. Ethnics with their knowledge of other languages and markets are envisioned as storm-troops (my formulation not theirs) for Canadian trade and export overseas. This brings to mind Sahlins' deft if whimsical observation: "... but Money to the West is what Kinship is to the Rest." *Cultures Canada* thus gives us an image of integration as visible ethnicity in a blue serge/grey flannel suit.

Secondly, ethnicity: diversity-as-unity, is viewed as a completed category which emphasizes the celebration of diversity over the re-creation of the various communities, cultures, inheritances, and projects that make such diversity possible in the first place. Thus it is not the development of a particular community of memory, intention, and expression but the fact that many such communities exist and can be apprehended and constituted as a totality, an ethnicity. Neither value nor investiture reside in the fact of community but in the fact of a diversity of communities. This is laudable. It is also strategic since it creates a synthetic tradition which is denied a basis for development as it denies development for its constituent parts.

Thirdly, ethnicity is considered as a bit of colourful exotica and a tourist attraction. In the celebration of this now homogenized and contained diversity is supposedly revealed another legitimation. This is the legitimation of the claims made by the dominant discourse to a free, open and equitable society. Ethnicity becomes the colour that is added to moose, the Rockies, and totem poles as expressions of the particularity that is Canada. Ethnic festivals are promoted along with simulacra historic sites in tourism brochures produced by various levels of government. Here again the ethnicity is an ethnicity that is limited to repetition of older forms (now frozen and turned into artifacts) and site and time specific to either the celebratory moments of community life or to an expression of diversity.

These then are some of the constituents of the synthetic configuration, the edifice that emerges out of the text of an official multiculturalism that produces this thing called ethnicity. If they be the components of a foundation, consider a figure that has strutted across it not long ago. Hunky Bill is a good ethnic. He is a good ethnic because he is a good businessman. He is a good ethnic because he has a sense of humour about a name ("Hunky") to which other Ukrainian/Canadians, being stuffed shirts, object. Hunky Bill does not discriminate. He will sell perogies to anyone at all who comes into Hunky's "Dover Arms" pub (emblazoned proudly with a Union Jack) in West End Vancouver. Hunky Bill has turned his ethnicity into a sign that sells well.

3. Hypothesis

Already written in the fate of communities of memory, language, and intention—so-called ethnicities—is a rehearsal of the fate of all "national cultures" in the age of mass communication and electronic techniques, in the post-industrial era.

An ethnicity, an ethnos with its ethos and ethics, is really only a micromorphological moment of what, when seen through the geopolitical arena of history, can appear as a people or a nation. That is, they and it are imagined communities. As Benedict Anderson has shown, this imagined community is based to a great extent on language, shared history, and the dissemination of shared cultural expression through the media, print in particular.

There are structural similarities between the efforts of ethnic groups to continue to function as living communities that express their relation to the world through arts of various kinds and the efforts at much the same sort of thing being made by Canada as such in the face of the American cultural industry's production and distribution.

Canadian cultural policy is no less heterogeneous than the ethnoculturality that it excludes from the realm of culture and the arts which the cultural policy as discourse itself produces. This heterogeneity derives from the essentially doubled tensions that the policy is confronted with. On the one hand, the policy seeks to facilitate cultural production arising out of the tensions deriving from the essential diversity of cultural particularities of the Canadian social fabric. On the other hand, the policy seeks to find a way to regulate the nature of the environment of the arts with reference to the influx of American and global cultural content and the economic and technological systems and structures that facilitate and enforce

9

such an influx. This regulation proceeds against the back-drop of the market as the privileged cultural institution.

The federal government's response to Book IV of the Royal Commission on Bilingualism and Biculturalism in October 1971 expressed these broader tensions at work within cultural policy.

> Cultural diversity throughout the world is being eroded by the impact of industrial technology, mass communications and urbanization. Many writers have discussed this as the creation of a mass society—in which mass produced culture and entertainment of large impersonal institutions threaten to denature and depersonalize men. One of man's basic needs is a sense of belonging, and a good deal of contemporary social unrest—in all age groups—exists because this has not been met. Ethnic groups are certainly not the only way in which this need for belonging can be met, but they have been an important one in Canadian society. Ethnic pluralism can help us overcome or prevent the homogenization and depersonalization of mass society.[7]

The tensions are internal and external—the heterogeneity that is Canada, and the fate of that heterogeneity-as-identity in a marginal relationship to the American media and cultural empire.

With respect to culture and diversity, the latter is expressed in terms of the bilingual, then the regional, then the ethnic, and then the indigenous diversity contained in Canada as a social community. This description is drawn from the AppleBert report. The report suggests that this diversity is not a problem to be resolved but rather a central cultural resource to be celebrated. Given that the foundation sign for both multicultural policy and the ethnicity that it produces is integration, the nature of this celebration vis-à-vis ethnoculturality is suspect. This is described even more clearly in the AppleBert discussion of multicultural diversity and ethnicity a fortiori.

When the AppleBert committee arrives at ethnicity and the multicultural discourse that sustains and creates such a state, an odd problem emerges. The relationship between multi-culturality and the place of ethnicity in it is problematic.

> On the one hand the committee note: Throughout its public hearings the Committee encountered considerable public confusion about this policy. Some measure of misunderstanding may come from the fact that, while the policy is described as being cultural in nature, in reality it is only partly so, since the Secretary of State's Multiculturalism Program has tended to take on a character of social rather than cultural policy.[8]

They go on to observe that there is added confusion in the policy because the "1971 policy is framed in relatively general terms." This is an interesting observation since in the entirety of Canadian cultural policy there is no clear, concise or concrete formulation of what Canadian culture is or how it might be framed in policy.

On the other hand, the committee goes on to argue that while ethnicity is an important aspect of Canadian cultural diversity, it is only one aspect and not the totality. They suggest that a government multicultural policy based solely on ethnicity runs the risk of ignoring the other types of diversity in Canada. Among these other diversities they list "those deriving from language, religion, age, place of residence and so on."[9] They conclude with the thought that:

> The federal government should therefore enlarge its present concept of ethnic multiculturalism, to take into account the many different types of cultural diversity that exist in Canada.[10]

This seems entirely acceptable in the context of the implications of the federal government's Neilsen report which suggested that funding for ethnicity and ethnocultural development be cut and that such development become market-driven, market-responsive, and market-funded or sustained.

The AppleBert report ends its discussion of cultural diversity with the problem of indigenous arts and culture. Here they recommend that the native artist be first thought of as an artist and then as a native one. This is an interesting twist given the nature of the ethnicity that multiculturalism sets out to produce and given the vacillation of the AppleBert report's language on where ethnicity fits into the resource of cultural diversity that is to be celebrated, not resolved.

If there is some confusion in this, there is no less of it when the cultural policy extends into the realm of the arts and Canadian cultural industries. This is the realm of the second of the two tensions at work in the cultural policy area—the problem of empire. Here the dynamics are tied up with the market economy, both locally and nationally as well as the flow of cultural resources and expressions across borders.

The economic climate of Canada since the mid-1970s has seriously endangered the fate of Canadian expression in Canada and in the broader world context. By 1978 the federal government, which had been providing sizable support to the arts,[11] found it politically expedient (if not necessary) to cut back on this support. Additionally the 1970s witnessed an increasing proliferation of communication technologies and program distribution formats along with an increasing centralization and concentration of production facilities, head offices, capital, and ownership.

Since the Massey Commission handed down its recommendations in the 1950s much government implementation of cultural policy has been oriented toward establishing the physical plant and developing the organizational aspects of Canadian arts and cultural industries. It is an odd irony that while Canada boasts some of the most sophisticated communications hardware in the world, over 80 per cent of Canadian TV viewing time is given over to American-produced TV programming. In short, while there has been a development of hardware it seems that there has not been enough attention paid to developing the software to go with it.

While there is debate and legislation in aid of ensuring some form of cultural autonomy, many of the cultural industries and most of the arts are importations. Parochialism does not motivate these observations. It is only a sense that much of what constitutes the Canadian urban environment hails from elsewhere. In cultural terms Canada is part of the Third World.

4. Deconstructing ethnicity

> The metaphysics of man is the same in the private sphere as in the public one. This is the great private problem of man: death as the loss of self. But what is this self? It is the sum of everything we remember. Thus, what terrifies us about death is not the loss of the future but the loss of the past. Forgetting is a form of death ever present within life. . . But forgetting is also the great problem of politics. When a big power wants to deprive a small country of its national consciousness it uses the method of *organized forgetting*. Milan Kundera

If ethnic meant dispossessed or alienated then everyone would be an ethnic in the post-industrial age, but it is exactly the opposite. The ethnic is wealthy in ethnicity. Indeed it is this very excess of cultural perception and conception that is at issue. Inheritance and project structurally denied are a disruption, a negation of this excess.

What is excessive is the scope of the experience of ethnicity-as-community. Community can be an oppression, a herd, institutionalized rechannelling of social violence. A community, the name it inscribes on body and biography, can be a burden, a blockage to social mobility. Life within a community can be a continuing, perhaps ever-expanding source for cognitive dissonance with reference to the dominant discourse and its norms.

So also is a community a knot of social pleasures, the *kosmeisis* of conviviality. It is the pleasures of living with people—the familiar syntax of embodied relations, the gestural play of shared speech. Community is the contentious and contested collaboration of received traditions and projects. It is the unfolding language and musicality of a people, a place, a time. A community is memory and time; extended biography. Even if in memory, it is a community of the embodied and interbedded which reproduces and celebrates this collaboration as its being. This is being when one is among those who are one's own. Schutz called being a "growing older together."

From the perspective of the dominant discourse it is the ethnic who must be dispossessed, disburdened of ways of thinking, seeing, understanding, feeling, and knowing rooted in ethnicity-as-community which exceed the codes into which this ethnic-as-immigrant arrives. Only when the ethnic has been dispossessed is he sufficiently liberated to be delivered into the cold hard light of modern alienation. This, too, is tactical. Once liberated from the tutelage of this excessive experience the ethnic is ready to participate in the dominant culture—its market and the bilingual and unicultural state. Though the economy is a crucial strategic resource in all this, it is hardly an issue of pure economics. Rather, it is an issue of the political economy, of the organization of memory and its claim on what we are to become.

If there is a deconstructing of ethnicity (as opposed to "Ethnicity"), then this deconstructing has been underway since the spread of industrialization and the market system. However, this is not the only deconstructing underway. The unicultural state, built on technical rationality, information, and an administrative culture, plays its part in the deconstructing, too. This is by means of the apparatuses and structures of cultural policy and multiculturalism.

Cultural policy produces a Canadian culture, Canadian art, or at least seeks to legislate the possibilities for and regulate the development of such a thing. It does so while assuming the existence of the American communication/cultural empire and suppressing ethnicity as culture. In the former case it confronts the logic of the danger of a shared language with the Americans. In the latter case the state encounters ethnicity as an internal scandal, as an extraneous community which, by separating it from art and culture, the state reduces to insignificance, to triviality.[12]

This gesture, trivialization is a component, is perhaps the genius of an organized forgetting. Here again is the deconstructing which is a two-fold de-realization of inheritance-as-project. First, the organized forgetting originates from tactical omissions in the narrative that grounds the state,[13] and secondly, by the trivialization, the dismissal of inheritance and project as entirely excessive, residual, incongruent, and irrelevant.

13

5. Post-modern or perednovok?

> There is no document of civilization which is not at the same time a document of barbarism. Walter Benjamin.

I began this by counterpoising two categories—one referring to stages in the development of Western civilization and culture and the other referring to cultivation of the earth and the culture of those things which, at the most fundamental level, sustain humanity. I chose these two because they also suggest an inflection: the post-modern with its reactive tone, and the perednovok with its troubled and anxious expectation intermingling with hope.

Were ethnicity a question of stylistic legitimation then the post-modern would be tailored for it. Consider the following from Andrea Branzi, an educator and designer:

> The present post-industrial model of society reveals a world in which industry has come to an end of its period of heroic growth, characterized by a rationalist and internationalist culture, and in which the homogeneous society of equals has been replaced by an assemblage of minorities, of conflicting groups no longer founded on different productive, economic and social functions but on different cultures, religions and traditions. A world which is seeing the return of culture, the transcendant and the traditional as great historical forces. As a result the myth of reason and egalitarianism, so vital to the whole of modern culture and architecture, has entered a period of crisis. The myth of the unity of all languages and technologies in the project has given way to a ''narrative'' process of discontinuity and partiality.[14]

However, this narrative process is neither a new Babel nor is it a refined polyglot. A unity of languages does exist. There is a logic which continues to ground all this discontinuity and partiality as such. That logic, specifically the logic of market-industrial relations, serves as a fluid grid which reformulates and restructures all partialities, discontinuities and diversities according to its own imminent imperative. Following the patterns of consumer culture, this new age resonates to the label of tourism where all ethnicities, all particularities, become just bits of exotica for the consumer-as-tourist-as-modern-citizen. It is just so much disposable entertainment and ultimately an addition to the store of recall kept at the ready for excellence at any Trivial Pursuit.

A perednovok is somehow different, for even through the emptiness of this time it turns itself toward what might yet be. The post-modern perhaps refers to an age and a civilization which yawn at themselves and their mutual boredom. Perhaps the perednovok refers only to the residuum that are called ethnicities.

Among the legacies of the Enlightenment are the philosophies of the individual and the group. Both have proven to be liberating and both have proven to be engines of domination. Perhaps a rehearsal of perednovok lies elsewhere in the account of community among communities. Perhaps it begins with an ethnicity located here between history and will, between memory and project.

NOTES

1. "Multiculturalism a Policy of Fusion or Fission?" *Globe and Mail*, 5 September 1984.
2. Albert Borgman, *Technology and the Character of Contemporary Life* (Chicago: University of Chicago, 1984), 196-210.
3. Many of the elements which constitute ethnicity as produced by multicultural policy are discussed at length by Karl Peter. I am indebted to his analysis and critique. Karl Peter, "The Myth of Multiculturalism and Other Political Fables," Jorgen Dahlie and Tissa Fernando, eds., *Ethnicity, Power and Politics in Canada* (Toronto: Methuen, 1981), 56-67.
4. An interesting question: why did this appeasement work in Quebec or elsewhere?
5. Kenneth Frampton develops the idea of a critical regionalism. I have extended his formulation to critical ethnicity. Kenneth Frampton, "Toward a Critical Regionalism: Six Points for an Architecture of Resistance," Hal Foster, ed., *The Anti-Aesthetic: Essays on Post-Modern Culture* (Port Townsend: Bay Press, 1983), 16-30.
6. See *Cultures Canada* V, 14, 15, and VI, 1 (1986).
7. Canada, Prime Minister, "White Paper on multiculturalism." Federal Government's Response to Book IV of the Report of the Royal Commission on Bilingualism and Biculturalism. (Tabled in the House of Commons, 8 October 1971), 8580.
8. *AppleBert 1982: Report of the Federal Cultural Policy Review Committee* (Ottawa: Information Services, Department of Communications, Government of Canada), 11.
9. Presumably the "so on" can be taken to refer to lifestyle groups and consumption communities.
10. AppleBert Report, 11.
11. An overall budgetary allotment of 1.9 per cent for the arts is pitiful (especially in light of a nearly 10 per cent allotment for defence), but it may be a great deal of money and support from the perspective of an ethnic who perceives far greater restrictions on aesthetic and cultural projects than those facing Canadian artists.
12. I have dealt with these themes at greater length elsewhere: see "Ukrainian Experience as Text: Toward a New Strategy," Manoly R. Lupul, ed., *Visible Symbols: Cultural Expressions Among Canada's Ukrainians* (Edmonton: Canadian Institute of Ukrainian Studies, 1984), 147-52.
13. For example there were foreign book-burnings on the grounds of the Manitoba legislature in the early part of this century which were to impress on the immigrants that the education system in that province was to be unilingual. See William A. Czumer,

Recollections about the Life of the First Ukrainian Settlers in Canada, Louis T. Laychuk, trans., (Edmonton: Canadian Institute of Ukrainian Studies, 1981), 96-136.

14. Andrea Branzi, *The Hot House: Italian New Wave Design*, C. H. Evans, trans., (Boston: Massachusetts Institute of Technology Press, 1984).

John O'Neill

Techno-culture and the Specular Functions of Ethnicity: With a Methodological Note

I begin with the proposition, argued elsewhere, that all technology is bio-technology.[1] I do so in order not to lose the connection between our technological culture and the life-world which it either seductively colonizes in the name of utility and practicality or else imperiously condemns to ignorance and obsolescence. Thus from the standpoint of the life-world, technology is anti-nature. As such it has preoccupied our greatest thinkers from Marx to Husserl and Heidegger. With similar boldness, I shall consider ethnicity as the shaping element or inscape of the cultures that constitute the life-world. I do so in order not to lose the point that, whereas our technological culture is relatively universal and homogeneous, the life-world is local, ethnic, and richer in meaning and values than our techno-culture.[2]

Next, I shall rephrase the relations between technology, the life-world, and ethnicity in terms of a classical sociological paradigm drawn from Weber and Parsons.[3] Thus we may consider a technological society to require of its members conduct governed by norms of rationality, universality, affective neutrality, and meritocratic achievement. Such a society will need to subordinate its own opposed tendencies to value non-rational, local, passionate, and kinship governed conduct. In short, a technological society strives to subordinate kinship or ethnicity to rationality and bureaucracy, and to represent the conflict between technology and ethnicity as a problem of social control requiring the imposition of homogeneity over difference.

Finally, in order to provide a key to the apparent arbitrariness of my use of the tourist, Kojak, and third-world fashion as figurations of ethnicity in the technological age, I shall translate my argument a third time into the language of natural symbols, as developed by Mary Douglas.[4] The effect I want to achieve is to show how technical rationality and ethnicity may be considered figures of opposition linked to the contrasting structures of mind/body, culture/nature, order/disorder. These terms are inextricably bound, however much we try to give hegemony to the symbols of techno-culture. Our civilization is neurotic about its body, its family, and its ethnicity, inasmuch as these become figures of disorder in an age whose faith lies in the smooth operation of a techno-bureaucracy far removed from such local impurities:

> According to the rule of distance from physiological origin (or *the purity rule*) the more the social situation exerts pressure on persons involved in it, the more the social demand for conformity tends to be expressed by a demand for physical control. Bodily processes are more ignored and more firmly set outside the social discourse, the more the latter is important. A natural way of investing a social occasion with dignity is to hide organic processes. Thus social distance tends to be expressed in distance from physiological origins and vice versa.[5]

By reconstructing the technology/ethnicity relation in terms of the purity rule, we can understand how technological societies treat ethnicity as "difference," or as "other" to the homogenizing processes of rationalization and bureaucratization that attempt to exclude all other forms of the life-world as alien modes of heterogeneity. Thus the ethnic, the native, the family, the feminine, the exotic, the wilderness become natural symbols opposed to the techno-symbols of the hegemonic culture of industry, science, and technology. In practice this contradiction is compromised. As I shall show, the techno-culture strips ethnicity in order to re-appropriate it in a secondary system of natural symbols floated in the "social imaginary" whose specular production is the primary function of the media. Tourism, crime, and third-world fashion can then be seen as figurations of ethnicity operating as the internalized/externalized otherness of the technological world order and its own desired specularization.

It is, of course, impractical to "un-think" our technology. What can we mean by such an exercise? What use, what good can come of it? Such questions themselves reveal the extent to which we have made technology our voice, our omniscient and ubiquitous sensorium, our pride, our morality. Indeed, we have no other point of view than the view we have of ourselves amplified and relayed through our specular technologies. Nor have we any history, society, politics or economy outside of our video terminals which now reproduce in light matrices that owe nothing to the womb, and less to our ordinary and divine memory. For the flash which places us at the centre of the screen renders us the outcasts of mankind's hitherto civilized incorporation and continuity:

> Television is our body, our vision, our mind, our sanity, our appetite, our will to live as we do. Television is our mother's body, endlessly materializing our appetite for security, nostalgia, and happiness. Television is our father's body, in heaven and on earth, patient and strong, loyal and free. Television is our brother's body, subversive and superfluous, the joker in the pack. Television is old bodies, black bodies, broken bodies, bodies resurrected, imprisoned and burned. Television is Christ's body sacrificed in the same way every day everywhere in the world with the same benign indifference to the local sufferings, ignorance, injuries, and fears that it takes upon itself *per omnia saecula saeculorum*. It is this god that we offer our detergents, our deodorants, our dog food, toothpastes, and beer that He take upon Himself our murders, rapes, deceptions, and insanity - *agnus dei televisionis*. Thus our metabolism turns symbolism in an unending Mass celebrating the bonds of everyday life before millions of families gathered at the altar of television.[6]

From the standpoint of the life-world, it is becoming apparent to us that the technological age is an age of death, an age whose end obliges us to review its origins. In short, our fire technology no longer inspires us with its Promethean revolt and even its domestic achievements have degenerated into the endless gadgetry of obsolescence and mindless consumerism. Whereas our technology once promised to make us lords of creation, we find ourselves cosmic aliens, polluters of nature, and barbarians of the galaxy. Our gods are the twisted creatures of that outer space which in our own inner space we no longer revere. Our ambition is to travel to the stars in order to extinguish them in the darkness our planet now casts upon the galaxy. Today's children know this lesson while their elders continue to run away from it. Meantime our children grow older than their parents in a world whose seductions deepen the exploitation of their minds and bodies, driving them into helpless narcissism and suicide on their own doorstep, while elsewhere condemning them to famine and genocide, short of musical relief.

To argue that we are "dispossessed" and are "disembodied" in the technological age, will surely seem perverse, if not fantastic. Everything, every machine, seems to tell us the opposite. For all our things and all our machines are talkative. They are the principal rhetorical agents for the view spectacularized in our media, in everything as a medium for the media, that we are in charge of things and of ourselves. In such a world it is the machine-less, the information-less that are the dispossessed, barely conceivable figments of history and nature before the age of the Coca-Cola bottle, before the gods had gone crazy, before writing and the American Express Card had permitted everyone to leave home. Thus all shrines lead to our technology and all our pilgrimages honour our ability to travel the earth and to compare its ethnic peoples to the image of history's most homeless citizen—the tourist. Tourists, of course, do not lack those practical arts which render them, however single or infirm, however ignorant or indigent, the temporary lords and ladies of the vacationer's empire. The tourist honours the world technological order. Indeed, the tourist is the world's inspector general, roaming freely in a Disney World of ethnic food, drinks, and crafts arrayed for his pleasure and profit. Nothing can be more curious than the annual flocking of American immigrants to their former homelands to discover the now omnipresent toilet roll, toothpaste, central heating, hamburger, and Coca Cola signs for which their ancestors displaced themselves and with which they identify their choice of America as the ultimate trip. What is sad in all this is that the real history of immigrant labour and political refugees recedes into the background of canned cultures created for the international tourist who travels as nearly as possible within the same technosphere as he or she enjoys at home. Today's tourists now spread around the world in a few hours with minimum discomfort and colossal self-confidence in the relative value of their national currency. Until recently, they were by and large a good-natured people willing to suffer strikes that often left them stranded before or after a holiday, not to mention the occasional hijacking and severe bouts of diarrhoea. Indeed, it once seemed that tourists could only be angered by those natives who short-changed them in a deal where their own honour as the cunning collectors of worthless things was at stake. Today, however, tourists are outraged to discover that they are pawns in a techno-order that has colonized the world pushing it into a picture book past (or the more insulting scenarios of the lost American Express card) which unaccountably explodes and rages against our obscene cameras. Thus tourism now meets its counterpart in terrorism which threatens to limit that thoughtless empire where travel narrows the mind.

Have I misplaced my observations upon the tourists, hitting at those innocents abroad rather than looking for their booking agents? Indeed, it might well appear that I have chosen sarcasm in place of criticism, enjoyed irony where I might have suffered the more laborious tasks of analyzing the political economy of multi-national corporatism and its hegemony over the earth and interstellar travel. Such an analysis is necessary and will appear in the closing pages. However, at this point I wish to add something that is just as difficult to capture because it does not seem to be part of the puzzle. The part we are trying to fit to the puzzle is the phenomenon of the specular ideology of technology, or rather, the practices through which we moralize the behavioral age and its specularization as an age of benign utilitarianism. The ideological production of the specular image of the technological age operates through the figuration of the citizen, the deviant, the consumer, the child, the tourist, the patient, the feminist, the ethnic, the handicap, and the transplant as celebrants of the social system that reproduces their identity and its supporting socioprosthetics.[7] We speak of the flotation of these figures because, although the fundamental drive of technological society is to subordinate all social relations of production to the basic operations of the forces of production as narrowly conceived in the laws of profit and practicality, on the cultural level the subordination of the social to the technical infrastructure is reversed, or floated in ideological discourses that figurate the individuals as the principal agent of social processes.

How is it possible for the work of justice, for the hard police-work of crime hunting, to be achieved by an ethnic in a city where "everyone knows" crime is produced and not solved by ethnics? How is the impartial, rational, legal-scientific work of the bureaucratized criminal system executed by ethnics whose values are inimical to such practices? Part of the answer is that in reality the police solve very few crimes. To reduce crime in any serious way we need massive reforms in the property system and its effects upon levels of education, housing, employment, urbanization, race, and ethnicity. What a capitalist criminal system needs to portray in its daily operations is the relatively honest efforts of the lower classes to police themselves by repressing ethnicity as the source of its troubles. This is the basic specular function of such series as *Kojak*. Because its expressive task is primary, the police movie needs to be guaranteed a modicum of success at the instrumental but secondary level of actual police work. The large amount of specular work devoted to expressive ethnicity is therefore redeemed through a benign technology (bugging and informing) which provides for the hunted to tell Kojak where to hunt for them. Here, then, are the two sides of the moral economy of police work. Because of an unfailing technology of disclosure (however little it transforms the field of crime), police work can be made to float all the other expressive values of the society which it represents as a moral order. Thus in the pastel world of *Miami Vice*, which avoids the earth tones of ethnicity in favour of the electri-city, America's doubly failed ethnic adventures at home and in Viet-Nam are refloated in the black/white police couple, Ricardo Tubbs and Sonny Crockett. Here the specularization of police work—which costs millions of dollars per show—exceeds the cost of much real police work. But since police work is not meant to solve the drug problem, its specularized functions are again primary and make it compatible with elaborate body advertisements for fast cars, yachts,

Italian tailoring, and the throb of ethnicity. Because the American Dream remains an exclusionary vision for the lower orders, the city is the perfect setting for the morality plays serialized in *Kojak*, *Police Woman*, and *Miami Vice*. This is why *Miami Vice* goes to such trouble to colour its world:

> The urban environment, and in particular the ghetto, is the prime target of effacement. It is saturated with signs that fixate and stereotype ready-made experiences, objects, and encounters that stylize the bodies, dress, and vehicular movements of city people. The aesthetics of the city are a flash-board of the exchange values and the icons of commodification that celebrate the commercial life of its denizens. By the same token, the practical aesthetics of the city are noisy, ugly, and hostile to those who are incompetent with the city's official uses and occasions. Everything that is contradictory and incoherent in the material basis of the political economy is reflected in the neonized iconography of the urban environment, in its wealth and poverty, its comforts and dangers, its crime, its sophistication, and its vulgarity. The city is hard on those who are not making it in the city: it crushes and silences them unless they are able to subvert it by creating their own style and unforeseen ways of holding out, getting by, and hitting back. Thus the city is open to the endless necessary profanations and effacements whereby persons otherwise excluded from its ostensible activities make a place for themselves, cut a figure, and hold out where they would otherwise seem to be submerged. It thereby furnishes a genre of television series, from *Kojak* to *Police Woman*, that serve to spectacularize the dream of law and order as an urban morality play.[8]

Is there any connection between the figures of the tourist and Kojak, and how can they reveal the life-world of the technological age? The question might be repeated to ask how these two figures provide any insight into the figure of ethnicity as the internal other, or the external other of the technological society and the world order it seeks to impose upon the life-world. The connection I am suggesting lies in the operations of the specular technology, or media of the technological society, which display it as a moral order which needs the Pax Americana at home and abroad. Thus it is now possible for the United States to treat terrorist attacks upon its military and diplomatic operations as attacks upon the outposts of American tourism. The American tourist is in turn capable of rebutting Italian protests against a McDonald's fast food pit adjacent to the Piazza d'Espagna with the rejoinder: "I have a right to have a Big Mac wherever and whenever I want to." This right to the great American fry is ultimately backed by firebombs, napalm, and the nuclear fry. Such is the moral order of the things we consume without any thought for how

22

it is we are dispossessed by the life-style with which they threaten the life-world. Meantime, while Americans play sheriff to the world technological order, at home one of their own terrorists turns a local McDonald's into a massacre reminiscent of Mai Lai. Worse still for the faceless family restaurant, the Chicano's turn it into a shrine, making memories somewhere that was forgettably nowhere.

I have now to draw together the way techno-symbolism and natural symbolism work together in the specularization of ethnicity as the underside of the world industrial order. I propose to do this by treating third-world fashion as a bio-technological integrator of the civil and savage bodies of international capitalism. I consider fashion a body technology inasmuch as it commits us to homogenized styles, cut, and colours which rule the seasons with an imposed "look," while simultaneously invoking the body's freedom and frivolity in the choice offered between the elements that compose the look. To achieve this, the fashionable body must learn to be alienated from itself through its desire to become itself by abandoning previous commitments to styles that always threaten to be out of style. Fashion, then, is a technique for the creation of comfortable risk and boredom through endless flights from the stylized body whose labour is freely engaged on behalf of the fashion industry. The world economy of fashion is in turn deeply committed to the ruthless exploitation of sweated labour, as well as the pillage of its cottons, silks, colours, and designs.[9] The expropriation of third-world fabrics, colours, and designs produces the natural symbols of the pre-industrialized body. Floated in the post-industrial semiurgy of classless, raceless, timeless, life-styles, the fashionable body of late capitalism denies the domination of its own internal and external ethnicity. At the same time, it entertains its repressed fears of the exotic cultures of poverty and colonialism symbolized in the Bazaar/bizarre world of aestheticized exploitation.

The operation of this aspect of the logic of late capitalist semiotics is nicely caught in Julia Emberley's remarks on the text and imagery of John Galliano's spring collection in *Harper's/Queen* magazine for February 1985. While seemingly far away from the pastel world of *Miami Vice*, Galliano's "Visions of Afghanistan: Layers of Suiting, Shirting and Dried-Blood Tones" in fact conceals the same violence, the same genocide, the sameloody bodies at the end of the industrial violence of the world's two major powers. What Emberley discloses is the double layering of textual and visual signs required to appropriate the broken symbols of colonized ethnicity in the forced alliance of tradition and fashion:

In the syntax of Galliano's title we find the heterotopia, a heterogeneous splitting and fracturing which is translated in the "world of fashion" as a multiple and spectacular field of types and tropes that circulate on the sur-

23

face of visual and textual representations. The fashion-effect of his title dismantles the narrative continuity of presentation because its syntax is broken, dismembered, shattered and replaced by a ''layered effect'' - a horizontal syntax, discontinuous and fragmented, gives way to a vertical effect of imaginary and semantic layers. In fashion, images cut across traditional barriers or limits of representation, effacing along the way differences and historical specificities and producing, instead, a unitary effect of congenial pluralities that apparently ''hold together'' without contradictions.[10]

Thus, as we observed in the beginning, the life-styles of the technological age turn out to be modes of anti-nature, styles of death that live off a degraded life-world pushed into the urban ghetto and the colonial slum. Third-world chic, punk, and the pastels of *Miami Vice* are merely the death masks of late capitalist history whose narrative fragments into the discontinuous lights and deafening sounds in which it records itself.[11] In turn, the layered poverty and masked pallor its unkempt youth turns against the world's sick and poor is its own mirror-image, embracing the world's children in the profitable protest of a charity that never gives away the game.

Such observations are difficult because they imply standards of reason and justice that reject the post-modern insistence upon the pluralization of culture. The latter confuses centre and periphery in the development of global capitalism. What I mean is that the plurality of cultures is available to us only as a result of the marginalization and fragmentation of local cultures in the face of the globalization and homogenization of late capitalist corporate culture. Curiously enough, the melancholia and eclecticism of the post-modern plurality saps its individual producers and consumers precisely because they have lost all dimension of oppositional culture—of ancient, distant, exotic, class, ethnic, and gender cultures. Within national cultures, the deconstruction of the law, of patriarchy and the phallus are therefore attacks upon the abandoned fortresses of late capitalism which is everywhere and nowhere. In fact, by allowing its loyal opposition to attack its presumed notions of authority, art, sexuality, and politics, late capitalism achieves a benign solidity and tolerance that in turn underwrites its post-modern university departments where such criticism flourishes. Thus post-modernism and feminism are necessary correlates since their celebration of the autonomy of signifiers naturally admits the expanded circulation of the now least valuable social signifier, woman, into its orbit.[12] We are referring, of course, to the reduction of the local, historical, cosmological value of woman's difference to her complete exchangeability in markets whose own discursive production is the feature that best exemplifies the direction of late capitalism and its recoding of the life-world and its human shapes. This is not to say that women are any less wise than any other minority demanding an equal opportunity to become unequal within a social system they do not otherwise challenge. Such an insistence, as Marx would have observed, merely deepens the levels of surplus value extractable from the free market operation of late capitalism which at the same time yields to various welfare and therapeutic demands as palliatives to the negative side effects of its overall operation.[13] What is peculiar to the feminist narrative is that it is floated in an imaginary universe of symbolic equality which forecloses on its own signified domination of those men, women, and children who live with the underside of success in executive suites, panels, committees, galleries, and classrooms. Thus the male gaze is not deconstructed by its female return so much as by its very absence from a world in which the human sensorium is subordinated to the look of things, or to the light-sound of events which constitute the disembodying information process of late capitalism.

Neither mastery nor victimage can be espoused in a cultural system that can recycle all of its class, sexual, artistic, and political symbols to re-embody atemporally and aspatially configurations whose social contexts no longer delimit the places of late capitalism. Thus a woman on the move, selling other people a move, can wear a perfume celebrating the flight of the Viet-Namese peasants from a murderous machine-gun fire that destroyed their villages and countryside, threatening to turn their land into a great American parking lot. Even this horror, captured in the photographs of burning women and children, can be expropriated as a challenge to American sentimentalism and its medicalized charity. The media exposure of the Viet-Namese mother is due to an imperialist system of pillage whose genocidal impulses put third world women well beyond the recycled emancipation of women in the advanced industrial countries. To speak of solidarity under such circumstances is merely to bring third world women under the gaze of women within the hegemonic world. Thus to speak of visibility as a male prerogative, or as a phallocentric practice which produces women's invisibility for herself, merely distracts from the invisibility of the socio-economic system which reproduces these and similar practices while leaving itself without a name.[14] To locate these practices in patriarchy when in fact the majority of men, no less than women and children, is powerless is a self-inflicted injury that further incapacitates families whose lack of authority marginalizes them and their political function.

In short, to sexualize the system of stratification and imperialism rather than to analyze how that system is productive of racist, sexist, and class

25

ideologies is really to be mesmerized by the surfaces of exploitation. Worse still, it is to risk co-operation through inclusion in the imagery effects of participation and visibility which is the prime effect of what I have called the specular ideology of the technological society and its effacement of ethnicity, family, gender, and locality.

This essay, then, avoids the conventions of ethnic studies because the latter are intentionally and unavoidably boring.[15] No offence toward honest practitioners is intended by this observation, nor any invidious contrast with, say, stratification studies or theoretical sociology. I simply remark upon an endemic and irremediable feature of the industrialization of the arts and sciences. For the same reason, their topics, methods, interests, and concerns are profusely available at every discourse level from what used to be called the "Ladies Home Journal" to television documentaries and science journals. From this perspective, ethnicity, inequality, poverty, sexuality, "ring around the collar," "twenty-four hour protection," and "multiculturalism constitute *melodoxies*, that is, staple concerns that feed the very worries they are intended to resolve. They recruit spectacular armies of producers and consumers, researchers, writers, readers, and listeners. All these people are busy, right-minded (even when leftists) and gainfully employed in the reproduction of society's concern with society.

This phenomenon is directly related to what I call the trivialization of social science culture. The interests served here are those of governments, legal, and welfare agencies and the entire social science disciplinary apparatus of the modern therapeutic state. The legitimacy of their concerns underwrites, in turn, the production of commercial entertainment scenarios in which the normal topics and procedures of the social sciences create endless pseudo-science soaps whose pursuit of human interest threatens to saturate even the most sentimental listener or viewer. Thus ethnicity, as well as sexuality, illness or a broken romance provide inexhaustible topics and resources for the soap production of trivialized science and entertainment, or rather, of trivialized-science-as-entertainment-as-science.

In light of the proceeding processes, we cannot expect normal social science to exceed the Mertonian ethic of consensus through conformity to anonymous general procedure. In this the scientific community reproduces the large founding community which it simultaneously claims is the object of discovery by social science methods. The general ideology of the social science requires therefore that specific social sciences, such as race and ethnic studies, document the degree to which social reality resists theory and ideology. To the extent that this is so, a number of sub-theorems may be derived. Thus ethnic studies are likely to:

(a) make unwarranted assumptions about the levels and sources of social integration;

(b) make unwarranted assumptions about individual tolerance for the industrialization of and homogenization of culture, mentality, and embodiment;

(c) be indifferent to the issue of political and moral accountability in the production and consumption of studies of ethnicity, race, and multiculturalism.

At the same time, the ideological assumptions in (a), (b), and (c), so far from being hidden, may be questioned without any theoretical resolve to move beyond them as an organizational analytic. The latter is preserved while its materials are rendered topical or contemporary or controversial.

How all of this functions may be seen from the "seventh edition million copy seller" of Broom and Selznick's *Sociology*.[16] We see that the analytic warrant for the construction of the chapter on ethnicity turns wholly upon the homogeneity/pluralism contrast. It is thereby possible to construct a material display of the discipline of ethnic studies as an object articulated through this contrast device. At the same time, the device is resilient enough to contain its utter relativity as an analytic artifact by, for example, literally subsuming its colonial and political history as subsections of the overall chapter-heading "Ethnic Pluralism" through which it displays its range of concern. The information thereby conveyed never moves beyond common sense knowledge nor outside of the design of other media formats. It is through and through reproducible or instantly "accessed" through its "key terms" (assimilate, stereotype, minority, affirmative action).

Practitioners in ethnic studies may need to rethink their basic assumptions about socialization, assimilation, individuation, and defamilization processes in contemporary western industrial society. Thus, it may be the case that:

(a) industrial societies no longer require their historical levels of socialization and internalization of benefits, values, and competence oriented to the production sphere;

(b) industrialization and urbanism, as contexts of ethnic experience, may be better interpreted as a universal semiotics of desire[17] in which all referentials (family, class, gender, race) are "floated" in life styles that feed on desire liberated from traditional communities of values and beliefs;

(c) because the universal semiotics of industrial and urban experience no longer require any referentials in the real world of work, class, family, and the body, the latter are now floated in spectacles which continue to portray them as the natural settings of desire and as failures or pathologies in race, illness, aging.[18]

Thus it may be the case that ethnic studies has no object, except as practitioners continue to reify collectivities of analytically constructed groups (Ukrainians, Italians, Blacks) into processes such as assimilation, accommodation, pluralism, etc. In my view, ethnic studies should be sold off to community and government agencies whose practical concerns already engage them in data collection and naturally organized inquiries that do not have to support the secondary processing of an uninteresting social science. By the same token, once relieved of the incubus of a postured science, then ethno-community directed studies of the practical issues, troubles, and coping strategies their members use against urbanism and industrialism, as well as shifts on the world political and economic scene, would remain within the naturally self-organizing competence of these groups democratically respected as communities of practical reasoners.[19]

Finally, I should say that if ethnic studies were generous enough to subvert itself in the way I am suggesting it would set a model for the rest of the sub-disciplines of the social sciences! I mean nothing destructive in this. I believe we have cluttered up the university with information gathering and dispersal activities which might more honestly be returned to the communities or markets they claim to service.

Notes

1. John O'Neill, "Bio-Technology: Empire, Communications and Bio-Power," *Canadian Journal of Political and Social Theory*, X, no. 1-2 (1986): 66-78.
2. John O'Neill, *Making Sense Together: An Introduction to Wild Sociology* (New York, 1974).
3. Talcott Parsons, *The Social System* (New York, 1951).
4. Mary Douglas, *Purity and Danger: An Analysis of Concepts of Pollution and Taboo* (London, 1970); *Natural Symbols: Explorations in Cosmology* (London, 1973).
5. Douglas, *Natural Symbols*, 12.
6. John O'Neill, "Televideo ergo sum: some hypotheses on the specular functions of the media," *Communication* 7 (1983): 221-40.
7. John O'Neill, *Five Bodies: The Human Shape of Modern Society* (Ithaca: Cornell University Press, 1985).
8. John O'Neill, "Looking into the Media: Revelation and Subversion," *Communication Philosophy and the Technological Age*, Michael J. Hyde, ed. (University of Alabama Press, 1982), 73-97.
9. Rosalind Coward, *Female Desire: Women's Sexuality Today* (London, 1984).
10. Julia Emberley, "The Fashion Apparatus: A Deconstructive Reading of Post-Modern Subjectivity." Paper presented at the Annual Meetings of the Canadian Learned Associations: Sociology and Anthropology Section on the Post Modern Scene: Fashion

and the Politics of Style, Winnipeg, Manitoba, 6 June 1986.

11. Dick Hebdige, *Subculture: The Meaning of Style* (London, 1979).

12. John O'Neill, "Defamilization and the Feminism of Law in Early and Late Capitalism," *International Journal of Law and Psychiatry* 5, no. 3/4 (1982): 255-69.

13. John O'Neill, "Sociological Nemesis: Parsons and Foucault on the Therapeutic Disciplines," Mark L. Wardell and Stephen P. Turner, eds., *Sociological Theory in Transition* (Boston: Allen and Unwin, 1986), 21-35.

14. John O'Neill, "The disciplinary society: from Weber to Foucault," *The British Journal of Sociology*, XXXVII, no. 1 (March 1986): 42-60.

15. See Merton's remarks on the trivial and the important in sociology in "Social Conflict over Styles of Sociological Work," *The Sociology of Science: Theoretical and Empirical Investigations* (Chicago and London: The University of Chicago Press, 1973), 59-62.

16. Leonard Broom and Philip Selznick, *Sociology* (New York: Harper and Row, 1981).

17. John O'Neill, "McLuhan's Loss of Innis-Sense," *The Canadian Forum*, LXI, no. 709 (May 1981): 13-15.

18. John O'Neill, "The Productive Body: An Essay on the Work of Consumption," *Queens's Quarterly*, 85, no. 2 (Summer 1978): 221-30.

19. John O'Neill, "The Mutuality of Accounts: An Essay on Trust," in Scott G. McNall, ed., *Theoretical Perspectives in Sociology* (New York: St. Martins Press, 1979): 369-80.

Alkis Kontos

Harvesting Ancestral Landscapes and Techno-Culture

Some landscapes live because they roam
Across the world rooted in dreams
C. A. Trypanis

Both papers traverse a common territory—the ominous, omnivorous nature of technological society—yet they diverge in scope and differ in style and temperament. They complement each other and provide a distinct, sound, and constructive orientation to the proceedings of our symposium. They constitute a fruitful departure.

Onufrijchuk's paper is epigrammatic, sensitive, and rich in suggestive allusion and explicit articulation. The paper is structured thematically on a minimal but penetrating, perceptive approach—two theses and a hypothesis. He places ethnicity in two distinct but interrelated contexts. The first is the post-modern era. This is the global, societal dimension which is constructed of technology, capitalism, consumerism, the lonely crowd, the world of video and television, and the culture industry that sells and consumes everything. Culture becomes the exterior, the appearance of the void, the empty interior. Culture is commodity. The post-modern era permeates everything. It levels. It imposes homogeneity. It devours indiscriminately, beastly, anti-aesthetically. The second context that he provides is the Canadian situation of the federal multicultural policy.

The first context is introduced concisely but precisely. It lingers in the background while it darkens the future horizon. In Onufrijchuk's view the global cultural dimension of the post-modern era frames the multicultural dimension of ethnicity. The former is the prison house of the latter. The era conditions and represses it.

Ethnicity is correctly viewed as a living, experienced communal rela-

31

tionship which is predicated upon history, culture, memory, and language all being treated as heritage. Language fuses, renders coherent and vibrant the whole. It bestows meaning and thus historical continuity. It sustains memory and thus ethnic identity. In addition to being a heritage, ethnicity is also a project. Ethnicity is past and future oriented. Its stream flows with receptivity and steady direction. Inheritance and project together constitute the ethos of a nation and a race. Inheritance and project are in tension when there is no homeland. The project demands greater dynamism and imagination than merely to safeguard and cherish the ethnic inheritance. In this brief definitional thesis he captures the dangers and potentialities of ethnicity, its collective condition and the individual, existential dimension of the self.

Ethnicity as a project—its energy, dreams, and uncertainties—is conveyed best by Onufrijchuk's suggestive agricultural metaphor of the harvest. It is the possibility of a future harvest and the danger of a failure at harvest time that inform the paper as a whole. A tamed tension between hope and resignation, between energetic optimism and melancholy, exists here. It is a realistic assessment.

Harvest presupposes collective and individual toil; hopeful tilling of ancestral landscapes; landscapes soaked with history; the life of the ethnos. Harvest demands direct interaction with nature and passion for the land. Harvest holds promises expressed in songs and dances, the initiation of the young, and the celebratory rituals of communal life. Harvest demands land to be cultivated. Projects away from the homeland can become illusions, abortive ventures.

Onufrijchuk turns to a critique of multiculturalism. He argues persuasively that multiculturalism is a grand strategic manoeuvre to absorb ethnicity, in its plurality and distinctiveness, into a synthetic edifice, ethnicity, which sterilizes, expurgates, and truncates the project. This part of the presentation is insightful and provocative. Multiculturalism is, potentially, the burial of ethnicity rather than its acceptance, celebration, and invigoration. The parochialism and complicity of ethnic leadership should not be ignored here. Narrow self-interest, constricted horizons, dwarfed visions, tend to celebrate ethnicity as heritage devoid of a dynamic project. They tend to forget the harvest, its toil and joy.

There is a veiled intimation that ethnicity and the post-modern era are locked in mortal battle. Ethnicity need not succumb but cannot remain pure, transhistorical. The wasteland of the post-modern era need not succeed in devouring everything. The hypothesis that "communities of memory" are the rehearsed casualties of a universal fate is disconcerting, yet the metaphor of harvest lingers on the distant horizon. Pessimism, cynicism, and naive optimism do not emanate from this text. With precision and perspicacity, with courage and insight, Onufrijchuk exposes hypocrisy, lies, and self-deception. He does it without bitterness or renunciation. He does it with the solidity of an existential identity firmly rooted in the dreams and landscape of his ethnicity. With voices like Onufrijchuk's, nurtured in the arable landscape of ethnicity proper, I suspect the harvest season is upon us.

O'Neill's presentation touches on a variety of issues that he harnesses under the rubric of techno-culture, the artifice, and ethnicity as nature. The rationalized technocratic society and culture are adumbrated in bold strokes by O'Neill. The emptiness, spiritual poverty, and misery of modern capitalistic, technocratic society are stressed as forces of homogeneity. Diversity, differentiation, and individuality are neither respected nor tolerated.

O'Neill focusses his analysis primarily on the scene in the United States and the overpowering culture industry there. He is correct in stressing the oppositional aspects of techno-culture and ethnicity, though he might be going too far when he insists on treating ethnicity as *the* natural. He is stretching a partial truth. He is seeking the polar opposite of a disenchanted mass culture. Ethnicity cannot be totally the other, but O'Neill's strained oppositional taxonomy points up the nullity of techno-culture and the specificity-particularity of ethnicity.

The treatment of tourism is insightful and significant. It highlights and complements Onufrijchuk's references to ethnicity as exotica. The power of O'Neill's scrutiny of tourism rests with the fact that the tourist encounters sameness instead of difference while travelling. The techno-cultural sameness reaches its apogee in its transformative impact on the ethnic tourist's homeland. This is the one and only, the ultimate trip, Americana as universal panoramic show, the American dream, the ultimate cultural nightmare. The terrorist as the tourist's counterpart is not developed. It is a complex issue that warrants more detailed and cautious dissection. An aspect of modern terrorists is the loss of their homeland. Exiled, embittered, young, nationalistic, even fanatical, they express despair and wrath. This alone does not tell the whole story, far from it, but without some comprehension of the pain and agony of non-immigrant ethnicity—the loss of homeland, not merely property—no meaningful story can be told. Fanaticism and derangement obscure rather than clarify the issues.

The absurdities and idiotic aspects of modern tourism capture fully the techno-cultural context of the modern state and citizenship. A de-historicized mass culture, oblivious to its pillage of the landscape of history, sends its mercenaries, the new barbarians, to roam the earth, desperately seeking joy and meaning in a meaningless and joyless social environment.

O'Neill's treatment of the television shows, *Kojak* and *Miami Vice*, is suggestive and intriguing. Police shows alternate between the tough law enforcing officer/hero—reminiscent of the macho western hero who declares war on evil doers—and the more sophisticated investigator. Kojak is a mixture of the two, tough but not physical. I have some difficulty recognizing Kojak as a Greek either by name or manner. Though the actor is Greek he is more a parody of the integrated, assimilated ethnic. References to his ethnic background are frequent and strategic.

O'Neill is absolutely right when he points out the contradiction between the ethnic law enforcer and the ethnic community as a crime centre. However, such shows might be suggesting more than simply the capitalist criminal system's need to portray in its operations "the relatively honest efforts of the lower classes to police themselves." The protagonist is portrayed as an ethnic who has managed to internalize the ideals and values of American society; who has left behind all the nasty aspects of the past; who remains vaguely proud of the ethnicity which culminates in the universal individualism of the American dream. This "ethnic" is America incarnate, the exemplar educator of the other ethnics who failed. As an officer, Kojak's success is the glorification of the system. That he is a law enforcer suggests his renunciation of the sociogenetic proclivity toward crime of all poor ethnics. He is the reformed, purified ethnic. He is the avenging angel who knows the satanic world of crime against the decency and dignity of a free market society, against the free and glorious America.

Miami Vice had a phenomenal impact. It is a sleek, mindless show. Form not substance or plot is its essence. It is a visual experience, a prolonged video, which accompanies two aspects of modern culture: song (music) and fashion. O'Neill treats fashion separately but I wish to combine them here. The show has no linguistic qualities to redeem it. The white-black duo is efficient and effective but they are too opulent to be policemen. The movieland unreality, Hollywood, is already in full strength here. The black is elegantly attired whether in the city or in the jungles. Like Kojak, he has left behind his natural fate. He is middle-class continental. The white is casual but fashionable. Each show parades the wardrobe of both. If the black is the success of the system, the confirmation of its openness, the white is the refutation of the sociological truth that the Viet-Nam war produced many tragic psychological casualties, drugs, and violence. He is confirmation because as a veteran he fights the war against drugs and crime. He is neither muscular nor extremely experienced, but he is phenomenally accurate with guns. With soldiers like him, what went wrong in Viet-Nam? The mythology continues.

Black/white has been exploited before in *The Defiant Ones* (escaped prisoners) and *I Spy* (spies in the service of good against evil). The duo's professional imperfections, human weaknesses, and occasional immaturity are moderated, rectified, by yet another ethnic, a Hispanic. Since most of the drug magnates are Hispanics, we are back to O'Neill's insights into *Kojak*. This ethnic is experience personified. He is efficient, authoritative, taciturn, and not eccentric. Attired in the dullest possible way, he symbolizes the true, ascetic fighter against crime. Lest we panic, the fashion show of *Miami Vice* does not permeate the whole of the law enforcing agency. America is serious. She means business and the superior in *Miami Vice* is meant to inspire confidence.

Such are the travesties of purified ethnicity. Moronic, ridiculous treatments of crucial issues, of painful realities, aspire to reach the level of serious social commentary. Italian police officers can fight the Mafia best since they know its workings instinctively. Rejoice.

Both presentations have the virtue of placing ethnicity in a techno-culture which tends, indeed seeks, to strangle it. Both authors, correctly, refuse to irrevocably declare the demise of ethnicity. The video is used by both as a sinister tool of transfiguration of the very essence, the physiognomy of ethnicity. The system wants to absorb and render homogeneous the ethnic as other. It also wants to tame and preserve the diversity of the other. This simultaneous, dual desire is a deep-seated contradiction. Part of its possible dialectical resolution is the ethnic's own project: video or action; amnesia or consciousness and memory; history or oblivion. The dangers, the promise, and the predicament of ethnicity in a technological age have been ushered in by these first two presentations.

René Char, the French poet and writer reminded his comrades and compatriots during the resistance against the Nazi occupation of France, "Notre héritage n'est précedé d'aucun testament." So it is with ethnicity, an inheritance and a project—"Our inheritance was left to us by no will (testament)." Let us pause and ask what forces, what events, brought about such destiny? Finally, what is to be done?

This symposium will provide a meaningful and unexpectedly rich harvest only if we manage to raise some of the vital questions and issues which capture the problems of ethnicity. The signs and omens are positive. Let us proceed.

Discussion

Technological Society

Jose Huertas-Jourda: On the one hand, we have ethnicity as distraction, while on the other we have technocracy as destruction. Both of these remind me of a machine newly devised by Japanese industrialists. It can reduce seven square miles of jungle trees to wood chip-board in twenty-four hours. Our whole earth's ecology is dependent on those trees for its weather patterns, and jungle forest once destroyed becomes hard stone. This brings to mind a remark by Simone Weil to the effect that the Roman Empire was a blight on the face of civilization. When I first read it, this shocked me very much, particularly since I am of Latin ethnicity. Of course, I rejected it outright, but now that one can travel from Hilton to Hilton and McDonald's to McDonald's, it seems far more cogent.

I am worried about the ethos of distraction. I am not worried about the ethos of destruction. I understand that one, it is clear, but from what is one being distracted? Is it the same thing as being destroyed? In that case, on what are we collectively turning our backs by allowing ourselves to be mesmerized either into distracting ethnicities or equally distracting technologies. This is the question with which I am left here. I think we ought to protect our human jungle by allowing, as Chairman Mao once said, "A hundred flowers to bloom." We must drop, as he diplomatically did at the time, the second half of the quote, namely, "so that we can weed out the old from the new." Let us not weed out anything. Let us celebrate

36

weeds with Pierre Brassens who sings, "I am a wild weed. Good people, good people, it is not me you harvest, nor is it me you put in bales." The lesson I derive from this is that there is a special relationship between weeds and what we are all about that ought neither to be distracted nor destroyed.

Leslie Armour: What is one saying when one is concerned with the extent to which ethnicity is covered up by something from which we are being distracted? That it is a kind of fiction? I think that is true, but it is much harder to say what ethnicity is. I think if one could cross technological society with ethnicity, then everybody would become an ethnic. George Grant, who represents the once dominant Scottish intellectual culture, feels as marginalized as any Ukrainian. It is not as if there were a body of people whose culture is the new technological culture. It does seem to be, indeed, a culture for imaginary persons who are represented on television. Everybody struggles to adapt to it and I suppose nobody succeeds. There must, therefore, be something which all these marginalized people have in common, which represents that alienation from this technological structure. It is certain that we need to try to identify it if we are going to make a fight of it and try to recover something from this mess.

Alkis Kontos: There is a common denominator in modernity, but there is also a fundamental difference. George Grant might be alienated from the predicament substantively, but his alienation is different from that of an ethnic because the context already fully subscribes to and honours his language.

Leslie Armour: Indeed, language is clearly a crucial linchpin, though I am not sure that it is George Grant's language. George Grant is hard to understand. Language has become technologized also, and the real language is not one that is represented by the technologized media. A real difference is developing between the language in which one could express the things that are being covered up by technology and that technological language.

Ian Angus: George Grant tells some wonderful stories about his rejection of the dominant intellectual and cultural scene, but I think that one of their common themes is that it was a conscious rejection and that he had the option. He had the option to fully participate and I think that is a big difference.

Leslie Armour: I wonder if anybody does though? I have always felt myself to be a marginalized person since I was thrown out of school in grade nine as being uneducable. [Laughter] I wonder if anybody who maintains traditional cultures, anybody who is intellectual, or anybody who meets other kinds of specifications with which technologized culture is really at war, really has that option. I think George would like to imagine that he gave up his heritage as Wittgenstein gave up his fortune for poor poets, but in both cases there is an element of imagination.

Ian Angus: If one is looking for what is common to these different ethnicities, it has to be attachment to particular histories. There are things that I care more about than you ever will, or need to, and vice versa. In what sense is that common? It seems to be necessary to start talking about histories rather than about history.

Leslie Armour: There is a certain view of time, for example, that goes with this, that is common to everybody who is being marginalized.

Alkis Kontos: In strict linguistics, an ethnic is a part of an ethnos which seems to automatically mean a people with a history. This transcends and can never be concretized in a state about which ultimately one can be a nationalist. There are people who are nationalists but who have no nation. The best example of this would be the Jews prior to Israel. An ethnos, that is how they saw themselves, but they did not have a state yet. All ethnics are fragments of a larger situation. The real issue is, how did it happen that the ethnics came here? This illuminates the difference between George Grant and me. There is a fundamental difference, which goes back to the choice: how did it happen all these people came here? If they came like the Argentines, the Chileans, and those from the Soviet Union who are political refugees, it is no accident that the most hostile phrase ever used is "go back where you came from." The assumption is that you can, but you cannot. If you could you would not have come in the first place.

Ian Angus: The notion of people coming here through various sorts of repression applies also to English-speaking people. It is not the same thing. The Scottish people of the late nineteenth century were English-speaking, and came here solely through political oppression at that time. The question of political oppression and refugee status is not exactly the same question as that of language.

Leslie Armour: Most people came for the same reasons. The French who came to Quebec were tired of being pushed around and found it desirable to accept even the harsh terms on which they could come. The Scots were being cleared out by the Highland Clearances. Even the English in British Columbia were remittance men—people who were paid money to stay out of England. People came, by and large, for the same kinds of reasons, and further, they came from the same kinds of groups. These were people who had missed the Enlightenment of the eighteenth century. The people from Eastern Europe were similar in this respect. The larger problem is how, having come for the same reasons, and often from the same background, the deck was shuffled.

Ato Sekyi-Otu: Consider Onufrijchuk's two categories, ethnicity as an inheritance and ethnicity as a project. I suspect that how one accentuates one or the other is related to the question of origins. I do not mean origins in terms of whether I came from Africa or somewhere else, but how I came here, why I came here, and the class position from which I came and into which I was condemned when I got here. The phrase "ethnicity as a project" is an intriguing oxymoron, but it can be redeemed depending on its connection with the material conditions from which you came, and into which you enter, into which you are put.

Roman Onufrijchuk: I say project because of my particularity and this particularity speaks a language and has a history. The people who came here, came here because, like everybody else, there were very good reasons to leave. One of those reasons was that people's history was constituted by its denial. If you can imagine, a minister of education for the Russian Empire remarked in the 1860s, when this country was being born formally, that "There has not been, is not now, nor will there ever be, such a thing as the Ukrainian language." In that one statement he dismissed the existence of forty-eight million people who spoke that language which had not, did not, and would not exist. There, inherent in my particularity, is a struggle to at least have a history that I can call my history. This is our history, not its denial. For over a thousand years history has been its denial. In that sense, I say ethnicity is a project for this particularity. It may not be that way for all particularities. I am not sure.

Dušan Pokorný: With respect to English and the particular conditions in which the English-speaking person could lose his cultural predominance and become an ethnic, the interesting thing is that English has historically become the language of technology. That is something which the people who speak the language do not always realize. When I was in India in the fifties, Indians made an attempt to substitute their own terminology for the technical terms in English. They published a book which was about 1200 pages long, translating all the technical terms into Sanskrit. What happened was, of course, that nobody touched those terms. Similarly, in France you have a special session of the Academie Francaise to deal with the problem of the invasion of technical language. Therefore, even granted what is said here, still the English-speaking world is in a predominant position vis-à-vis the others.

Quite apart from history in a much broader sense, there is also the history of the language. English is one of the European languages closest to

Chinese in that it has very little in the way of morphology. What we do in Czech or in Ukrainian by means of suffixes to the verb, is done in English by a combination of verbs. Which means there is a sort of machine where you can put things together. You do not have to morphologize the structure. That makes it easier to learn at a certain very elemental level. That also makes it almost impossible to learn at the real level at which the language is used. When you learn English you acquire a layer of the language which is very easy to acquire. Later, you progressively realize that above that layer there is an extremely complex structure which is accessible to you only within certain limits.

John O'Neill: If one looks at English from the point of view of the accomplishment of university people, the real bilingualism is those who speak English with approximately 200-400 words, and those who speak it with more. Consider the massive investment in talking machines. What makes the talking machine possible is that we have produced a population of people who talk using so few words. In effect, instead of this whole mythology of the mass and equal society, what we really have is a society that operates where it is very good for capitalism. In England people went through something called elementary education which was meant to be enough. Most people in the street used very, very few words. So few, that in fact you could have talking machines. We object to talking machines, but we always presuppose our level of linguistic competence. The way for linguistic expropriation has been elaborately prepared by the public education system of mass culture. The working business of the society is done so simply that it can be reduced to a machine language. That is very important history. We do not have that history written, though there are bits and pieces about the way in which a national language like French or English is created for state purposes. For the sake of the economy, it always wants a very simple command system, and the fewer the words the more likely you can appropriate a yes/no system.

I live with six teenagers, as a function of two marriages, and the emotional chaos in which I live is incredible. It is all created because they do not know how to say what they mean. They always mean more than what they say, but they do not know how to say it. The teenage language culture is incredibly restrictive. Any idea of mass culture, or the mass media as levelling, is a myth. It actually creates greater and greater inequality provided you take a bench mark. My kids, the kids in the house, and the kids they deal with, have no way of dealing with me as an older person. They have no way of dealing with me as a professor. We are seen as the same, but of course that makes me all the more powerful.

Ian Angus: Inarticulateness leads to a certain kind of frustration so that one looks for an image on which to release that frustration, precisely because words cannot be given to this amorphous lost something. It seems to me the way people are attached to these things now usually does not have to be good literature. It does not have to do with writing at all. It has to do with images and signs.

John O'Neill: The family sitcom, of course, does what I call specularizing, the thing I have just described endlessly. We can all see ourselves in that. In this sense, techno-culture does make us all ethnics. We can watch *Kojak* and *Miami Vice*, and so on, because we all know that we are being chased by something and that we are not quite sure what it is. Occasionally it is benign. Occasionally it is not so benign. We are willing to see ourselves in these figures of the child and the ethnic because otherwise we have to formulate the problem in language, and the necessary languages are very complex—economics, the history of language itself, a theory of the media.

Myrna Kostash: I would like to say something about these levelling capacities that come with high tech. It seems that something else might be happening. I was just at a conference in Slovenia, which is a nation of perhaps two million people with their own language, and they are a people who are speaking very optimistically and hopefully of the possibilities available in video cameras, VCRs, software. They speak of being able to publish a book on your own personal computer with the kind of instant communication between Slovenian speakers which seems to completely bypass the imperialist communication structures. This new high technology is manufactured in sweat shops outside the unions. It is being financed and capitalized by overnight capitalist sensations, excluding the Americans and Japanese. It may eventually be swallowed up within international capital, but the whole thing has been initially capitalized in an entrepreneurial way.

Patricia Mills: Think about pre-school children in impoverished home environments going to school without learning skills, and then having access to something like *Sesame Street*. That has its bad side in terms of the way it teaches, but it also gives some children access to information that they would not otherwise have.

Roman Onufrijchuk: The other side of that is the struggle in the making of multiculturalism and the struggle that ethnics went through over the CBC. These people were not stupid. They wanted the CBC because they understood what was happening. Implicitly people understood that there is a media environment, and ethnicity excluded from that environment—not only being spoken for and represented but not being able to represent itself and speak for itself—would create a certain kind of environment in which children, young people, would have an image of what it meant to be ethnic. To be ethnic was somehow to be not normal, not in the normal flow of things.

Manoly Lupul: This is one area we have been almost totally unable to crack. There have been all kinds of goodies in the way of programs from government, provincial and federal, but almost nothing on media.

John O'Neill: You have to ask what the media is for. The basic question here is: why is watching the media free? There is nothing free in this society. You really ought to have to pay. All the media either convey market messages or government messages, and there is a relationship between the two. Ethnic cultures could not conceivably, in the positive sense of ethnicity, survive in the market box. They must go to the government box.

Leslie Armour: Ethnic programming does now appear on cable television, but what is doubly fascinating about it is that no money is invested in it. The Polish community is allowed to have little Polish programs, but they are not professional. I talked about this with the vice-president in charge of programming on CBC and he said you have to realize that television is a professional's game. In the days of radio, anybody who had something to say and a decent speaking voice could get somebody to listen to him. You are absolutely dead if you go on television and you are not professional. Ethnics are being made to look, in Ottawa anyway, extremely foolish all day every day by being given free time on cable television.

Roman Onufrijchuk: If you know how to get along inside it you are ok, but if you do not. . . Take the Hunky Bill episode in Vancouver as an example. This is a classic. Bill Konick is his name and he is a professional. He is an ex-broadcaster who used to do talk shows. He is a writer, so he is quite comfortable in the media. He is a promoter, a salesman. When he goes on television, he is in his own medium. The Ukrainian community tried to take him to court for using the work "Hunky" in his promotion. They hauled him into court over discrimination, and he said: "Look, do you have green money? I take green money. I don't care if you are orange, or purple with polka dots. If you have green money you can come and eat my perogies in the Dover Arms Bar, which I own." It is a very English pub where he sells perogies. The government gave the Ukrainian community money to prosecute him for discrimination. The people who opposed him wore shirts and ties and were very sincere and very intense about their grandfathers being called Bohunks and having their noses rubbed in that. Konick understood the media very well, and you do not get serious on the media. He turned the agenda, which was an attack on him using that sign, around to: "Bunch of stuffed shirts, no sense of humour, a bunch of turkeys who are picking on me." Their concern was

42

very elegantly subverted by the government, ultimately, because there was no way they could ever prove that Konick discriminated against anybody. The only way they could have gotten after him was to prosecute or to sue the government itself, for authorizing the trademark. What he said was: "Look, why pick on me? They said the trademark is ok." The government said: "We gave you $10,000 to prosecute him, so you cannot prosecute us." End of story.

Ethno-Communities

Alkis Kontos: One comment I would like to make concerns a tendency to polarize reason and passion. While there is an earthy dimension to ethnicity, it is constantly on the verge of being turned into vulgarity by the dominant culture. It is not the passion that is respected. It is a strange otherness, therefore ethnicity must be understood in its authenticity. It is not just any otherness, but a specific otherness. I have some reservations about any fully phenomenological approach to it, because it is this specificity that is meant—where I come from; what I was; what I am; language; religion; interaction. Ethnicity itself has suffered severely because fundamentally it is a form of exile. It is transplanting a flower of the plant (to return to Jose's agricultural metaphor) from its natural soil and climate. Therefore in sustaining it, we are endangering it, yet it ought to be sustained. I am not against it. I am not saying we should surrender, but there is a tendency internally, a dialectic, to freeze it because it is stuck in the memory of the past. Therefore it seems to me that history, language, literature, and memory must remain constantly as alive as they can be. It is precisely this inner propensity within ethnicity to suffer its own demise that enables multiculturalism to kill it from outside.

John O'Neill: We want some positive term for what I call ethno-communities. We want to remove the "nic." The term ethno-community is a way of treating the notion of "folk" as a set of regulative principles that a group needs to exercise. To be a person within the folk community, you must have a set of competencies: able to recall the past; having a sense of your immediate environment; having a sense of the future; and knowing how to do what you need to do. The fifth principle is that you need to know how to deal with other communities that have similar sets of rules—a super rule for interaction. One could say an ethnic is somebody who asks four question. What has been my past? What is my present situation? What is my present environment? What will my future look like? The ethnic will also have instrumental knowledge that translates these questions into practical matters and will ask what sorts of things are necessary to be able to interact with similar collectivities. Of course, then, there is always a state and corporate level, as well.

Ian Angus: What we are complaining about here is the fact that the only super rules we know now are government and economy.

John O'Neill: We live in a techno-professional culture. It lays out rules for the environment. They are usually de-spatializing practices, de-historicizing practices. At the same time, they re-collect us in roles. While their super rule is profitability, the next close rule is that there must be a certain kind of order, because you cannot make profit in a totally disordered society. It has certain functional rules like that. Now if ethnicity could be seen in similar terms, including the questions of who will represent us and what is it we want represented, with something about place and time where the place is articulated, we could re-spatialize and re-historicize the thing.

Dušan Pokorný: I think there is some virtue in distinguishing very sharply between formal rules of technocracy which are efficient given certain criteria, and the normative structure which is characteristic of the ethnic by virtue of the fact that ultimately ethnicity is a matter of the ethic, of the norms which we have accepted, and these norms are not formal. They are substantive. The relationship of the notion of belonging to a nation has always been associated with belonging to a whole which deals with problems of ethics, whereas that is totally missing in the technocratic side. Therefore, just as a tool of making things more precise, one may distinguish sharply between one kind of rule which we may call formal rules, and the other kind which we might term ethical rules.

John O'Neill: There is an extraordinary myth it seems to me, permeating ethnic concerns, that there would be a place in the world, made up of all other places in the world, that would be absolutely transparent to all members the day they stepped off the boat. Now, I have a son who is wealthier than I am as a function of my labours. He lives better than I do, and all his friends are millionaires, but he is terribly anxious about his life in Canada. He is not sure what he will become. He does not understand how the country operates. Yet we have a thing going where someone gets off the boat and wants to know why he is having trouble with the society. Think how long any member has to grow up in a society to be competent with its ways and its problems and its troubles. It seems to me there is an Enlightenment myth pervasive in ethnic studies, that there ought somewhere to be on earth a place where human interaction could be transparent, unproblematic. Even a society that is relatively homogeneous, with classes that are relatively homogeneous, has great trouble understanding itself. We have created the idea that Canada is somehow a kindergarten, in which the minute you enter, it is easy for you to understand how the country works.

Alkis Kontos: You are right, but you have to see the other side. I do not know how many of you have seen the movie by Elia Kazan, *America, America.* It is at Ellis Island that you are transformed, and not because you do not know how it works. You state your name and they change it immediately, because it is not possible for them to deal with the name. Automatically it is the first rape of your identity. You say your name is Roman, they say, "no, you are Roland."

John O'Neill: You ought to have welcomed this removal of your name at Ellis Island, because you were coming into a land that gives its streets names like First Street, Second Street, Fourth Street, Fifth Street. People live at First Line, Second Line, Tenth Line. Now they do that because of the Enlightenment striptease. The idea is that everybody is nobody. The ethnic in some sense wants that and does not want it. We come back to the phenomenological issue of "the life-world wants the techno-world, and it does not want the techno-world." If you want a techno-world, there must be a certain socio-striptease.

Manoly Lupul: It is easy to understand this in terms of the immigrant, but how can you apply it to a third-generation person? How do you apply the word ethnic in terms of identity? You say, they start to "strip" you. Well, can I see myself as having ever been stripped? I have grown up in Canada. I understand the technology and all that, but in terms of ethnic identity, nobody ever did anything to me. I grew up here. Already there are problems. I can see that they did, but what else could it have been? After all, I do live in a territory which is not Ukrainian. It is called Canada. It has some kind of content, therefore supposedly some kind of identity which is more than trees, rocks or moose. What should have happened?

Alkis Kontos: What has happened is that while you could not be in Ukraine here, nowhere here are you ever permitted to be fully Canadian. That is what they did. You are suspended, if not stripped.

Manoly Lupul: That is my point. They say, "enter into it fully, and embrace it."

Alkis Kontos: You cannot enter. It is not open to you. The truth of the matter, which might sound too bitter but it is the truth, is that an ethnic is defined from the non-ethnic self. The ethnic is not terribly competent in common life. In other words, the measure of the ethnic becoming less ethnic is the degree of competence in society. Therefore, if that is the case, there is a bizarre contradiction here that the more I try to cling to what I was, the more obsolete I must appear. This is where the confusion is for the ethnic. I will give you a simple example. In the United States, Belafonte is immensely efficient in the life of America, but he is immensely conscious of being black. There is no contradiction. He can be both, but here in Canada, you really cannot. The leader of the Greek community is some pitiful creature and you do not want him to represent you for anything. That is the point, that is the tension, because that is what they want. The more such leaders appear in national presses, the more secure the establishment is.

Jose Huertas-Jourda: I disagree. We spoke of something related to this topic yesterday, dealing with the question of the good use of surrealism by some black poets of French extraction under the heading of Negritude. To re-discover this deeper layer, this spiritual essence of who they are, they use surrealism instead of the conceits of French prosody. The magnificent result of this is the most fantastic poetry every written by anybody. Sartre has a long essay on this topic called "Black Orpheus." The project of being who one is, independent of place and circumstance, is a perfectly valid one, so that there is nothing oxymoronic about endeavouring to be here and yet be a Catalan, Ukrainian, Ashanti or whatever, on one's own terms. Though it may be perhaps in a limited and not very public sort of way in the sense that I do not expect to see a Place Charles de Gaulle in Toronto any time soon.

John O'Neill: Negritude certainly was not a Canada Council or CBC project. [Laughter] Part of the ethnic problem, as I understand it, is the requirement that government deliver what the government officially says it will not deliver. It is not for that. The history of nation states, any way you look at it, is unified language, unified currency, and unified laws built for the infrastructure of an economy.

Leslie Armour: Surely there is no necessity in those things, is there? Canada was founded on the premise that it was possible to be an anti-nation, because it was not made up of this modern nationalism that we are talking about, which is a product of the seventeenth- and eighteenth-century Enlightenment. Canada has always been a kind of anti-nation.

2. MARGINALITY AND OTHERNESS

Jose Huertas-Jourda

Estrangement and Telos: On the Existential Ground of a Universal Polity

The present essay travels a spiral road in order to bring recent developments in phenomenology to bear on the formation of intersubjective symbolizations. The existential encounter with intrinsic worth occurs after the experience of estrangement, which might be termed the very doorstep of phenomenology. The life-world of intended objects and constituted meanings is the beginning situation of the involved consciousness. From here, a disengagement must be accomplished in order to describe and study this world of meaning. The hunger for intrinsic worth is inherent to consciousness, or inwardness, and sates itself through symbolic representations of intrinsic worth. Thus, intrinsic worth beckons inwardness to its innermost telos. I will begin by tracing the outlines of the phenomenological approach in order to place the problem posed by ethnicity and otherness within the description of a worldly awareness.

Husserlian phenomenology is the stepchild of the nineteenth-century discovery of the world of consciousness or inwardness.[1] Husserl was a student of Franz Brentano who is one of the major figures in the above-mentioned discovery, through both his own work and that of his students.[2] Epoch-making for our purpose was Brentano's definition of psychical phenomena as distinct from, and not simply reducible to, physical phenomena.[3] With it, the world of inwardness or consciousness received its "lettres de marque" as it were, being thus clearly recognized in and for itself in its major feature. It remained for Husserl to show in what way this new source of data could be brought under the sway of rigorous

49

scientific description, and for this he devised the phenomenological method. It would be tempting to engage in a discussion of the epistemological foundations of this method, but it is sufficient to show how he used Brentano's discovery of intentional relatedness as the hallmark of the world of consciousness in order to distinguish further between intentions of signification, their "aim" or "sense" or "intentional objects" on the one side, and acts of fulfillment, or the intentional *encounter* with a perceptual support for the act of signification, in an objective referent for the sense or aim thus signified.[4] Now that those features of the world of consciousness Husserl found most useful while devising his phenomenological method have been recalled, I may proceed with a summary description of those features of the world of consciousness pertaining to the general topic.

First of all, I must note here that the world of consciousness, or inwardness, was named the life-world by Husserl late in his career, especially to mark the intentional or inward dimension which differentiates it from the inert world of mechanical physical processes. This distinction parallels a similar one made independently by Kurt Koffka to differentiate the realm of Gestalt occurrences[5] from the realm of simple stimuli. According to Koffka it is necessary to distinguish between the behavioural environment and the geographical environment.[6] Although this distinction has sometimes been conceived as that between the subjective and the objective worlds, it is preferable to suggest a third characterization, namely, the intentional or interpreted world versus the world of uninterpreted stimuli. In this manner, it is possible to specify the way in which the world of inwardness or life-world transcends, and is not tightly reducible to, the physical world of mechanistic exchanges. In this connection it is necessary to open a parenthesis in order to stress those features of the life-world which have a direct bearing on the topics of telos, estrangement, and ethnicity.

It is necessary to return briefly to the distinction made earlier between act of signification and act of fulfillment, and, this time, to mark the epistemological priority of the act of signification over the act of fulfillment, and especially the independence of the former compared to the latter. The relationship between the two is asymmetrical in that the act of fulfillment depends upon a prior act of signification, which the primal perceptual upsurge, permeating the field of presence,[7] answers as best it can with whatever perceptual support it can provide. The act of fulfillment is therefore the experiential positivist moment in Husserlian epistemology. In it a "sensile *hyle*" provides stimuli which organize themselves (that is, blend, fuse or *verschmelzen*) into figurative aspects or Gestalt quasi-qualities which perceptually support the apperceptive, appresentative symbolic presentation of the signification intended. Thus they provide it with an objective referent. Here, then, at the level of acts of fulfillment, phenomena occur that are peculiar to the life-world alone. These are the figurative aspects, Gestalt qualities, blendings, harmonies, disharmonies, and *Verschmelzungen*. Here it is necessary to bear in mind Husserl's two-tier epistemology and remember that all these unitary phenomena appear as an answer to, but are not caused by, a unitary act of signification. That is, an intention of signification, having for its intentional object a unitary apprehension of some kind of which the Gestalt quality provides perceptual support in a symbolic presentation, announces the objectivity it presents but does not present it "in person." In other words, something is aimed through the symbolic presentation which gives it meaning but which it only represents, albeit adequately. Hence we have to recognize here a mode of appearing transcendent, even to the transcendental level within which life-world appearances take place. Acts of signification may aim directly at this level through life-world appearances. These in turn answer as best they can with an appresentative, apperceptive adumbration of some aspect of the intended aim, with the help of perceptual support figurative aspects can provide. Phenomenological description of what takes place here will perforce have to do justice not only to the operation(s) performed in the act of fulfillment, but also to those performed in the act of signification and to the objective signification intended. This task of description is performed in what Husserl called the *Ruckfrage* or retrospective question which is the hallmark of genetic phenomenology.

To be sure, in order to better study the life-world, one must somehow step out of it or suspend participation in it or put it in parentheses. This Husserl calls the *epoche*, borrowing a term from the elder Stoics and the skeptics. By this they meant a suspension of judgment. However, since the life-world is the world of intended meanings and acts of fulfillment, with the *epoche* what is suspended are the acts of signification. Through the *epoche*, one finds oneself confronted by what William James termed "a buzzing blooming confusion." The field of presence becomes once again the open well from which the flow of "physis" emerges in all its serendipity as primary primal perception (*primare ursprungliche Wahrnehmung*) in a living present. The *epoche* thus immediately results in the most radical estrangement since it suspends all worldhood from the life-world, all intended signification, hence all answering Gestalt fusions including the ones which habitually structure the cohesive whole we call the world of everyday ordinary living. So philosophizing philosophers performing this phenomenological experiment find themselves confronted by an ongoing primary primal perception to which they are passively receptive but toward which they refrain from extending the ideal tentacles of acts of signification. This predicament merits close observation. All ideally possible acts of signification are essentially available to the philosopher, as the essential appanage of a live awareness, by virtue of being a live awareness. Any live awareness as validation of the essential "live awareness" is in principle ideally capable of enacting any act of signification whatever. It is also free to enact any one of them or even to try not to enact any at all. This last statement has clearly gone beyond what is phenomenologically admissible here. As a matter of simple *cogito* the live awareness is not free not to enact any act of signification at all. For, in doing so, it chooses to be a merely passive receptor. Paradoxically, it would actively will itself passive, an essential impossibility similar to Descartes' inability to doubt that he doubted, even under the hypothesis of the evil Genie. Here is the most crucial point in the phenomenological experiment so far, the point which corresponds to what Unamuno would call the confrontation with the Sphinx.[8]

The bracketed world is a temporally marked "hyletic" presence to which a seemingly uninvolved live awareness bears uninterfering witness. Thus one reaches the recognition of what Husserl named "the living present," with its retentive points of lingering data, and its protective inertial opening to the permanence of whatever data are presented. This living present is itself collapsible into a "living now," the "true origin of time," the *ninc stans* recognized by both Husserl and Boethius, which Husserl described as *stehend-stromen* and as the "absolute flow of consciousness" (which is a flow only metaphorically).[9] With this living present comes the true beginning, the true point of entry into the science of consciousness. It is the point from which all constituted meanings eventually originate, the point at which world-awareness and live or aware world are nakedly present each in its indissoluble unity with the other. At this particularly sensitive point it is necessary to proceed especially carefully since whatever is done will ground and overshadow all structurally derived or subsequently constituted formal meanings. Moreover since this is not only the point of entry into the life-world but also the source from which all meaning constituting intentionalities originates, it is desirable to attempt to discern if possible whatever motivation there is toward meaning constitution or life-world constitution on the part of the live awareness as it is encountered here. First, it is necessary to determine that this is truly the naked point. Here Husserl's embarrassed phrasings give warning that if one tries to adjudicate what is the proper province of the *stehend* aspect and that of the *stromen*, one finds that both aspects are mutually referent and mutually exclusive. In the "field of presence" the primal perceptual upsurge either monolithically passes unavoidably and unchangeably into the "stream of lived experiences" which is passively receptive of it, much as the Whiteheadian superject simply registers all change or, on the contrary, is an unchanging Aristotelian subject. Being bears quiet witness to an ever-variegated spontaneous upsurge, the hyletic flow. Further, between stasis and flux a foreground/background discrepancy unavoidably presents itself, try as one might to suspend it. A foreground flux is "haunted" by a "background" stasis, or vice-versa, but in no way can one perceive both on an equal footing of presentness or reality. I call this the Law of Partial Actualization,[10] according to which, of the two ontic aspects under which the real may be lived, only one may be really present in any one living "now," while the other haunts it or hovers behind it in the background/foreground dichotomy previously mentioned. Even labelling those points stasis and flux means lapsing into the use of constituted meanings, whereas the discussion is focussed on the point of emergence of these meanings. A thoroughgoing *epoche* must resist these temptations and note that at this lowermost level of pre-verbal consciousness the live awareness is equally open to both stasis and flux. The aim or telos of this primal intentionality is a harmonious balance between these two aspects. However, the law of partial actualization clearly states that this primal intentional aim is doomed to partial fulfillment, at best. Actually, something far more dramatic than mere partial fulfillment is taking place here. The primal perceptual upsurge announces itself as all there is and the live awareness experiences itself as denied and "de trop" in an essential aspect of its most fundamental hunger. As intimated earlier with the reference to Unamuno and the Sphinx, the choice is not simply a metaphysical one, nor is it primarily gnosticism, far more fundamentally than either one of these options from the genetic point of view is the existential dimension of this choice.

Existentially, the *epoche* rather collapses upon itself. Not only does it issue from the ineluctable necessity of action in the guise of the choice to will oneself passive or in enacting one, or another, of all the possible interpretative acts of signification of which the live awareness is by essence capable, but also it presents the live awareness which has phenomenologized this far with the choice of suppressing itself in front of the primal perceptual upsurge, or of maintaining its own presence despite that upsurge as something other and more meaningful than a mere passive receptor. Here the *epoche* reveals its deeper intentional aim. In putting out of commission all previously enacted acts of signification, it initiates a deeper, more sweeping question about the legitimacy of all enacted acts of signification with respect to their existential comparison to mere passive receptivity. Thus, pursuing the *Ruckfrage* to its deepest existential roots, one finds a demand for legitimacy, for validation. The live awareness perceives itself here as this demand, as this hunger. Looking now towards the aim or telos of this hunger, one finds that it is nothing other than what is in itself self-legitimating, self-validating. It is essentially worthwhile existence or intrinsic worth itself. In other words, through the

53

epoche, the live awareness apperceives itself as agent through which intrinsic worth may be symbolically represented, as well as agent to which intrinsic worth may symbolically be presented, through the primal perceptual upsurge. To summarize, one may say that the live awareness at the moment of the *epoche* knows itself through an existential *cogito*, as the a priori, apperceptive demand for the symbolic appresentative apprehension of intrinsic worth through whatever perceptual support the primal perceptual upsurge and the field of presence may provide—even if this perceptual support is the meditative one of the live awareness itself in its choice of acts of signification. This last brings us to the most important feature related to ethnicity.

Further remarks must be preceded by the observation that the life-world of any live awareness is essentially horizontally open to all alter egos, hence the self-estrangement and the self-categorizing just described are horizontally potentially intersubjective. Thus, an awareness that chooses passivity is intersubjectively apprehensible by any other awareness to whom this choice was essentially equally possible and who may have refused it in the face of the existential relatedness to intrinsic worth described earlier. Each live awareness is in its choices of acts of signification both self-categorizing and open to categorizing by all alter egos in light of the privileged essential relatedness to intrinsic worth which is theirs qua live awareness. Here it is necessary to remember that the *epoche* is also the discovery by each live awareness of its a priori essential freedom of choice with respect to the act of signification with which it intends to represent intrinsic worth (with the possible exception of passivity, since paradoxically choosing passivity is self-refuting in this instance). All that is existentially prescribed here is that the choice exhibit adequately and symbolically a presentation of some aspect of intrinsic worth, aimed at through the choice but in person nonetheless. Now it is possible to turn to a phenomenological treatment of ethnicity.

Through its choices of acts of signification, a live awareness chooses itself as agent through whom intrinsic worth may be apperceptively, appresentatively apprehended, symbolically and by adumbrations. Such an awareness thereby also defines horizontally an open group of alter egos which may, through their own choices, fuse themselves in assimilation (Gestalt fusion) to the first one as exemplary of the whole group and symbolically representative of them all. This process is summarized by popular wisdom in the proverbs "like likes like" and "birds of a feather. . . " This generative process of ethnic typification defines an ethnic grouping as one created when a group of free live awarenesses adopt communally the same concatenation of acts of signification as symbolically representative of intrinsic worth. Two things have to be remembered here. First, the "ratio" of the whole series of grouped alter egos is such that each has a privileged, fundamental, and ontic relatedness to intrinsic worth in total and has inescapable freedom of interpretation. Hence, second, anything short of this relation, any peer coercion whatsoever, will be a severance of the only essential feature under which the group might legitimately be assembled. The practical consequences of this are worth dwelling upon in a form of conclusion to this phenomenological exploration.

First of all, any polity made up of the agents just described, must itself preserve its own relatedness to intrinsic worth, and must ipso facto also preserve the privileged relationship of each of its members to intrinsic worth. The most glaring immediate consequence of this is that the melting pot, or crucible, societal model does not fulfill this requirement. Hence, a polity which understands itself in light of phenomenology will have to view itself as a mosaic of free agents, not as a melting pot. Here, however, lurks kitsch, a danger which must be immediately pointed out, lest we be victimized by it.

One must not mistake the merely signitive or symbolic representation itself for the signitive representation through which intrinsic worth is livingly intended, and may be said to be livingly present (though symbolically so). Empty signitive intention is what is defined as kitsch. Previous symbolic representations are accepted as an acquired capital to be squandered at will, without the existential tension of the confrontation with the sphinx. One may then attempt to teach virtue or beauty, through supposedly sure-fire recipes, having thus forsaken Dionysus for Apollo. This is to use Nietzsche's terminology for his fight against the technologues of kitsch or engineers of virtue by whom he felt his age was stifled. None of these remarks should minimize the importance and the relevance of the context within which the choice of acts of significations must be made. On the contrary, the context preserves its limiting and potentially deforming powers, but these add to the challenge, as it were, and to the unbridgeable gap between alter egos, even those collectively assembled in one polity. Each individual remains alone in its confrontation with intrinsic worth, just as each polity remains thus alone both in spite of, and through, its individuating circumstances. Thus Canada, which has the privilege of being educationally, and to some extent technologically, part of the so-called developed nations, remains nonetheless marginal with respect to them since it cannot compete with them in terms of economic and technological advances. It must thus find its destiny in terms other than those the developed nations have chosen. I venture to suggest that these terms deal with the realization of a polity truly representative of intrinsic worth, one in which all flowers may bloom without fear of the technological kitsch of a cultural revolution or a melting pot. In my opinion, Canada's destiny is to experiment with and elaborate the future polity of the closed world we share, our so-called global village.

Notes

1. From Rousseau's *Reveries* and *Confessions* to Senancour's *Obermann*, the new awareness of the world of emotive response makes itself manifest in the literary world. In philosophy, the 1807 question posed as a competition theme by the Berlin Academy heralds an attempt to confront philosophically the hiatus perceived between stimulus and response by the later Philologues such as Cabanis. Later in the century Kierkegaard's discovery of inwardness and Nietzsche's discovery of *resentiment* both widened the perception of the new field of problems; but the culminating discovery was left to Franz Brentano. See note 3 below.
2. A number of whom were indeed signally connected with the exploration of the world of consciousness. From Carl Stumpf, whose discovery of *Versmeltzung* to his *Tonpsychologie* prefigures that of Gestalt qualities by von Eisenhanz and materially helps Husserl discover *figurale momente*, to Sigmund Freud, by way of von Elsenhanz and Edmund Husserl. See on this my *On the Threshold of Phenomenology: A Study of Edmund Husserl's PHILOSOPHIE DER ARITHMETIK''* (Ann Arbor: University Microfilms, 1970), 1-32.
3. Franz Brentano, *Psychology from the Empirical Standpoint*, Maurice de Gandillac, trans., (Paris: Edition Aubier Montaigne, 1944), 102.
4. Edmund Husserl, *Logical Investigations*, J. N. Findlay, trans. (New York: The Humanities Press, 1970), 725 sqq.
5. This discovery occupies much of Husserl's second posthumous treatise *The Crisis of the European Sciences and Transcendental Phenomenology*, David Carr, trans. (Evanston: Northwestern University Press, 1970), 103 sqq.
6. Kurt Koffka, *Principles of Gestalt Psychology* (New York: Harcourt, Brace, 1935), 704, 709.
7. Here I collapse together many different and longer developments in the phenomenology of internal time-consciousness and in the genetic phenomenology of pre-predicative experience. Compare on this Edmund Husserl, *Erfahrung und Urteil* (Hamburg: Classen Verlag, 1954), 74-7 and *Phenomenology of Internal Time-Consciousness*, James Churchill, trans. (Bloomington: Indiana University Press, 1964), 105 sqq.
8. Miguel de Unamuno, *Selected Works*, vol. 4, *The Tragic Sense of Life*, A. Kerrigan, trans., Bolingen Series LXXXV (Princeton: Princeton University Press, 1972), 48
9. See the references in note 7 above. Also see section 31 of *Phenomenology of Internal Time-Consciousness* and Claus Held, *Lebendige Gegenwart* (The Hague: Martinus Nijhoff, 1966), 115 sqq., 124 sqq.
10. See, for a longer exposition, Jose Huertas-Jourda, "The Genetic Constitution of Reality from the Innermost Layer of the Consciousness of Time," *Cultural Hermeneutics* 1, no. 3 (November 1973): 225-50.

Myrna Kostash

Domination and Exclusion: Notes of a Resident Alien

The concept of otherness—social, political, sexual—is freighted with prejudice. It is broadly assumed that an individual who bears the characteristic of an "other," that is, someone who lives outside the norms of the social, political or sexual standard suffers accordingly. Such a person—a woman in patriarchal culture, a worker in a capitalist political economy, a Ukrainian/Canadian in WASP society—relegated to the margins of power, experiences the anomie of the outsider: inconsequence.

It is true that this condition is deeply wounding, even crippling. We are only now beginning to understand the costs to mental health and social cohesion of our culture's deeply-embedded hostility to women, of the exploitation of labour, of the assimilation procedures of mass culture. However, the history of social movements also reveals to us the capacity of the outsider to fight back against marginality, pain, and inconsequence. To be an alien, then, is not a simple condition.

As a writer who identifies herself as an ethnic, a feminist, and a socialist, I for one experience a whole complex of exclusions, but paradoxically, in these excluded cultures I also find the means to resist the dominant ones. They give me a place to stand, from which to launch salutary barbs, critiques, *and* visions, but there is a price to pay. In trying to reconcile all the elements of my alienation into a critical whole, I discover new marginalities and new exclusions. Such is the dance of the dialectic!

Since ethnicity is the glue to which the other components of my critical otherness adhere, it would be appropriate, before proceeding further, to say something about the way I use that word. Not long ago I had the occasion, at another conference, to make the following assertion about the notion of Canadian identity: "The label is far too reductive," I wrote. "It speaks to a sense of self that claims no Old World antecedents—as though we were all cast from a new mould in a refining process which burned off the impurities of our earlier selves—and promotes a sense of identity to which a dizzying diversity of ethnic and racial components can be melted down into something that looks Anglo-American with a Gallic twist. A 'Canadian,' it seems to me, is a creature of the Ontario-Quebec heartland, an anglophone, a WASP, and latterly a functionary in Quebec, a creature, that is, of the liberal genius which supposes all we 'Canadians' are the same sort of folk, mutually intelligible, from sea to shining sea."

This sort of statement has got me into trouble with some of my friends who would argue that "Anglo" is also an ethnicity, and so it is, in the sense that everybody has one (or several) just as they all have a gender. Ethnicity as I use it is also a conscious identity. One can be born of Ukrainian ancestry, say, but take absolutely no interest in that fact. One can, for instance, identify instead as an Anglo, speaking English exclusively, living in a style indistinguishable from that of the masses of one's North American peers, and holding values squarely conformist with the middle-class Anglo-American ideal. In this sense, Anglo identity is also conscious, is *chosen*, irrespective of one's ethnic origins.

"Anglo" and "ethnic" have become politicized designations in the same way that, thanks to the women's movement, the designation woman has become politicized and represents a world-view critical of and alternative to male-dominated identity. So it is with ethnicity vis-à-vis Waspishness. When I call myself an ethnic I am signalling that I situate myself obliquely in relation to Anglo-American culture and that I am interested in uncovering modes of being which represent values and dreams subversive of the dominant culture. These alternative modes may be linguistic or folkloric or not. They may be emotional or critical. The point is not their ethnocultural purity, that is Ukrainianness, but their capacity to generate opposition to the oppressive and repressive status quo. Because the word ethnic is not culturally specific, it means that it can include the struggles of all kinds of other peoples, or at least the possibility of being in solidarity with them. For me it is a definition suggestive of the dynamism of the process in which all we aliens are engaged in Canada. That process is the construction of an identity generated right here, in our hometowns, from the lives and memories of people from the wrong side of the tracks.

I am, however, aware that the identifier ethnic has been emptied of its specific Ukrainian content and that an ethnicity, in this less than perfect world, still refers to one or another origin, not all at once. So I use it as a hopeful word, a word referring to a process of mutation and synthesis and accretion, a word on the road to "Canadian." In the meantime, it might be more reflective of the nature of the experience I have of living in Canada to call myself a Ukrainian/Canadian. It acknowledges explicitly the sense of duality inherent in the being of anyone who is conscious of her origins in a people who had a history and a definition prior even to the drama of emigration. The compounded tag does not represent, as some fear, a diluted Canadian but rather a doubly-endowed one, a person who is rooted in two historical narratives. This is exciting stuff but still has its limitations. The graphic egalitarianism of the compounded term Ukrainian/Canadian belies the fact that in Canada Ukrainians are a minority, are in many respects disadvantaged, and are increasingly served up, thanks to the ethos of multiculturalism, as mere colourful relief to the main business of society, which is Canadian. It also fails to reflect the complexity of ethnic derivation as we move beyond the second and third generation. What are we going to call all those people whose mothers are Ukrainian-German-Polish and whose fathers are Anglo-Franco-Celtic? More to the point, what are they going to call themselves? What about the tendency (my hope at least) for all these discontinuous units of identity to fuse one day into a brand-new historical and cultural creature known as a Canadian?

If this sounds exploratory, there is a reason. I have only recently been politicized as an ethnic. As a student in the sixties, I was politicized by the New Left. As a woman in the seventies I was politicized by the women's liberation movement. But it has taken me until the eighties to understand that ethnicity too can be a liberating, vivifying politics. It took this long because, except for moments in the development of multiculturalism as federal policy, there has been no ethnic movement as such that has taken to the streets to contest the homogenization of popular culture and to demand a revolutionary program of heterogeneity. What are its slogans? Where are its headquarters? People have tended to view their ethnicity, when they are conscious of it, as a private and domestic affair, best expressed in time-honoured custom and evocative ritual among relatives and close friends. That is, they have viewed their ethnicity and its components, language in particular, as belonging to their intimate life. The English language and Anglo manners and mores have been ascribed to the public realm out there where the majority lives.

This was how my grandparents and even my parents lived and this is how I lived as a girl. I went to language classes in the church basement and to the church-based youth group. I learned to dance and to sing, to paint eggs after a fashion, and to make cabbage rolls. I even had a Ukrainian boyfriend for a while. What I did not do was learn to speak Ukrainian. There was no percentage in it and so I learned to speak French instead. I was vaguely embarrassed by all this Slavic foreignness in my life and so, when I left high school for university, I dropped it all and never thought about it for the following twelve years. Instead, rather perversely, I studied Russian for five years.

In 1964 and 1965, as an undergraduate, I was thoroughly taken up by what was happening among my peers over the whole continent—the civil rights movement, the anti-war movement, rock and roll, drugs, and sex. This was where the action was. This was public culture and here I was among my own people.

The people among whom I had grown up, the non-Communist Ukrainian/Canadians of Edmonton, had nothing to say about this, absorbed as they were by those private and intimate affairs of the self-reliant, increasingly petit bourgeois ethnic group. This involved getting ahead without betraying too much the ancestors whose shades hovered wherever their progeny still gathered communally. When they did notice what was going on in the streets beyond their neighbourhoods, they were more or less hostile. Wave a literal red flag in front of them and they respond like the proverbial bull. They were stalwarts of anti-Communist sentiment and, not unrelatedly, of deeply-felt but ambivalent ethnic pride and solidarity with the oppressed nation of Ukraine. As they saw it, Bolshevism was inimical to Ukrainian national independence and so Reds, even Ukrainian/Canadian Reds, were the enemies of the Ukrainian people. One could not be on both sides at once. One could not be for revolutionary socialism and for the liberation of Ukraine. The one betrayed the other. History had spoken thus.

Was it any wonder then that when I became interested precisely in the ideas of rebels and revolutionaries (Che Guevara, Martin Luther King, Jean-Luc Godard), I concluded that I could not identify with them and be a Ukrainian/Canadian at the same time? As my elders put it: Which side are you on? There was no contest. I would choose the liberating and challenging and visionary New Left and leave behind the Ukrainian/Canadian self who could see nothing ahead of her, in that identity, that was not compromised and parochial.

So I lived for years, until I wrote a book about Ukrainian/Canadians, discharging all my anger about what had happened to them and to me as their daughter. Then I was taken up by Ukrainian/Canadians from coast to coast as one of them. I might have thought I was no longer a Ukrainian/Canadian but the people who read my book certainly thought I was. While some thought I was a bad one and some thought I was a good one, they all called me one. For my part, knowing what I knew at that point about the catastrophes that had befallen them—their immigration into hardship and poverty, the destruction of their organized protest, the suspicion and hostility and prejudice they had fallen under, their shaping into self-loathing and diffident "bohunks"—I could not, as a writer on the left, deny it. If to be a Ukrainian/Canadian is to be conscious of my relatives' origins, to speak up against the honeyed deception of New World success, and to imagine an uninhibited ethnic creativity and activity in a post-Anglo world, then I am a Ukrainian/Canadian. In a word, my ethnicity became essential to an elaboration of my New Left politics. To repudiate that ethnicity, that Ukrainianness even, was to cheapen and enervate those politics.

How did I come to understand this? How did the New Left, that consummately public politics, come to intersect with ethnicity, that private practice, to produce a highly-charged consciousness of resistance? It began with the lessons of movement politics and actions in the sixties. Let me recapitulate them. We learned that collaboration among the state, the military, the corporations, the multiversity, and the business-as-usual unions makes it all but impossible for people to have control over their lives. In examining the record of the Old Left (the Communist Party and social democratic parties), we learned that they were incapable of taking up the challenge of social change because they were too compromised by reformism, bureaucracy, centralization, ethnocentricity, and sexism to be able to fashion a society in which we would want to live.

From our own experiences in movement activities, we learned that there were alternatives to authoritarian and hierarchical organization, namely a process called "participatory democracy." While organizing in the communities of the poor we learned three very important things. First, direct action—direct confrontation of bureaucrat, landlord, and employer—was effective. Second, the social minority group—the coloured, the ethnic, the unemployed—provided a ready-made protest group. Third, and most important, it is all right to fight in your own interests. In our co-ops and communes, in our festivals and be-ins, in our ad hoc committees and editorial collectives, we learned there is not much point in talking about the construction of a new society without including within it the construction of a new culture. Unless our politics integrates the issues of family life, sexuality, health, ecology, education, art, and ethics, we will just reproduce the same old insecurities and alienations.

You can begin to see what the consequences of this learning were for young ethnics. It gave us the tools to analyze the structures of our community. We understood that our second-class citizenship as ethnics or immigrants has an economic base, as the hewers of wood and drawers of water for the Anglo-Celtic elite. Because we had experimented with radical democracy in the movement, we chafed at the undemocratic procedures of the established ethnic organizations. Because we had some understanding of how the education we had received mythologized the calamity, the deprivation, even the heroism of so many North American lives, we began to see how our own community propagates its own self-serving mythologies. For example, one is that ours is a saga of stoical and tractable peasants and workers who slowly but surely reaped the rewards of private enterprise through patience and diligence. Thanks to the explosive ideas of the women's liberation movement, we learned to train a feminist eye on the Ukrainian community, to strip away the sentimentality surrounding the figures of baba and the good Ukrainian woman and to inquire at what cost in female personality the community has renewed itself.

In the second place, the values of the counterculture in the sixties and seventies validated certain so-called ethnic values. Suddenly it was all right, even necessary, to be spontaneous in one's behaviour and gestures, to be open emotionally, even extravagant, to live in extended families of friends, to express oneself in music and dance, to hug and kiss each other. All these were things we ethnics had been doing all along in the privacy of our ghettoes. (As an aside here, when my first book was reviewed in the press, reviewers frequently referred to its earthiness and foreign exuberance. That is something to think about. Is it possible to write English like a Ukrainian?)

In the third place, because we had been touched by or were active in the New Left, we saw that we were new creatures, progeny neither of the Ukrainian right wing nor of the Ukrainian Old Left. Paradoxically, what this amounted to was both the de-ghettoization and the re-nationalization of our politics. On the one hand, we felt a solidarity with all peoples who are waging a popular struggle to find out the truth about themselves and to repel their enemies. On the other hand, we repudiated the phoney internationalism of the Communist Party which obscured the abuses of Russian chauvinism. We insisted on Ukrainian specificity. To paraphrase Emma Goldman: "If we can't be Ukrainians, we don't want your revolution."

This was heady stuff but I soon became aware that my excitement about the liberating potential of a conscious ethnic self acting in concert with other aliens, especially with feminists and socialists, was not shared by them. I always used to wonder, looking about me at the various events and meetings in the sixties, where were the Ukrainian/Canadians I had grown up with in Edmonton? At the time I explained their absence in terms of their upwardly-mobile identification with the program of right-wing America. I still think that is partly true but I now also understand that, for those to whom the Ukrainian Question had become a burning issue (that is, who understood Ukraine to be an oppressed nation and who accepted the need for Ukrainian/Canadians to keep the vision of a liberated—socialist or not—Ukraine alive), the New Left had nothing to say.

Of course, the New Left had a lot to say about very many things. My point here is that, in my memory, I never once heard the Ukrainian issue raised among New Leftists. I heard a lot about the Prague Spring, and something of the student riots in Warsaw and Belgrade, and about the Praxis Group in Dubrovnik and Marcuse's visits there. All of it was mentioned with a great deal of sympathy as being representative of the ideas of protesting youth everywhere—ideals of grassroots democracy, decentralization of authority, empowerment of the people. That there was a sixties generation in Ukraine (a little older, but dissident for all that), that there had existed for hundreds of years the dream of "national liberation" (from Pole, Lithuanian, Russian, Romanian, and Austrian overlord), that Soviet hegemony was maintained by means of the deployment of the Red Army and Russification, that there was a tradition, completely suppressed, of indigenous socialism was either unknown or of no interest to the New Left in Canada. As for these same leftists in the eighties, there seems to be an assumption that to be an anti-Soviet Ukrainian patriot is to be an hysterical right-wing creep, in the manner of Igor Gouzenko. To be an anti-Soviet Polish patriot, however, in the manner of Solidarity, is to be somehow sexy and heroic.

There are many reasons for this kind of unsympathetic thinking. One is the bitter quarrel of the New Left with Reaganism and its version of the Cold War. The need to counter the propaganda and sallies of the recrudescent Right is felt to be so urgent and so demanding that niceties of analysis, like the nature of the nationalities policy of the Soviet Union, are foregone. Who has the time to sort out the various strands of Ukrainian nationalism when our very neighbourhoods are being ransacked by the cowboys from Supply Side? That is fair enough, but under this rationale I sense a more disturbing tendency. In the showdown with Reaganism, nothing that could give comfort to the enemy will be deployed. If that means refusing to challenge the superpower politics of the Soviet Union, and turning a blind eye to the death of a dissident generation of Ukrainians in the gulag, and trivializing the nationalist aspirations of Ukrainian/Canadians as crank, then it will be done. The aspirations of the Ukrainians are as nothing compared to the travails of the North American Left.

As for that other moment of radicalism in my generation, the women's movement, an analogous process took place. I, and others with me, began with seemingly untenable notions. Either we repudiated the Ukrainian/Canadian community in order to live and breathe apart as independent women, captains of our own self-directed ambitions, or we embraced our ethnicity, smothering them in that embrace. Many, many of us left the community to become feminists and wondered, in the flush of our new analysis, if we could ever be ethnic again. Some felt not. Others, like

63

me, have been able freely to reforge our attachment to the ethnic community because, secure in our feminist politics, we need not fear that we will be repatriated into the stereotype of the "good little Ukrainian woman" who serves family, church, and ancestors without complaint or question. Thanks to the women's movement, I can now declare myself a Ukrainian/Canadian woman on my own terms, not the least of which is to demand the recovery of the history of Ukrainian feminism. This is a demand I would not have even been able to imagine, let alone formulate, without the women's movement. However, having found a way to be a feminist among Ukrainian/Canadians, I now ask myself, given the apathy at best, suspicion at worst, of non-ethnic feminists to the ethnic fact in their midst, is there a place for me as a Ukrainian/Canadian among feminists? For someone who has felt safe declaring her ethnicity only because she was already at home among feminists, this is a painful question.

I broke with my ethnic community in late adolescence. For the child, there were no negative consequences attached to her gender in that community. For the young woman, however, there certainly were, and I could see them coming.

The ideal of Ukrainianness meant preserving the culture which is transmitted by institutions. These institutions are the church, the language school, and the family. The Ukrainian family meant an authoritarian father, obliging mother, and respectful children. I intuitively understood that at the heart of this ideal, of the concerned attempt to preserve identity and resist assimilation, of the revivalism that is ethnic pride, lay the oppression of women. To serve my people in their struggle for cultural specificity, I would have to live as a traditional Ukrainian woman. That woman goes directly from her father's house to her husband's, devotes her time to the rearing of Ukrainian children and the keeping of a Ukrainian home (for this it helps if she is constantly in attendance), provides her husband with an oasis of serenity, deference and loyalty, and goes to church where she is reconfirmed in her chaste, selfless, and complacent Ukrainian identity. I turned and ran.

Yet I have rejoined. I found my way back. Just as the Left's recovery of the history of ordinary people's lives and the celebration of their survival (material and psychic) against great odds had shown me how I could re-identify with Ukrainian/Canadians, so did the propagation of "herstory" among feminists teach me that even among Ukrainians and Ukrainian/Canadians there had been forbears of feminism. There had been women of remarkable talent and courage and masses of anonymous women who toiled so their granddaughters could read books. The feminist re-creation of pre-patriarchal myth and ritual aroused in me a sympathy for the folkways of Ukrainian peasant women, which had been long repressed in us as shame of the primitive. The feminist validation of the intimate and confessional and sentimental in personal relations reminded us that we had lived like that before, as girls in an ethnic family and community. To declare oneself a born-again ethnic, then, was not to rebind the foot, to rewind the chador. It was to intervene in the community with all the brazenness of women who know they have, to back them up, the moral authority of millions of other feminists.

However, having declared myself, I am then forced to ask: How interested is the women's movement in us, the Ukrainian/Canadians? We ethnic feminists have been doing our duty for years—going on the IWD marches, financing pro-choice campaigns, writing for feminist publications, volunteering at the bookstores—but, when it comes to that other question, the Ukrainian Question, where is everybody else? To cite one example, we put on a conference celebrating one hundred years of Ukrainian feminism and, except for those expressly invited to give a paper or chair a panel, no non-Ukrainian feminists attended.

There is a perception, I believe, among non-ethnic feminists, that our ethnic or minority or nationalist politics are not fruitful for feminist politics. What, for example, are the consequences for a political practice which eschews working with men to be confronted by ethnic feminists who, to pursue their program, must and often want to work with men? Because many ethnic feminists leave the feminist group at the point when they raise ethnic issues—for example, the crisis in the Soviet dissident movement, or the campaign for bilingual schools or the record of Ukrainian "war criminals"—ethnic consciousness is seen as divisive of feminist consciousness. Yet women leave at this point precisely because the feminist milieu is seen as hostile or, at best, indifferent to these issues. Some of the reasons for this are the overwhelmingly Anglo-American content of contemporary Canadian feminism, residual resentment of uppity minorities, and suspicion by leftists and liberals that Ukrainian nationalism is crypto-fascist. Consequently many Ukrainian/Canadian feminists join forces with their men and male colleagues when it comes down to the Ukrainian Question.

For the ethnic feminist as well there are resentments and suspicions and ambivalences. When feminist theory resuscitates the notion of matriarchy, an ethnic feminist can be forgiven for wondering if this is the same matriarchy that male leaders are so fond of evoking when they talk about the power of the ethnic wife and mother. As for herstory, is not the notion that history can be read from the point of view of anonymous women's lives likely to distort our view of Ukrainian and Ukrainian/Canadian history? History, of course, is a male-oriented distortion, but we are not much further ahead when ethnic and nationalist political activity is dismissed as male or when Stalinism is analyzed as a crisis in male politics. Can Ukrainian/Canadian feminists find out all we need to know from such herstory? Finally, because herstory tends to conflate all the texts of female history into a primary text of gender oppression, it obscures the class question in our feminist historical narratives. This makes it all the more difficult for an ethnic feminist to see that our history is not just a history of men and women but also of farmers and workers and housewives, all sharing exclusion from Anglo-American privilege.

I said near the beginning that I feel I am a doubly-endowed Canadian, one who is rooted in two historical narratives. By this, of course, I mean that I come from a European people who, not very long ago, uprooted themselves and resettled in western Canada, here to begin a story that runs alongside that of the family left behind. The Canadian story is fresh and inventive. It has never been told before and its tellers are a new kind of person, bred in Canada from far-flung antecedents. It is something to anticipate, this ethnicity which is neither the melancholia of the ghetto memoirists nor the unthinking assimilation of the denatured suburbanites.

Some of the options are minority group strategies, anti-imperialist strategies, alternative life-styles, feminist culture, and regionalism. This last option exists because Ukrainian/Canadian identity cannot be separated from the whole drama of the colonization of the prairie. In this way a new kind of ethnic consciousness may be taking shape, a consciousness which takes account of the moments in our history on this continent when we were militant, for in those moments we demonstrated our fierce appetite for control of our lives. The new consciousness likewise goes on the offensive. Here is the outside agitator with a vengeance. Our ethnicity in itself is a proposal of options to wasteful, mechanical, and alienating mainstream culture. I am thinking of our familial and tribal interdependence, our sense of responsibility for each other, our graceful ritual, and our sense of being home with each other. This new consciousness does not stop with multiculturalism, which accepts the social hierarchy, nor with conservation. It proposes a struggle for a social existence based on humanizing relations. Those of us engaged in the development of this new consciousness may have begun with our particular ethnoculture, with ancestral memory, with historical grievances but we end in the action of the dissident alien *in this place*.[1]

Note

1. An earlier version of this paper was delivered at the "Second Wreath" Conference at the University of Alberta in October, 1985.

Patricia J. Mills

A Return to Reconciliation?

In "Estrangement and Telos" Jose Huertas-Jourda analyzes "otherness" in philosophical terms whereas Myrna Kostash, in "Domination and Exclusion: Notes of a Resident Alien," analyzes otherness in social, political, and sexual terms. Huertas-Jourda speaks of the necessity to rethink the philosophical problem of the relation between estrangement and telos without any reference to the problem of power which is the underpinning for the exclusion of those defined as Other. Kostash speaks of power relations without reference to the philosophical foundation of the problem of otherness. Given these two analyses it is important to think them together in an effort to understand, and perhaps reconstruct, the relation between theory and practice.

Kostash points to the capacity of the outsider, the Other, to "fight back against the experiences of marginality, pain, and inconsequence," but this fight requires that those who suffer the condition of exclusion be able to name their experience. In the 1960s Betty Friedan wrote *The Feminine Mystique* in which she described the domination of woman as the "problem with no name." Thus, the first task of the women's liberation movement was to describe and name the experience of male domination. What emerges here is the question of who names the experience. Is the experience to be named by those who suffer the exclusion and domination or by those who exclude and dominate? I see this symposium as an attempt to have those on the outside speak and name their exclusion.

Huertas-Jourda attempts to name the experience of otherness as primordially an experience of the relation between stasis and flux—a dualism that is resolved in the telos of reconciliation through a "Gestalt law of fusion." There are several questions that emerge when we try to think the two papers together. The first is the question of whether an ontological dualism of stasis and flux can address the multiplicity of otherness referred to and described by Kostash. The second and more important question that is raised is the question of the relation between particular and universal. For Huertas-Jourda all groups are particulars and are defined in such a way that their actual symbolization as a group is *contingent*. Any given group has no necessary link to the symbolization of the good, the symbolization of the universal. The instance that defines the group, whether an instance of race, sex, ethnicity, religion or class, is seen as inadequate in terms of the telos of symbolic presentation of intrinsic worth.

Beginning from the ground of stasis and flux, Huertas-Jourda claims that we can live only one aspect of the real and that we perceive the other in a background/foreground relation. That is, we can live either stasis or flux, and consciousness is the proto-symbolization (the basic, pre-conscious symbolization) which attempts to reclaim the missing aspect of the real. The fact that I can live only one aspect of the real leads to a primal absence of the Other. This primal absence, according to Huertas-Jourda, is the origin of my experience of death in life and the origin of my sense of exclusion or estrangement.

When the reclamation of the missing aspect of the real is successfully realized through the process of proto-symbolization, then I feel "at home" rather than excluded. Thus, the sense of at home or exclusion is based on the adequacy of the symbolization of the missing aspect, not on a necessary connection to the universal. No group is *necessarily* an instance of universal freedom, of the telos of the symbolic presentation of the good. For Huertas-Jourda the telos of the symbolic presentation of intrinsic worth (of freedom, of the good) occurs only at the epistemological/philosophic level, not the socio-political one.

Now, I read this as a critique of the early Marx's understanding of the working class as the class with radical chains, "a class which has a universal character because its sufferings are universal," a class which "can only redeem itself by a total redemption of humanity."[1] In a similar vein, it is a critique of that part of the women's liberation movement which thought that the liberation of women would lead to the liberation of all humanity. (Marcuse's analysis of the "feminine principle," as the definite negation of the male performance principle, came out of such an understanding.) Given my own perspective, which is rooted in the analysis of social and self-domination done by Horkheimer and Adorno, I am sympathetic to the critique of the necessary connection between any particular group and universal freedom. However, since not all particularities are the same, there is a philosophical-political question that emerges. If at any given historical moment a given group *might* symbolize the good, might symbolize universal freedom, how would we know it?

For Huertas-Jourda the relation between particular and universal seems to be one of mutual exclusion. Therefore, if I embrace and claim my particularity I have no connection to the universal since the instance that defines the group is contingent. My connection to the universal can occur only at the level of my consciousness of the relation between stasis and flux. This relation between stasis and flux might be a useful analytic concept for understanding the relation between immigration and ethnicity. Immigration may create a state of flux, a state of uprootedness, in which the experiences and memories of the homeland prevent one from ever being truly at home in the world. The attempt to come to terms with this situation may lead to a focus on ethnic identity. However, ethnicity can become a static and reified cultural form. Here it is important to consider the difference between the Canadian mosaic, in which ethnic plurality is idealized, and the American melting pot, in which ethnic identity is meant to be subsumed within an *American* identity.

The primary concern in Huertas-Jourda's work is with the concept of the universal once the particular has been consigned to its place as merely contingent. For Adorno, who is also critical of any necessary relation between a given group and universal claims to freedom, the project is to rescue the particular from domination by the universal.[2] Kostash, as I read her, is claiming a third relation between particular and universal. For her, it is only *through* the particular that we can get to the universal. Through the particulars of our otherness we may reach an understanding and realization of the good. If we annihilate or dismiss the particular as merely contingent, then we may never reach the goal of freedom.

Given these very different perspectives on the relation between particular and universal, the question we must ask, I think, is whether the facts of my contingency, my particularity, necessarily preclude a relation to the universal. Or perhaps the question is really whether contingency is the same as particularity. Does contingency mean mere immediacy and therefore if, as Kostash describes it, I intentionally embrace one or more aspects of my otherness (my ethnicity, my sex, my sexuality, my race, my class, my religion) have I not gone beyond mere contingency? For Kostash otherness as estrangement is crippling, but it is also an intentional act of resistance, a critique, a vision. When viewed this way, the forms of otherness are shown to be somewhat different. Ethnicity, class, and religion can be ignored or overcome in a way that race and sex can-

69

not.[3] In any case, the most significant questions that emerge here are whether particularity can be rescued through a moment of intentional reclaiming and whether this intentional reclaiming of my particularity gives me access to the universal.

The relation between particular and universal raises other theoretical and socio-political questions which need thinking through. The universalization of capitalism as a socio-political-economic system entails both direct and abstract domination. The direct form of domination as revealed in the Marxist analysis of the master-slave relation gives way to the abstract form of domination in which labour power as a commodity is exchanged in the market. Capitalism initiates a universalization of society through the equalization of abstract labour. However, it does not, therefore, eliminate all forms of direct domination. In a capitalist-patriarchal society women are beaten, raped, and sexually abused by men. And the abstract forms of patriarchal domination mean that even if a woman is not beaten or sexually abused by her father/lover/son/brother the threat of male violence still hangs over her and she is structurally disadvantaged by a system of domination in which she is defined as different, as Other, and less than man. The domination of ethnic and racial groups also takes both direct and abstract forms. Given this, I look with some suspicion on the ontological and epistemological claims which focus on a universality in terms of the concept of freedom but, in fact, have never yet meant *my* particular freedom. The structural forms of personal and abstract domination are embedded in philosophic discourse. To assert oneself, to speak, to name an experience, has been a male privilege, a privilege with class, race, and ethnic components. I would argue that it has been contingently rather than necessarily so, but any theory of liberation must focus on this contingency rather than consigning contingency to insignificance.

Kostash again raises the question of the relation between particular and universal when she describes the problem of how to relate her Ukrainian/Canadian otherness to her feminism. The women's liberation movement began as a call to all women ("Sisterhood is Powerful"). It began with a critique of woman seen in universal terms as the Other, as different from man, and as the ontological principle of difference itself, to be dominated and excluded. De Beauvoir articulates this most brilliantly in *The Second Sex* where she details the ways in which woman has been feared, idealized, and negated as the Other. Thus, the analysis of woman as Other became the starting point for an understanding of what all women shared, the starting point for a universal understanding of the experience of male domination and for a politics based on shared oppression and domination. However, this framework does not account for the present situation in which women are exploring differences among ourselves.[4] It

70

is not only, as Kostash observes, that an ethnic identity means that one is working with men which causes friction between one's feminism and one's ethnic identity. More importantly, there is a process of political disintegration involved in the shift from the shared politics of sisterhood to the present allegiances within the women's movement which produces ever smaller and more exclusive groups. From thinking and acting on the belief that all women are sisters, women have regrouped into specific forms of separatism based on race, sexual preference, religion, and ethnic identity. This multiplicity of otherness challenges the solidarity that once made the women's movement powerful, even as it discloses the importance of understanding the non-identity of women.

The problem of solidarity based on exclusion emerges here. Kostash describes her experience in the New Left as a discovery of "her people." I think that all of us who were in the streets together in the sixties and seventies felt as if we had finally found our people, as if we had arrived home in the world. It was not long, however, before we were confronted with the internal problem of difference as well as the external problems of co-optation and infiltration. Is it that a group identity based on domination and exclusion is not enough? What is the character of the solidarity that I share with others who struggle against domination?

Along with many other feminists I continue to believe that sisterhood is powerful and that the Ukrainian/Canadian woman, the working-class woman, the black woman, and the Jewish woman are my sisters. Now, this claim may be a mistaken claim to name a universal experience, but it is also, and more importantly, a declaration of solidarity. In the same way that the statement "I will" or "I promise" entails certain actions on my part, so does the assertion of sisterhood. Through these actions I lay claim to the bond I am asserting. If my actions are not in line with the assertion then the assertion is an empty ideological abstraction. Thus, the claims of solidarity I make with other women are to be verified by my political practice. However, my affirmation of sisterhood, my declaration of solidarity with other women, is in fact different from my declaration of solidarity with other dominated groups such as the blacks in South Africa or the people of Nicaragua. My assertion of sisterhood does assume a common social position which the other declarations of solidarity do not. It does assume all women experience male domination in either or both its direct and abstract forms.[5]

Interestingly, both Huertas-Jourda and Kostash refer to the concept of fusion as some sort of solution to the problem of otherness. Huertas-Jourda claims that the "Gestalt law of fusion" reconciles stasis and flux. Kostash says that the goal she hopes for is one in which "all the discontinuous units of identity [will] fuse one day into a brand-new historical

71

and cultural creature known as a Canadian." For her, the motive for such fusion (and the motive for social change in general) is the disruptive aspect of ethnicity. She writes:

> Our ethnicity in itself is a proposal of options to wasteful, mechanical, and alienating mainstream culture. I am thinking of our familial and tribal interdependence, our sense of responsibility for each other, our graceful ritual, and our sense of being home with each other. This new consciousness... proposes a struggle for a social existence based on humanizing relations.

Here, the elements of the private world, the realm of the family, and the pre-capitalist world, the tribal world, are asserted to challenge the larger, public world, the world of the patriarchal-capitalist, military-industrial complex. The private realm, however, is often a realm of pain and domination for women, a world of direct patriarchal power. Kostash herself had to take a "leave of absence" from the Ukrainian/Canadian community in order to find herself and it was the power of the women's liberation movement that allowed her to do this. Is it possible to return now to reclaim *only* the virtues of the private-tribal world in an effort to create a political challenge to the public world?

While Huertas-Jourda and Kostash both see fusion as the goal, it seems to me that the socio-political problem of the multiplicity of otherness described so eloquently by Kostash is not well served by a philosophy of reconciliation in which freedom at the epistemological/ontological level has its counterpart in the socio-political realm in a return to humanism (Kostash) or the existentialism of individual choice (the only politics I can see emerging from Huertas-Jourda's analysis). The sixties generation moved beyond the preceding generation, beyond vanguardism, in its political practice. Now we have to assess and move beyond the philosophical concept of reconciliation in light of our political struggles. Theoretical reconciliation has too often masked and/or been the ground for social domination for it to seem like a new promise of freedom. The consideration of otherness presented by Huertas-Jourda and Kostash points most urgently to the post-modern project as the reassessment of the concept of reconciliation.

Notes

1. Karl Marx, *Karl Marx: Early Writings*, T. B. Bottomore, trans. and ed. (New York: McGraw Hill, 1963), 58.
2. Theodor W. Adorno, *Negative Dialectics*, E. B. Ashton, trans. (New York: Seabury Press 1973), 8. Adorno writes: "...the matters of true philosophical interest at this point in history are those in which Hegel... expressed his disinterest. They are the nonconceptual, the individual, the particular... What Hegel called 'lazy Existenz'."
3. Even the male-identified woman remains identifiably female as the white-identified black remains identifiably black.
4. Judith Butler, Response to "Women: The One and the Many" by Elizabeth Spelman at the American Philosophical Association, 29 December 1985 in Washington, D.C. Butler summarizes de Beauvoir's analysis and claims that the hostility to separatism, the fear of factionalism, within the women's movement is fundamentally an ontological "dread of the differentiated." She distinguishes her analysis of this dread from de Beauvoir's analysis of the "dread of the Other" by arguing that de Beauvoir confines her analysis to a form of binary opposition.
5. Sandra Bartky, Response to "Women: The One and the Many" by Elizabeth Spelman at the American Philosophical Association, 29 December 1985 in Washington, D.C. Bartky articulates most clearly and cogently the concept of sisterhood as a promise of action and distinguishes the solidarity of women from solidarity with other dominated groups.

Discussion

Figures of Ethnicity

Ian Angus: There is something very central that underlies this set of questions. It has been called a number of different things in our discussions. Kostash began by talking about defining ethnic identity as *conscious* identity. What Huertas-Jourda was after with the term protosymbols was explicitly not a self-aware symbolization of belonging. What seems to reside in here is the whole problem of articulation—who speaks, in what situation one speaks, and what is involved in the assertion. Mills called it the promise, the assertion of "I will." This brings us back to another question that has been haunting us, which is the problem of time. How do you achieve historical continuity? As Onufrijchuk says, it is a project, which means it is an "I will." It is not just there, but is a problem of articulation.

Alkis Kontos: Mills' synthesis is a miracle. There is one particular point with which I personally agree very strongly in the way she presented the papers. Huertas-Jourda gives a precondition of whatever is to happen, whereas Kostash's universe emerges, but Huertas-Jourda's description is de-politicized and therefore a problem. Kostash's comes subsequently and is intensely political as it should be, but there is one thing in Mills' synthesis that I do not think you can get from Kostash's paper. I do not think it is a leave of absence. Rather, it is a continuous integration of her identity. By calling it a leave of absence you alter the coherence of her analysis.

Ian Angus: I understood Kostash to be saying these were different discourses and indeed the problem was that she moved from one discourse that is essentially a New Left discourse, and into another one, which is a feminist discourse. She is saying that in fact it does not seem to be possible to integrate them or put them together, except perhaps in a serial fashion or in a narrative after the fact.

Alkis Kontos: The climax of the paper is the way it ends with a synthesis. In other words, she says, "I always thought that if I am a feminist, I cannot be an ethnic Ukrainian female. Now it is, I can be both." It is that that is the power of the paper.

Roman Onufrijchuk: It seems to me that that integration is what I was trying to get at with the idea of the project. That integration of the project is localized and embodied in Myrna Kostash. That is the origin of that discourse and that is where it is being fought out internally.

Myrna Kostash: I am concerned with the notions of integration, synthesis, and reconciliation. Mills' critique of the ideal of reconciliation I take very much to heart because I think any notion of integration, given an unintegratable universe, becomes a reconciliation of irreconciliables.

Dušan Pokorný: Mills asks whether identity based on exclusion or sisterhood is likely to be a permanent one, or whether it is incomplete. Is this a question of exclusion, or rather a question of an unmediated universality? One can in certain extreme situations identify oneself directly with the universal, for example in the case of a revolution. Sometimes, some people may identify themselves with the cause as such, but that identification cannot last. It is not permanent. It cannot be permanent without some intervening particularity, because once the battle is over I return home. There is my sister or my mother. There I belong to a community. Therefore, rather than the problem being exclusion or universality which excludes, is it not the attempt to bypass particularities and jump right into universal which causes the problem? Ultimately what we have in the Soviet Union is precisely that sort of thing. One deems that the momentary identity of the individual with the universal can last forever, but it cannot. The result is that you suppress all the particularities in order to get to these unmediated universalities.

Patricia Mills: I think there is a difference between the kind of revolution you are talking about and the situation between men and women. The momentary overthrow would be nice, but I do not think that is what we are talking about. I think that is a difference and I do not know that you can use one to metaphorically describe the other.

I was asking the question of universality as a question. Is the identification from exclusion part of the problem? It is not that I was offering an answer, but certainly the beginning stages in which de Beauvoir and people in the movement were saying, "we all share this as women," was an important place to begin, because without that we had not had a name for the experience. We were all walking around thinking that we had particular and individual problems, and yet, in fact, as a group we did share something. The problem came into existence once we identified that we also had problems that we did not share. Then we began splitting first by gender, then by race, then by ethnic groups and religion. The hyphenated feminism can go from socialist-feminist-lesbian-black-vegetarian-Jewish. It goes on and on as the groups become smaller and smaller, and the initial solidarity which was important for millions of women all over the world now is an anguish for people who do not live it. I teach women's studies and women say to me, "I feel all this and I have nowhere to go."

Jose Huertas-Jourda: With respect to Mills' comments on fusion, I do not view it necessarily as a reconciliation. It is simply a Gestalt law of perception at this level of awareness. This is how the particularities transform into the general rather than the universal.

The other point I want to make is that it is *through* the contingent that one aims at intrinsic worth. The contingent is only perceptual support for the apprehension of intrinsic worth. It would seem to me that Kostash describes her present as feminist, as Ukrainian, as Canadian, each time in the light of intrinsic worth. I have to respect her as manifesting intrinsic worth through these different contingencies, but it is at that infinite point of intrinsic worth that the reconciliation occurs, not in the fusion of all three which may be clashing with each other within her. Some of these things simply may not be compatible, in the way stasis and flux are not compatible. This is where the perceptual data simply is not sufficient to answer your rule-constituting act, project, telos.

Insofar as I adopt a certain description for my present, I do provide the possibility of a grouping which somebody else may decide to use as his or her own perceptual support. At this point I venture into the kind of exclusion that different contingent configurations have with each other when they are not compatible. In this sense I cannot at the same time be pro-Nazi and pro-Jewish in the same Germany. This is indeed for me to reconcile in the light of intrinsic worth, if I can. No choice, as Kostash beautifully pointed out, is anything other than contingent. So the existential problem I face in describing my present is always *ab initio*, always at the beginning. My discoveries are only a *problem* for you who have to make your own discoveries on your own. I cannot impose a resolution on you. All I can do is respect your posing and your initiating, which is a problem for me in light of your apprehension of intrinsic worth. This kind of mutual respect for each other's ability or independent relationship to intrinsic worth, seems to me to be the only solid ground for a universal polity. Anything less than that may be restful in a kind of bad faith sort of way, in the sense that I become Sancho to your Don Quixote and you relieve me of having to formulate my own world view. However, that still does not remove either the problem or the possibility of somebody digging out this thing and making it a choice again. That somebody may say: "You were the enemy of humanity, they were the saviours."

John O'Neill: That way of looking at it has a certain kind of monadology. It makes history look like a choice, a reversibility, and worse still, a moral reversibility. That most people would not allow. It is as if people were trying to claim that Nuremburg was after all the problem and not Auschwitz. On the stasis side, those judgments have sufficiently settled down so that the second time around it would not be a viable option. That would be destructive of that individual's sanity, morality, sanctionably so. We would declare them insane the second time around. Husserlian phenomenology makes it look as though one has that sort of radical choice with history. I would think not.

Dušan Pokorný: If I make what appears to be the choice of either living in marriage or outside of marriage, then am I making an actual choice in the sense that I am outside the framework of my choice? Is it rather that I am in a situation in which I am denying that institution, denying it in a manner which presupposes the existence of a framework in which one can live together on a different basis. Am I not in a situation which Marx once described by saying, "If I negate a powdered wig, I still have the unpowdered wig." In other words, is the framework not there already? Therefore, is not the choice limited by the framework even if I negate that?

Jose Huertas-Jourda: These are fundamental, very difficult questions which Husserl addresses in a different context when he talks about the logic of worth. At some point we do want to be able to say: "This is clearly a negation of intrinsic worth. This particular action is clearly and distinctly and obviously bad without any further need of truth or discussion." You have put your finger on a very difficult source of potential conflict in the position I outline for the ontological freedom of interpretation which the *epoche* opens for all of us. Kostash's presentation seemed to me to be specifically an example of the exercise of the *epoche*, the detachment from the constricting circle of meanings, in order to be able to view them from a distance instead of simply living them. This freedom which the *epoche* both requires and grants is such that, even if I want to say to Monsieur Himmler, "what you did was unconscionable," I have to have a slight pause there. It is, in my estimation, a clear contradiction between intrinsic worth and the holocaust, but I do not want to go that far into being tied up to the logic of a particular meaning, because I know I can always get out from under this particular meaning. At this point we have the problem of Camus as pacifist. In the fourth letter to a German friend he discovers that whether he stays at home or takes up arms against the occupying murderers, he is none the less participating in some form of murder either as accessory or as active partner doing it himself by fighting the Germans. I am forced to say that although killing seems to be the epitome of the negation of intrinsic worth, here is an example where, of two choices, one killing was better than the other in that particular circumstance. Camus' choice is defensible in light of intrinsic worth. That is why I have to maintain the possibility of the *epoche* against this logic of the particular thing. I must admit it is not a very comfortable philosophic position.

Alkis Kontos: We can view ethnicity as a prism and/or a spiral. The existential decision, which is beautifully presented by Huertas-Jourda, indeed is grafted upon the prism or the ascendancy of the spiral *ab initio*. Each new individual grafts it on, but not *ex nihilo*. Hence there is the structure of the base, hence ethnicity. That is the tension here. In Kostash's narrative of her biography/history the particular preceded her, but the existential appropriation of this meaning is her achievement. Those two things should be neither fused nor confused.

John O'Neill: In our thinking we have a synechdochic problem. Every time we use the term outsiders they are completely outside, but the outsider is always inside, and from there he or she draws a sense of outsideness. In that moment the inside turns outside. It turns other. It is this switching for which Huertas-Jourda gave a phenomenology. In Hegel there is a christology that Hegel and Marx historicize in the theme of "the first shall be last, and the last first." The anthropological switching point for them is the debased proletariat, or the broken figure on the cross, that will be resurrected. What we want is not any total solution of that. Between Benjamin and Joyce we seem to want only epiphany. We want finite epiphanies of the whole in the part and the part in the whole, but we never seem to want the fusion vocabulary, the integration vocabulary. We do want at times to be able to see a part in the whole and the whole in the part. There are a number of vocabularies for that. Bisexuality is a metaphor for that. Socialism is a metaphor for that. The church is a metaphor for that. Ethnicity may be a metaphor for that, too.

Manoly Lupul: Kostash made a reference to fusion toward something called Canadians. I sense the longing. "God, I wish it were so already. It would be so much easier to find oneself there." It would be so much easier to pursue those useful humanistic values which you connect with ethnicity. At least we would have more people to talk to in sharing that, or learning from it. I am wondering therefore why you do not leave the group and join the thousands of students that I meet who feel the same way as you, and do not like me. There is such a longing for that in Canadian society per se, especially among the young. I sense a longing for there to be a day already when we are all just Canadians.

Myrna Kostash: There was one moment when I sensed that I did in fact have that longing, and that was when I was heading for the Olympia with a Greek who called himself a communist. He took me to see this place and it was an exquisite afternoon. It was absolutely peaceful with the smell of the pine. It was wonderful. We were sitting on a broken piece of marble and he was surveying all this. He said, "I'm not a nationalist, but I am a Greek." I was so jealous because I cannot say that. There is no such person, a "Canadian."

Internal Division

Leslie Armour: It would appear that the nature of our present society is such that it creates problems which in turn creates causes. When you align yourself with these they have a divisive effect on you. It is obvious that we have the kind of social problems that cause feminism. If you become a feminist, though, you are divided within yourself in an interesting way that reflects on your background. I do not know to what extent the whole problem of ethnicity is also like that, but since there is an urge toward integration and reunification, it suggests that perhaps ethnic causes, as Kostash was suggesting, divide you in a way that becomes very puzzling when you take up public political causes, such as socialism. A very interesting feature of our society seems to be that it has these free floating clusters of ideas that you have to choose between, and by choosing you are divided. That, in turn, returns us to Huertas-Jourda's starting point, which is really inside the individual experience. However, within individual experience there are intrusions of the structure that we cannot overcome. When you try to make your free choices, you are fragmented. If anyone could find out precisely what it is about contemporary society that creates the kinds of problems, which when you try to solve them turn out to create causes that divide you against yourself, then we might be on the way to having a really genuine social theory.

Ato Sekyi-Otu: Kostash's exits and entrances are not simply the consequence of an embarrassment of ideological riches, or due to a failure on the part of theory to master experience. They are a consequence of the polycentricity of social existence. I am a black person in Toronto, an African, and a socialist. This is not just a matter of consciousness, it is a matter of social existence. They call for different forms of discourses. I have to deal with very conservative, reactionary, black people, with reactionary Africans, specifically reactionary Ghanaians. Socially I have to deal with people with whom I share a certain political discourse. One cannot ultimately reconcile these various social vocations. It is impossible to centre social identity. Social existence is polycentric and calls for different strategies of attachment, speech, and commitment.

Leslie Armour: Ethnicity divides one against oneself. It is very easy to be an American and absolve oneself of responsibility for blowing up children in Libya by announcing that one is not a Reaganite and one is opposed to these things. It is much more difficult to be a Zionist, for example, and dissociate oneself from what happens to the Palestinians. Somewhere in the middle of those things is the problem of ethnic identity. If you identify yourself with a certain ethnicity, you take responsibility for what the group does. It is a different kind of commitment. We have designed some political institutions, like the United States Constitution, for example, precisely so that people can divorce themselves from responsibility for what the government does. Once you have announced you are a Ukrainian, you do not have a similar way of divorcing yourself from whatever Ukrainians do. It is a claim you are making to be with them, and this causes great problems for everybody who is involved in those identifications. It divides them against themselves in a way that the other kinds of allegiances and discourses that you are talking about do not. You can be a socialist and divorce yourself easily from responsibility for what the Socialist International says tomorrow. In fact, most socialists do not even know what the Socialist International is. Once you say, "I am a such and such," whatever those people characteristically do is somehow your boundary.

Roman Onufrijchuk: At the same time, it is the nature of the "we." There were Ukrainians in the Second World War who were characterized by anti-Semitism, and there were Ukrainians in the Second World War who were not. Currently in the press, especially in eastern Canada, that has become a very hot issue. To what extent does the "we" require that I identify with those who wore the Waffen uniforms? As an American you can say, "I did not napalm kids in Viet-Nam." I did not burn Jews, but yet surely I share language.

Patricia Mills: The active protest against it is what is missing here. The political responsibility is not only to say, "I am sorry. I am not part of that." Those of us who were objecting to the war in Viet-Nam were in the streets trying to stop it. That is a different kind of "we" than those who say, "I am sorry. I do not really think that is I."

Can Ethnicity be Subversive?

Ato Sekyi-Otu: I understand Kostash is saying that ethnicity can be revolutionary, whereas it has been in the past a mere decorative component. Can ethnicity be subversive? If it can be, how can it be?

Manoly Lupul: Ethnic people are less than full Canadians. That is why they are subversive. This is why they are bad. They are necessarily less than full Canadians. They have given away something. You have given away something because you are Ukrainian/Canadian. Obviously because you are in Canada you have given away something already, that is true. Why do you not give it all away?

John O'Neill: It is not as bad as you are saying. The technology we are opposed to no longer requires us to melt. We do not have to internalize. You may be dumping your Ukrainianism, your Italianism, your Irishness and blackness, at exactly the wrong time. My argument is that the technology of early capitalism was uneducated. They had to melt down minds and bodies. Now it is highly educated and highly embodied and it leaves us around as men, women, blacks, Jews, Ukrainians. We can get on with it. Technology no longer needs us to work using many workers. Look at the big projects built by guys who speak twenty or thirty languages on the job and none of them English.

Patricia Mills: In the private realm there were disruptive family forms inherent in being at home, having intimate relations, and practicing rituals. That is what I read as being the disruptive element. The question is how you take these things now and bring them to the public without being co-opted.

Leslie Armour: It is subversive in all those ways. Black consciousness gets in the way of black consumption. They do not consume the same things as other people. That is why it creates problems. The reason there is a tendency to suppress it is that we live in a society which has been based until recently on the idea of mass consumption, both of goods and ideas. Our political system is based on national political parties that require a large proportion of the populace to swallow the same ideas at the same time. If we cannot have a Conservative landslide, we will have endless minority governments. Precisely the reason that you give for retaining your ethnicity is that it does get in the way of those things. We do not want to live in a country where everybody swallows the same political ideas on the same day. We do not want to live in a country where the Italians give up espresso coffee, or whatever they must, to become more efficient. Clearly the reason you do not give up all your Ukrainian background, but only some of it, is that just keeping it, opens the options for you and everybody else.

John O'Neill: One of the arguments in the current free trade debate is that the lower classes, by and large ethnics, would freely sell Canada down the tubes for a job. It seems to me it is exactly the other way around, that the lower classes want an ethnic Canada and they are willing to pay the price for it. It is the middle professionals and the upper owners who have already sold the country. That is another framework of this debate, too, and it is going to be very important.

Leslie Armour: It was the ethnicization of the Liberal party that caused the Liberal party to become the party of protectionism, leaving free trade for the Tories, which was the historic Liberal concept. That is a phenomenon that is very interesting.

Ian Angus: I would like to try and say something about this from a completely different angle. One of the things that is interesting about Kostash's different discourses is that they are all characterized by a certain form of communicative relationship which is oppositional in a contemporary situation. The New Left, feminist consciousness raising, and ethnicity are all rooted in face-to-face oral communication. There is a moment of similarity there. It is also rooted in Innis and the Canadian intellectual tradition, which is a recognition of a certain social history. That is important, and it may be something to examine for a clue which would explain why through all this Kostash felt there was something the same at issue, because precisely what characterizes oral communication is an engagement of the whole identity with its history and capacity to articulate. As soon as you name, you both make something possible and you exclude. What happens in oral tradition and oral communication is you are able to name for yourself. All of those political experiences were about being able to name for yourself. What ties these things together is not the common thing, the common content, but rather the commonality of the way it engages. There is something in the way orally-based political experiences engage the person as a whole which is different from what we experience in society generally.

3. ORIGIN AND IDENTITY

Alkis Kontos

Memories of Ithaca*

*And the sun set, and all the
journeying ways were darkened.* Homer

When Odysseus sailed away from his beloved Ithaca, leaving behind family and friends, he had a specific purpose in mind. To conquer and return home was his plan. Twenty years elapsed, years full of adventure, agony, and intense nostalgia. He returned to Ithaca an older man, unrecognized. The departing Odysseus did not have the slightest premonition of what was in his unborn future—Cyclops, Circe, Sirens, Nausikaa, and much more. His plans and expectations did not command his future. Odysseus wandering, longing for Ithaca, always hopeful, moved on to realize the desired homecoming. Odysseus was never a hopeless exile. Age and adventure, pain and fear, nostalgia and memory, rendered him unrecognizable, yet reminiscent of the other, earlier, younger Odysseus, the conqueror-to-be. An old scar of his was the tangible link between the departing and the returning man.[1] It was a scar and Ithaca. Odysseus derived his identity from Ithaca and disclosed it through visible signs from the past. A scar and memories detailing intimate moments were things which twenty momentous years did not manage to erase. Two decades veiled the past but did not erase it.[2]

In Horkheimer and Adorno's treatment of the Homeric tale, Odysseus was cast in a distinctly different light. He became a palimpsest upon which the essence of bourgeois existence could be inscribed. He was the prototype of what the frenzy and deceptively luminous reason of the Enlightenment could fashion—hollow victories, self-denials, and renunciations. A vanquished conqueror, a transfigured, estranged Odysseus

87

would return to Ithaca. It is a powerful reconstruction of the Homeric epic. Odysseus also appeared in another guise. James Joyce in his European exile unfolded structures, events, and moods of Dublin in excruciating detail, as if to erase the actual, foreign cities in which he lived. Dublin and Ulysses were a microcosm of life, of the world. This was a monumental activity of the mind, informed and sustained by the heart. Ithaca comes in many shapes and colours, in the myriad forms of homeland.

The many Odysseuses and Ithacas[3] are intriguing and fascinating. They constitute the enigmatic territory, the complex domain of homelessness and nostalgia. Ithaca as home; foreign lands, exciting, spell binding, and dangerous but foreign. Together they capture the dialectical tension between the familiar and the other, the alien. They are the kingdom and the exile. They disclose the vicissitudes of the self, the limits of identity and its profound expansiveness. They disclose the fragility and resilience of identity and the impulse of the human spirit to reach out as well as its desire for roots, its memory of the topography of the self, including childhood and more, much more.

Ithaca is a prism displaying multiple visions, dreams, fears, many colours, voices, nuances, eloquent gestures, and silent postures. Ethnicity must be unfolded, like Joyce's Dublin, in the context of Ithaca, in the dialectical movement between Odysseus' old scar and his nostalgic memories of his island Ithaca; between choices made and their consequences and conditions which are not fashioned by conscious, free choices. Between hopeless departures and hopeful returns we must decipher agony and resignation, defeat and spirited endurance. We must recognize crucial distinctions between those who returned, those who did not return, and those who can never return. Ethnicity as relocated community, active and thriving, is a lie. That is the Odysseus of the dialectic of the Enlightenment—a cunning, resilient survivor who pays with self-deception and self-renunciation. Survival requires the denial of the self. It is this topography and dialectic that I wish to explore here. The motif is derived from, and the text is placed in, a context of moods and elusive moments. It is the journey away from Ithaca, with its mystery and power, its irrevocable impact on the self, and its invisible scars and secret wounds. Joyless it might not be, but estranging it is.

Ithaca is the metaphor for the topography of the formation of the self. It is the particularity of space experientially appropriated. Ithaca is space and time meaningfully integrated. It is first biography and then history. It is not any place or merely a place but rather the place, the window through which we render the world familiar to us. Ithaca is not the world, nor is it an Archimedean point. It is the umbilical cord which connects us to the world. A great deal of the world we tend to take for granted because of Ithaca. We thrive in its familiarity. It is a mixture of habit and security;

blissful unawareness of danger and adversity. Faces, patterns, sounds, and colours constitute the canvas of our being. A common culture, a history, and a mother tongue integrate and render coherent the world of Ithaca. Yes, Ithaca is not the world, but the world without Ithaca is a heartless landscape.

I

Ithaca is not a paradise on earth, not the Garden of Eden. Life's anxieties, miseries, and tragedies afflict its inhabitants. Simply, Ithaca is the familiar, recognizable flesh of the world. Through it we experience life, self, and others. Ithaca is simultaneously an idea, an image which possesses the mind, and a concrete reality of memories and actualities that stirs the heart. It is neither a fiction nor a mental, conceptual abstraction.

Ithaca is the externalized mythopoesis of the ontological need of belonging; the desire and need for roots, continuity, and identity in the flux of time. Ithaca is the face of the world. Just as the faces of friends and lovers render anonymous, faceless humanity concrete, particular, familiar, and desirable, so it is concrete and tangible. Places, faces, and moments are the vivid flood of memory. However, Ithaca as retrospective and introspective reflection can never be fully exhausted, defined or crystallized. Concrete, yet with extreme plasticity, Ithaca adumbrates the boundaries of the self with its shifts, adventures, triumphs, defeats, glories, and despair. Like Ithaca, the self never receives its final, definitive form and meaning, yet it is never amorphous or nebulous. Ithaca is inherently an unfinished entity. It is the particularization of existence. The ocean of time, the currents of history, and the vastness of space are domesticated, humanized by the metaphor and reality of Ithaca. It is a home, a perspective from which to decipher the meaning and scope of the totality of our odyssey. It bestows meaning, significance, and unity to our otherwise endlessly meaningless, insignificant passage through time and place. Ithaca's truth cannot be proclaimed absolutely, axiomatically. It is situational but not relativist.

Gender, race, and ethnicity gain their full prominence not in isolation but in interaction, in cooperation, and in hostile, antagonistic circumstances. The female, the black, the ethnic are always that, but what precisely that is shifts and changes. Stereotypes, prejudices, and self-images emerge. To moderate and rectify this powerful mixture we must always re-open the question of history. We must re-interpret the past, redeem the future, and emancipate ourselves from the destructive, coerced self-images which protracted, chronic, external situations generate, sustain, and validate through introjection. Fanon's evocative narrative reconstitutes matters. It unveils the dynamics of racial colonial exploitation and dehumanization. Feminists are immersed in history as they should be. It is not simply a fierce battle over control of the past. It is not a struggle for the monopoly of the past, which is what Orwell's Big Brother desired in *Nineteen Eighty-Four*. It is the need for historical roots, the indispensability of the historical dimension of human identity. The quest for truth about origins is inescapable.[4] To articulate, to breathe life into the dead past, out of time, out of mind, is to reflect, to think, to seek Ithaca, to remember Ithaca, and to speak in the language of our Ithaca.[5]

II

The silent voices of the past and modern times

The human mind does not perceive the passage of time as an amorphous, indiscriminate sequence of events or as a process. The human journey through time is our history. Reflecting on time as history, demands, indeed forces, qualitative distinctions, differentiations, structures, and inevitably, meaningful interpretation. We are self-interpreting creatures. We bestow meaning on events. We demand a meaningful existence. When we reflect on the human predicament we set boundaries and demarcations to the natural, neutral flux of time.

From a specific, particular moment in time, a present moment, our present, we engage in a backward look, a retrospective look. We seek a view of and an understanding of the irreversible past. We seek the inner structure of our being where essence and existence meet. We also look forward toward a future horizon holding unknown possibilities and desired promises. It is as if we were permanently standing between past and future.[6] This existential in-between is neither an Archimedean point nor a vantage point for a panoramic spectacle of truth. It is at this point and juncture which is devoid, in and of itself, of topography[7] or geographic location that humans are tested, moulded, enlightened, and blinded.

The perspectives on and tensions between past and future are many and varied. Prototypical attitudes are a nostalgic vision of the past and a euphoric celebration of the future as a new era. These polarities bespeak two major human tendencies. The first is to seek refuge and solace in the past by regressing to what no longer exists and by exhibiting extreme and fierce hostility toward and contempt for the novel and current. The second tendency is to embrace the future as an emancipating dimension, as freedom from all the inadequacies of the past by seeing the future as the obliteration of all human weakness and by anticipating the future as the total, absolute transformation of human existence.

The immense polarization of the past-future juncture goes back as far as Aristotle and his castigation of idealist-utopians such as Plato. It should be noted that this double look is backward toward the past and forward toward the future. Aristotle cautioned us that the truth of nature, a normative category in classical Greece crystallized in the truth of experienced historical practice, does not exhaust human potentiality. Aristotle wrote: "We are bound to pay some regard to the long past and the passage of the years, in which these things [advocated by Plato and other idealist-utopians as new discoveries] would not have gone unnoticed if they had been really good. Almost everything has been discovered already; though some of the things discovered have not been co-ordinated, and some, though known, are not put into practice.''[8] The teaching of experience, the wisdom of the past generations as reflected in institutions and practices, must be heeded, Aristotle insisted. Reason censors, guides, and illuminates. It does not create *ex nihilo*. Reason must restrain experimental flights of the imagination toward horizons beyond the joys and sufferings of the earth.

Aristotle stressed the supremacy of the truth of the past, but this truth-bound past must be understood in its essential dimensions. It is the product of the practical wisdom and experience of many anonymous individuals, our ancestors. No genius, no demigod produced it. Trial and error, human essence in its collective expression and manifestation fashioned it. Reason affirms its truth while the passage of time and institutional endurance confirm it, corroborate it. Reason illuminates and reveals the truth of our empirical reality.

This Aristotelian past as normative truth does not insist that we be chained to ancient traditions and modes of existence. It only argues the continuity of human wisdom which sets limits on the possibilities held by our unknown future. Moderation as virtue is precisely the awareness of limits which should not be experienced or perceived as a crushing, humiliating defeat of human creativity. Proud we should be, but excessive pride, just like anything else to excess, is an imbalance in the natural order of things, in the natural cosmic order and harmony. Excess is a derangement. Aristotle did not view this excess as exclusively the intellectual vice of future eras. He believed it was a constant temptation. If contempt for the past is a vice rooted in ignorance, we should not assume that Aristotle endorsed the past in its totality. The past is not a sacrosanct universe, frozen in time, inflexible and rigid as a corpse waiting to be resurrected. It is truth and the normative principles of past experience that are stressed by Aristotle. The teaching of the past as lived wisdom rather than as formal, immutable doctrine is the heart of the matter. That is why reason, for Aristotle, was neither omnipotent nor impotent and superfluous.

Aristotle held firmly to the essential character of past experience and argued for a sustained, continuous presence of that essence in the face of new developments and changes. He did not celebrate the past nor did he deny the future. He did object to fundamental, radical changes which were, in his mind, cataclysmic discontinuities, assaults on the very flesh and spirit of human practical wisdom. Aristotle wished to conserve what is valid in our past. It is the truth of the past that must serve as the fountainhead of our socio-political world. The past is neither a place to return to nor a specific, structured, ritualized tradition. It is a moral and theoretical self-understanding and orientation toward the fulfillment of our future potentialities. Life is past and future in a reasoned, natural, developmental rhythm. We do not live in the past when we honour its truth in future time. To deny the future is to pretend that time can be arrested. To deny the past is an immoderate, ignorant, self-inflicted amnesia. Either past or future as choice is a mutilation of our historical reality, of the dynamism of time and human creativity.

It was Edmund Burke who sanctified the past as tradition, though the genesis of tradition and a healthy attitude toward it were Roman virtues. Burke, unlike Aristotle, dwarfed reason and in a mystical, providential tone fused the truth of past experience to past practices and prejudices. The Aristotelian clarity is obscured under the burden of ideological rhetoric. Burke was confronted by the deluge of the French Revolution while Aristotle was confronted only by the turmoil, strife, and anxiety of a shifting socio-economic structure in his Athens.

If Aristotle and Burke insisted on the virtues of the past from their distinct perspectives, it was Marx who spoke of the total emancipation of humanity from its past. The future held promise and prophecy. The past was a dead burden weighing heavily on present generations. So radically opposed are the two dimensions, past and future, in Marx, that he declared all pastime as pre-history. Truly human history is posited at a future time. It is a secular millennium, according to some.

Polarized and antagonistic, past and future are pitted against each other. It is so polarized into a horrendous either/or that the past denies novelty. It tames future time by rejecting its individuality. It renders it predictable, acceptable, and capable of incorporation into the precious past. The future obliterates the burden of the past and its wisdom while it transvaluates and de-historicizes. Future time so monistic and intoxicated refuses to be contaminated with the deadly passivity of the past, the used, the worn out, the obsolete. Vulgar Marxists, not Marx, hold views close to this. Orwell's *Nineteen Eighty-Four* captured fully the climax of such attitudes, with a twist toward totalitarianism. The past must be re-written, forgotten, extinguished. No trace of it must be left. Total control demands the reversibility of the past. Unobstructed entry of the new must be secured. Clearly a simple compromise between these two extremes, past over future, future over past, cannot be struck. Standing between past and future, between their claims and counter claims, between an old, if not ancient, world and an unborn one, is to stand between the past and modern times. That is a time, a present, distinct in texture both from past and future, a crossroads. It is backward and forward looking.

Since the present, our era, is located on the extremity of time, we do ponder and reflect on the origins of our circumstance. We speculate and seek demarcations, precursors, crucial turning points which would aid us in understanding and defining our predicament. Modern times are a mixture of the old and the new. Though perhaps all ages might have perceived themselves as modern, none appears as modern as ours.

Perhaps the genesis and origin of things modern reach back into ancient times, to time immemorial. Perhaps all things, events, and consequences blend or are woven into a grand web and therefore any determination of origins, of cause and effect, of necessary and sufficient reasons and conditions, of intended and unintended consequences, is an intellectually necessary but artificial demarcation. Yet reason and intuition point to certain factual configurations. If all major turning points have their origin in some totally imperceptible process, still, beyond a certain point in time, specific conditions and structures become more visible than others. They manifest themselves as more crucial and dominant, even if they are perceived so only retrospectively.

"Modern times" is used here to designate the segment of modernity in which we live. Modernity is a specific socio-historical, cultural term designating a qualitative, normative difference between the ancient and modern way of life and mode of thought. It is interesting to recall that historically, prior to the use of the term modernity, the term moderns was employed. It was meant to designate that modern faith, Christianity. The moderns were Christians while the others, the pagans, were the traditionalists. Modernity deals with the emergence of modern society represented by urbanization, science, technology, commerce, capitalism, new modes of thought and being, new self-images, and new dreams and fears. The Renaissance, the Enlightenment, and the scientific revolution are its demarcations. I speak of modern times because the term is more applicable to the sense of novelty in the present historical epoch and also because it fits into the larger historical unit of modernity. Finally, it echoes that masterful movie, *Modern Times*, in which a delicate, comic, sensitive Charlie Chaplin is aware of the peril and attempts to break out of the iron cage of industrial society, relying on nothing but his inner resources. He had the desire for gentleness, meaning, and beauty which are endangered qualities in our world.

III

In political thought many tend to attribute the origins of modernity in general and our times in particular to Machiavelli and Hobbes. Our century, itself so volcanic and monstrously catastrophic, can be traced in two events—the fire and smoke of Auschwitz and the luminous mushroom of Hiroshima. These horrendous events mark the century, disclosing its brutality and cynical decadence, but they did not give it birth. The prophet of the age is that mad genius, Nietzsche, who dared pronounce the murder of god and the unbearable freedom and loneliness of the murderers.[9] Without strength or a moral compass, we navigate in our world. Nihilism levels all criteria, all norms. It unhinges the human universe. We have a cosmos without courage, without axis, and without purpose. It is a bottomless abyss.

Well before Nietzsche uttered his fateful and frightening words,[10] Machiavelli sought to harness divine authority to political power in order to render it expedient but subservient. Machiavelli argued the truth of the past, the glorious historical past. He urged his demoralized contemporaries to recapture the glory of ancient Rome. Human achievements and greatness could be initiated and repeated. Machiavelli fixed his eyes on the political horizon, on this world. Humans need a homeland before they can achieve anything. The passion for politics, the political necessity for violence and fraud, the potential triumph, are the transformational, creative forces in the world. That is why Machiavelli could say in utter seriousness that he loved his homeland more than his soul. For him, soul without a terrestrial base, a habitat, was nothing. His soul became his true soul through loving his homeland, his Ithaca.[11]

Restoration and reinvigoration of a whole society is the grand task of a prophet, a political prophet. This prophet, armed with national armies and a nationalistic populace, is also armed with great political visions. Machiavelli's armed prophet, his great, talented, skillful prince, transforms, creates, and moulds. Dexterity and virtuosity are his. Omnipotence is not. Machiavelli, by calling his prince a prophet, captures the need to transcend the merely human. He evokes primordial images of divine mission and commission. The prince stands before the people in alliance with divine authority. He arouses a deep-seated fear, the fear of power, of omnipotence, of divine wrath. Machiavelli's prince, however, is not a prophet of an other-worldly order. He does not represent god nor does he believe in god.

The prince does not mediate between his people and god. He is not god's instrument. Instead, he brings the idea of an omnipotent god to earth in order to strengthen his military and political position, and to facilitate effective control of the people. He brings the fear of god to earth. He manipulates the divine in the human mind. The prince himself is fearless. He is not god's agent. He makes god his ally, his agent, his servant. God is an immensely effective tool. Machiavelli's prince is a godless prophet who utilizes and sustains his people's belief in the divine as a kind of psychological superstition. Unlike Marx who saw religion as ideology and in direct opposition to his historical goal, Machiavelli read in religion not a necessary evil, but a useful political tool, an extraordinary opportunity.

Machiavelli's political and ethical stance is a complex one. It fused nobility of spirit and action with sinister, perverse methods. Whatever the truth about his views and his significance, the crucial issue here is that Machiavelli effectively dethroned god but refused to permit the total leveling of human values. Something of extreme significance, something collective and national, not only remains erect and monumental but it is advocated, demanded, expected, and promised. Rome in her glory dazzles the human eye. Lest we forget, Machiavelli reminded us by unveiling before us the necessary horror, the bitter truth. All Romes have their origin in a murderous Romulus. There can be no exceptions.

That an extraordinary creature, who was a founder of a nation, a leader, a redeemer, solid, beyond corruption, would wield power, absolute power, with skill and knowledge, with wisdom and passion, might be the most romantic dimension in the thought of this otherwise realistic thinker. Nevertheless, Machiavelli's theoretical landscape is not one of total desolation, sterility, and futility. Fortune and human action, the prince, have political, existential, and sexual encounters. Neither omnipotence nor impotence constitutes the human predicament. The glory of politics is the possibility of ephemeral human success, the creation of a nation-state. The self does not disappear in the collective. The self blossoms in it. Power is indispensable but it is not an end in itself. It is a creative force.

It was Hobbes who stripped power of all creative dimensions. Politics was reduced to the function of the policeman—law and order. Glory, excitement, and positive passion were dethroned. Security was the ultimate value. Machiavelli's armed prophet was transformed into an absolute sovereign, a mortal god overseeing a congregation of atomistic creatures. These possessive individuals inhabited the ordered battlefield of the market place without a sense of belonging. Motion would be their characteristic, possession their essence.

Such are the precursors to Nietzsche's will to power and murder of god. If Machiavelli wanted to utilize divine authority, if Hobbes wanted to incorporate it into his sovereign, his mortal god, and if Nietzsche declared god's violent death, it was our contemporary writer, Albert Camus, who wished to reinstate gods to their supreme power only in order to challenge humans to a momentous rebellion against them. He wished to invite humans to a momentous awakening against nihilistic nothingness.

Nihilism distorts the natural tension between past and future, between existence and meaning. It devalues the past and yet it does not celebrate the future. Nihilism is a transfiguration and a fragmentation. Nietzsche believed that nihilism should be seen as the occasion of its transcendence. It was the transvaluation of all values, the song and dance of the new man (or is he a new god?) whom Zarathustra proclaimed and announced.

Nietzsche spoke of the death of god and the ensuing crisis, which we do not seem able to overcome with the facility and ease some had promised us. Camus, however, seized on nihilism and insisted on pointing out its logico-psychological and philosophical consequences. He argued against the intoxicating euphoria of an illusory blissful future and against the glorification of a sterile past. Vitality, moderation, joy, suffering, a tragic sense of life, consciousness, and conscience were propounded and demanded.

Neither despair nor resignation were recommended. We were to create in the midst of our existential desert. We were to come to terms with the fact of our mortality. We were to struggle against meaninglessness and death, injustice, and indifference. To humanize the world was to grasp the contradictions, paradoxes, and riddles of life. Confronting death, Camus believed, was the royal road to a meaningful life. He interpreted modern history from the French Revolution to the horrors of the concentration camps, as an obsessive drive toward power, a deification of man by man, and the grand denial of mortality. The murder of god had solved nothing. We had to start once again with caution and lucidity, with imagination and reason.

Camus' sober and eloquent voice must be understood as a call for limits. The loss of limits and meaning, the despiritualization of life, which is not identical with secularism, has been articulated by the great twentieth-century social thinker Max Weber. Weber spoke of disenchantment, the loss of enchantment, which is the magical mystery, the source of wonderment in the human heart. He also spoke of actual, protracted historical changes. These were external, structural changes. A host of circumstances and factors joined forces to generate the modern predicament, our modern times.

Such factors included science and technology with their primary emphasis on utility, functionalism, efficiency, the conviction that the mystery of life and nature can be comprehended rationally, and the idea that the world is an object of mastery. Bureaucracy is another major factor. Bureaucracy asphyxiates creativity, spontaneity, and passion. Routine, rules, organization, and systems prevail. Capitalism is another factor. Systematization or rationalization of all aspects of life, religious belief included, is another. Urbanization and the massive scale of modern social existence contribute their negativism. Finally, human beings tend to become indifferent, passive, and unwilling to or incapable of struggling with the central and fundamental issues of life—freedom, justice, human suffering. Human beings lose their autonomy and recoil from the glorious and humanizing responsibility of making choices, ethical choices. They subscribe to formulas and doctrines while they enslave themselves to simple, non-agonizing solutions. This Weber saw as an ultimate abnegation of humanity and the height of irresponsibility.

To re-enchant an already disenchanted world might be impossible as long as negative external, structural factors militate against it, but Weber was convinced that a partial re-spiritualization and re-enchantment of the world was possible.[12] He did not believe in the magic of Machiavelli's prince nor in divine prophets. Nor did he have any tolerance for secular prophecies of a future paradise on earth. He called them a fool's paradise. He believed that difficult, crucial choices had to be made in order to escape a future nightmare. His images of it are haunting: iron cage, petrified forest, polar night. Courage, heroism, and personal integrity were indispensable, in his view.

A philosophy of history, an understanding of past events and future possibilities, is most desperately needed. The past is neither burdensome inert matter nor a self-evident directive. The voices of the past are many and silent.[13] They are to be found in the ruins of the past and in ourselves. History, memory, and recollection do constitute the indispensable starting point of self-identity. Only if we are equipped with the voices of the past, and not the past itself, can we proceed toward our modern times and future.

Camus wrote that he used to return to a site of ruins by the coast, Tipasa. There he would, in utter silence and solitude, hear ancient voices which taught him what he knew, what was dormant in him. They would leave him fortified, aware, human. We must all find that secret place and time so that the voices of the past silently can awaken us.[14] Then and there we will fully understand that time past and time future are one,[15] only in this mysteriously paradoxical way. It is a primordial human activity to journey toward the unknown future with the courage and the wisdom of past navigators. We realize as well that no one can make the journey on our behalf and that each ocean we sail is a new and an old ocean.

The fusion and diffusion of time and place, of past and future, and the vantage point and vicissitudes of all modern times, perhaps amount to nothing more than one statement. It is that the human journey in time is a journey toward the inner world, the vast landscape of the human spirit. Though the journey is primordial, its specifics vary. This is why the voices of the past are needed. This is why standing between past and future, we stand between possibilities, lost opportunities, temptations, and dangers. There are no guarantees. Such is the nature of the ocean of time. That is why we must accept, indeed welcome, the challenge of change. We must go forth not only toward potential victories and triumphs but also toward potential defeats and betrayals. With sorrow and pity, but without bitterness and resignation, we must proceed.

Max Weber was correct when he said that those who ate from the tree of knowledge must create their existential meaning. This does not mean that meaning is a private, subjective issue, far from it. It is Weber who said that politics, as the art of the possible, must realize that the possible is never so declared *ab initio*. The possible is born out of the pursuit of the impossible, which is distinct from the illusory and unrealizable. We must have the strength to dream.

Such is the fate and destiny of those who wish to be alive and not simply pretend to be so. It is the fate of those who care about the world and the gift of life and of those who dare without recklessness but with danger. Go forth and become the salt of the earth. Fly toward the luminous sun, but be faithful to your inner strength. Be loyal to those who have been condemned to a life of silence and darkness. Speak on their behalf. Aristotle said it best. There is nothing more horrible than humans when they fail their humanity and there is nothing more beautiful than humans when human. Such are the most vital and most crucial choices that confronted and still confront our race. Such choices stand beyond time but assume the guise of each historical era. They manifest themselves in modern modes and visions before they are admitted once again into the eternity of the past, the possibility of the future, and the very flesh of the human spirit.

IV

Ithaca, Ethnicity, and Modern Times

If a conceptual moment, a juncture that had no solidity, no exterior, was standing between past and future, the voices of the past could not be rendered audible, meaningful. That juncture would have no authenticity, no stature. It could be an illusion, but standing between past and future is crucial not simply as a metaphor for the meaningful passage of time, of time as history, but also because the external reality, the world, is part of it, is incorporated into it. The past-future juncture is rooted in the interior of the self, in its biographical vicissitudes and history. As historical time, the flux of time has demarcations. Events, occurrences, the very process of the aging self and the social transformations of the world are there. The very natural, progressive, evolutionary changes of human existence suggest that time past and time future cannot be absolutely identical.[16]

The inner domain of the self pondering the past-future nexus is itself concretely immersed, rooted, and embedded in the territoriality of Ithaca. The self has a home, a base. Had we lived the whole of our life span in Ithaca, we would not have been immune to the negative aspects of life and modern times. The life experience would have been mediated by the positivity of Ithaca—the familiar, exteriorized, acculturated territory of the self. Thus, even with serious discontinuities, an infrastructure of meaningful continuity exists. Ithaca is not, then, a shell, a prison of extreme parochialism. Ithaca is not the arrest of time, a dream world unchangeable or untouched by history and reality. Ithaca as a home is a point of departure and a point of arrival. All journeys, all roads, lead back to Ithaca. All journeying gains its meaning and loses its horror precisely because it is an adventure, an exciting exploration of the world's other places, cultures, colours, and faces. It is so only because it harbours in its very being the idea and desire of homecoming.

Ithaca knows no ethnicity. Ethnicity does not exist because in Ithaca you belong to a homogeneous totality, to your people.[17] Precisely because Ithaca is a belonging, exile is such a fierce punishment, a form of death since time immemorial. Exile meant and means the sudden total uprooting of the individual. It is sudden severance from all that sustains the self. The exile, uprooted, transplanted, and abandoned is tossed in an alien ocean. Forced to sail the seas, the exile is not allowed to return to Ithaca. The horror of exile is captured in the repeated desire of exiles to be buried in their homeland. It is not ashes to ashes, nor earth to earth, but a belated homecoming to the soil of Ithaca. It is a return to the soil where flesh and spirit were nurtured, a home after homelessness, rest, tranquility in the bosom of the familiar and beloved. Since exile is a form of death it calls for a proper burial at home in Ithaca.

To understand ethnicity we must understand this. Departures from Ithaca, permanent or lengthy, are alienating forms of existence. No one leaves Ithaca voluntarily. We say farewell to beautiful Nausikaa and we escape the Sirens but we do not give up Ithaca. To get a last glimpse of Ithaca and die is Odysseus' final, ultimate compromise. Ithaca calls us back because Ithaca is in us. Without her we are incomplete, mutilated, disoriented. Without her we have the trophies of ethnicity—self-denials, insults and humiliations, false triumphs, hollow victories, amnesiac existence, dehistoricized life, a high standard of living. To live through memory, in memory, is exhausting, distorting. Life without memories, without dreams, is not worth living, but a life of only memory and dream is a wasted life.

Milan Kundera says, with accuracy and without compromise, that a person who longs to leave Ithaca is an unhappy person.[18] It is unnatural to leave, hence exile is punishment. The exiles, the political immigrants, the refugees, whatever ill fate awaits them, whatever their sorrow and tragedy, love Ithaca. She is never renounced or betrayed. Coerced departures do not kill love. There would be sorrow and tears, perhaps suicide and insanity, but never renunciation of the beloved land. Exiles are like orphaned children who never turn against the dead mother or father. Normally immigrants leave home for economic reasons—work, a better living, a better opportunity for themselves and their families. There is a great deal of truth in the reality of a superior standard of living, of improved material conditions. The Sirens of the market society, the dream of possessions, vie with Ithaca, but there are yet more temptations, more difficulties.

Technology, capitalism, consumerism, the world of domination and one-dimensionality, opulence and narcissism, Hollywood, the mirage of earthly paradise, and the necessities of industrialization combine to erode the prevailing pattern of existence.[19] By attrition Ithaca changes and so do we, away from Ithaca. Technology, more precisely the constellation of technological, political, and cultural forces, is the great leveller. The global village is the result. Ithaca and the self are under siege, under attack.

Ethnic communities away from Ithaca, whatever their material success and euphoria, begin to experience the problems of their existence in their children. It is not a merely natural generational conflict. The children are the first casualties, the first tangible agents, of assimilation. Customs, manners and, above all, language begin to crumble. The battlefield of ethnicity is now the family. The foreign culture has penetrated the domestic scene. It has infiltrated the sanctuary of character formation. The impulse of the immigrant ethnic community is to freeze time. Culture and customs become museum pieces, reified, worshipped. Ithaca is no longer a living, vibrant reality, an actual realistic memory. It is immortalized in an alien context. The immigrant wants both the material world of his new country and the human texture of his past. Parochialism, traditionalism, ossified ritualism versus cosmopolitanism, individualism, mass culture are all at war. Back in the homeland, armies of tourists celebrate sun, sea, and gastronomic delights and pretend to have grasped the spirit of the place. The natives become court jesters without either irony or wisdom.

To come from one culture and live in another is to progressively become a stranger in both. The crisis of ethnicity is that objectively no tangible Ithaca is possible. The community centres are artificial units, illusory islands of continuity. We must understand that ethnicity outside Ithaca cannot be a slice of Ithaca, for Ithaca and the ethnic community abroad develop, breathe, suffer, betray, and thrive in distinct climates. Their landscapes are no longer homogeneous.

Immigrant life is a form of exile which can be modified, but it cannot be transformed because to do so we must totally forget Ithaca. We must forget what we were and renounce history and authenticity, reflection and consciousness. We must empty ourselves totally. Living away from Ithaca undermines and enriches. Ithaca is never the same again, nor are we. Yet the memories of Ithaca are there in us and they silently beckon us to return, to come.

V

Memories of Ithaca

Perhaps the estrangement of immigrant life cannot know true solace. What I have presented here is a preliminary attempt to decipher the complexities of time and place as past and future, as history, and as homeland and foreign lands. I sought to point out how, in defining and redefining, in revising and articulating the landscape of the self, we must have a notion of identity and past as inviolable. This enables us to receive the future as an open-ended possibility. Past and future must be balanced. Ethnicity without Ithaca is decentred and the delicate balance of the old and new, of the familiar and the unfamiliar, is distorted, accentuated, aggravated.

Those of us who are still in the midst of their odyssey, those of us who lost their Ithaca because of circumstances beyond our control, should know that the mythic and the real, memory and actuality, will always haunt reason and mortify the heart and soul. There is silence and poetry.

Ithaca as a metaphor veils reality but is rooted in memory, a real memory: "and the summer Mediterranean lies before me in all its magnetic blueness... memory of friends, of incidents long past."[20]

With Ithaca on our mind and in our heart, with old scars and new, we move on. As Weber tells us in the concluding paragraph of "Science as a Vocation," "nothing is gained by yearning and tarrying alone... we shall set to work and meet the demands of the day." [The reference is to the Hebrews.] Perhaps ethnic communities survive by doing just that.

Poets know best. Durrell tells us:

In an island of bitter lemons
Where the moon's cool fevers burn

. . . . . .

And the dry grass underfoot
Tortures memory and revises

101

Habits half a lifetime dead
Better leave the rest unsaid
Beauty, darkness, vehemence.[21]

Memories of Ithaca is only a beginning. It is better to leave the rest unsaid, for the silent landscape is the capital of memory and the heart of exile.

*For Nicos Poulantzas, in memoriam.
Desperate moves far away from Ithaca;
public triumphs close to Ithaca.

Notes

1. Odysseus resembles, is reminiscent of the real Odysseus in physical appearance and age, but he denies he is Odysseus. He is recognized by his dog and then by his trusted servant who sees the old scar. On Odysseus' scar, see Erich Auerbach's masterpiece, *Mimesis: The Representation of Reality in Western Literature* (Princeton, 1953).
2. It is Homer's insistence which permits Odysseus' reintegration. He returns and he resumes his old life. Obviously his identity has not been shattered, undermined or transformed. What his odyssey had done to him rests deep inside him. It is totally internalized. This is the case with all survivors. Their story is locked in silence.
3. Nikos Kazantzakis in his *Odyssey: A Sequel* refuses to domesticate Odysseus who, restless that he is, seeks adventure beyond Ithaca. Though Kazantzakis celebrates the heroic, inadvertently he points out the fact that prolonged absence might render impossible the resumption of a normal life. Odysseus would be a stranger even at home. The metaphor of Ithaca abounds in literature. Alexandria for Lawrence Durrell; Tipasa for Albert Camus; Florence for Machiavelli; see C. Cavafy's poem "Ithaca". Also the work of Czeslaw Milosz and V. Nabokov is relevant here. Perhaps we should recall the movie *Citizen Kane* where in mythic opulence, in a castle, utterly alone the old billionaire holds only one memory, happier days, his Ithaca— "Rosebud."
   In this essay emphasis is placed on Ithaca rather than Odysseus. I do not view Odysseus as the archetype of the immigrant life. He was king; he left intending to return; he was with his comrades. He returned. It is the odyssey as a metaphor-reality of the loss of Ithaca that I wish to stress. Odysseus struggles with nature, not alien socio-political forces. I treat Ithaca as the metaphor of the familiar, desirable. For the ethnic it can be concrete; an actual lost homeland or imagined ancestral land and heritage; second-generation immigrants have no original memory of homeland like their parents have. Of the Ithacas mentioned here, though all relevant existentially, only a peopled homeland is the immigrant's Ithaca, the native land. The imagined and the actual are fused in a powerful emotional and mental mood that defies a permanent crystallization. Ithaca is the eloquent and grand metaphor of the human desire for a homeland, a cry against exile. It is only in this sense that the immigrant and the true

exile can be compared; immigrant life in extremis is exile, life away from Ithaca. Odysseus' nostalgia must be understood etymologically: *nostos*, return, homecoming; *algos*, pain, grief. Nostalgia is the grief and pain of the desire to return home, the haunting, painful memories of homeland away from home. Homesickness is a pitiful translation. On Penelope and female destiny in the Homeric epic Horkheimer and Adorno write: "Prostitute and wife are the complements of female self-alienation in the patriarchal world: the wife denotes pleasure in the fixed order of life and property, whereas the prostitute takes what the wife's right of possession leaves free, and—as the wife's secret collaborator—subjects it again to the order of possession: she sells pleasure." *The Dialectic of Enlightenment*, 73-4. It should be clear that Ithaca is neither a paradisiac locale nor a name for self-delusion. It is memory, desire, and imagination allied against an alien, hostile world; it is the heart of human identity.

In this essay I move from Odysseus to Ithaca and the metaphor of odyssey; I end with El Greco, a solitary, silent painter; in him I see the ultimate starting point, the founding of life away from Ithaca. He is the existential canvas. Others, community, language must follow. El Greco is, metaphorically, the silent nostalgia for Ithaca that screams in colours and forms to a world which would not understand him in Greek. El Greco and sunset. The foundation.

4. R. D. Laing, F. Fanon, and Orwell argue the need for origins and history. Octavio Paz and, recently, Eduardo Galeano are brilliant in their poetised web of history and existence. G. Seferis is the master of this in Greek literature. Feminist literature is rich on history and identity.

5. Language as sound and meaning, as flesh and music of the spirit is the least studied aspect of exile and immigrant life. When the vital nerve of existence is severed, language, the mother tongue begins to be bastardized among the ethnics. Writers in exile know it best: language is a living thing, it needs human interaction to survive meaningfully.

6. See Arendt's *Between Past and Future*.

7. See below, section III where the past as Ithaca, life in Ithaca, achieves corporeality.

8. *Politics*, Bk. II.

9. Nietzsche died on 25 August 1900. His mind entered the darkness of insanity several years earlier. In 1889, in Turin, the famous incident with the horse took place.

10. Heidegger "The Word of Nietzsche: 'God is Dead'" in *The Question Concerning Technology*.

11. The famous lines are "I love Florence more than my soul." There is a sophisticated tension in Machiavelli between Florence that he loves and Italy that must recapture the glories of the Roman empire.

12. He speaks explicitly of the re-enchantment in "Politics as a Vocation" and in "Science as a Vocation."

13. Alexis de Tocqueville spoke of the light of the past. Andre Malraux spoke of the voices of silence.

14. Tipasa is for Camus the equivalent of my metaphoric use of Ithaca. Tipasa is his Ithaca. Machiavelli has his Ithaca while Hobbes does not. This is the beginning of modernity.

15. Here I allude to T. S. Elliot's opening lines in his "Four Quartets":

> Time present and time past
> Are both perhaps present in time future.
> And time future contained in time past.
> If all time is eternally present
> All time is unredeemable.

Note the crucial word perhaps and recall that the motto of the poem is from Heraclitus.

16. Tonnies, Durkheim, Weber and so many others starting with Aristotle, point out the gradual transition, the shifts, and changes that beset social existence. Change takes place in the village, on the island, in the city, in the neighbourhoods of the metropolis. Lawrence Durrell captures it beautifully in his *The Alexandria Quartet* when he narrates in his letter to Clea the changing life on the island in the concluding pages of the novel.

17. The national Greek poet, Solomos, has said that language, religion, and homeland constitute the world of the self. This is the extreme of homogeneity and the solidity of communal life.

18. *The Unbearable Lightness of Being, 27.* Kundera understands the loss of Ithaca in its fullest bitter truth and pain. Lives interrupted by historical convulsions. There is pain, loss, the desire to forget the unforgettable past.

19. On domination, see Marcuse's *One Dimensional Man* and *Eros and Civilization.* Also *Domination* (Toronto: University of Toronto Press 1975), Alkis Kontos, ed.; "The Dialectics of Domination: An Interpretation of Friedrich Durrenmatt's *The Visit*" in *Powers, Possessions, and Freedom: Essays in Honour of C. B. Macpherson* (Toronto: University of Toronto Press 1979), Alkis Kontos, ed.

20. Lawrence Durrell, *The Alexandria Quartet.* Durrell speaks of Alexandria as place and history thus:

> I return link by link along the iron chains
> of memory to the city which we inhabited
> so briefly together: the city which used us...
> precipitated in us conflicts which were hers and
> which we mistook for our own... I see at last
> that none of us is properly to be judged
> for what happened in the past. It is the
> city which should be judged though we, its children
> must pay the price. Capitally, what is this city
> of ours?

Later on he will call Alexandria the capital of memory.

21. Lawrence Durrell, *Bitter Lemons.* George Seferis puts the mythic thus:

> on sea-kissed Cyprus
> consecrated to remind me of my country,
> I moored alone with this fable

Who returns and who does not return to Ithaca and why should be registered. Odysseus upon his return sustains his pretense that he is not Odysseus except when he encounters his father who laments the loss of his son. There is a belated but happy reunion. In *The Iliad* two scenes involve less happy encounters between fathers and sons. Hector bids farewell to his wife and young son on his way to the battlefield where he will be killed. It is a tender family moment for the warrior. Hector's father pleads with Achilles for his son's body. Achilles knows he is next to die. He gives up the body as if he is giving his body to his father for funeral. Odysseus returns and embraces his father. Hector's son, Hector's father will not embrace Hector again. Neither would Achilles be embraced again. The spoils of battle and conquest. Wars, memorials, a tomb for the unknown-soldier.

C. A. Trypanis in his poems *Pompeian Dog* writes:

> I was Ulysses, saw many lands,
> Spoke many tongues, made friends,

But every landscape melts and ends
In rock and blue-veined sands

Return. Where to? The sea-full storms
Over that naked island home,
Some landscapes live because they roam
Across the world rooted in dreams

Sun flooded sails, masts, roofs that seep
Into the new, a world that strays
Soft like the rest on children's eyes
Who wept for long then fell asleep. (31)

I think of El Greco—a solitary figure. He went from Crete to Venice, then to Toledo, Spain. The Greek—no name, no community, no illusions of having a slice of Greece there; a labyrinth without Ariadne; Dante's odyssey without beloved Beatrice. Alone, he was without illusion or self-deception, without false hope, without bitterness and resignation. Solid, authentic, and free stands El Greco, the son of distant lands. Colours and visions, echoes of the past pour forth on the canvas. Monumental but most human he stands, and:

Remember, trees die standing.
Standing they watch their blossoms fall,...
in a supreme dignity the trees die standing.
(C. A. Trypanis, 54)

Standing high above Toledo, El Greco—Domenicos Theodocopoulos by name—at sunset, caresses with his eyes the town, the landscape. Is he thinking of Venice, of distant Crete? Are there perhaps melancholy regrets? Visiting his house, paying homage to him, I salute a solitary human figure, a Greek in distant lands, and I believe I know. During those sunsets El Greco is immersed in memories of other sunsets, sunsets of his island as I remember the sunsets of my island—memories of Ithaca—and I recognize the truth of Homer's words:

And the sun set, and all the journeying ways were
darkened.

Yearning and tarrying; we must meet the demands of the day. Yet you ask: What of ethnicity?

"Better leave the rest unsaid." Poetry and silence.
For now, merciful silence—"tears unshed".
(Durrell: last words of the poem "Bitter Lemons")

Ian H. Angus

Displacement and Otherness: Toward a Post-Modern Ethics

Once upon a time, there was a continuity of belonging: place, sacred locations; rites of passage, time out of mind; world extended, thick with meaning. Displacement from this encircled world is the condition of our modernity. It is a schism in time which gives rise to history; a cut in space that amputates an individual from the social body. Pain of separation, an individualized fear, in response to which our modern projects are elaborated.

Yet through this pain there remain memories of the enfolding world. Often idealized, it is as if this world were only a comfort. Utopias of beginnings, of returns, or recreations of the end exist in a world without the pain of displacement. Ethnicity is our modern name for the memory of when place and time were indices of belonging rather than arbitrary modes on an infinite continuum. Still and all, the present historical situation may now allow ethnicity to become a project, the institution of a new belonging. Ethnicity is an "other" to the modern project of autonomy. It is a memory of that which is unchosen, but enfolds and demands. It is that which claims us, which we may only create by re-creating, and refuse only with an inner tremor.

Involuntary belonging, a claim from without, must seem a scandal given our devotion to autonomy, but there are other "others." Race, gender, and class all raise the figure of that which cannot be made uniform, that which is not equally available to all. So, in devotion to autonomy, to equality, we hide from such differences, which is not to say they all are identical. Race and gender are ineradicable, while class, perhaps is not so, unless it becomes just a name for division of labour. Some are invisible. White ethnics of the second or third generation have no trouble learning to pass, at least no trouble we can see. Yet all of these figures of otherness remain, signs of an involuntary claim, a question for the modern project of autonomy, a hint of other responses to individualized fear.

The encounter with otherness is constituted by a border, a boundary, that divides a self from an other, a here from a there, and connects them in a relationship. Most primordially, one human encounters another.[1] Founded on this are the levels of cultural groups, intercultural communication, and universal civilization. Like the figure mentioned above, these founded levels of self/other relation have their distinctive characteristics, but, in both cases, there is a core of meaning which bears investigation. Without a universalizing inquiry into the self/other relation, its various modes cannot be understood together and we are left with the inconclusiveness of social scientific methods or casual observation. Thus, we must risk inquiry into the ground of otherness, in the hope of gathering these concerns in the context of contemporary culture.

This essay begins with the project of modern ethics in order to clarify the sense in which its metaphysical basis has come to an end. It describes three main modes of self/other relation, rooting them in the primordial encounter, and concludes by exploring the ground for a contemporary post-modern ethics in a double non-reciprocity of self and other. If we are to found a new possibility of belonging, it will be through considering the claim of the involuntary, which, at bottom, is the body in its essential tension between empathy and display. For it is clear enough that the end of modern ethics has made homelessness universal in the name of autonomy.

The End of Modern Ethics

Throughout the history of modern ethics, recognition of all as free and equal subjects is the *telos* of ethical and political action. This ethical project encompasses two related aspects. Ethical action requires the self-identity of the subject and the reconciliation of all subjects in the ethical universe. The metaphysical telos of modern ethics is the synthesis of identity and reconciliation. In this respect a crucial aspect of modern philosophical articulation was discovered by Kant, who clearly recognized the essential ethical form that is compatible with and gives meaning to the domination of nature initiated by Bacon and Descartes.[2] The utilitarian strain in modern ethics, which posits the happiness of individuals as the paramount ethical goal, is in tension with the claim to autonomous subjectivity that arose from the new science. Either it merely reproduces heteronomy, in which case the individual ultimately becomes the mere object of a social-scientific calculus of desires, accomplished in practice by the marketplace, or happiness must be founded on autonomy, a task taken up by Hegel. The relation between happiness and autonomy devolves upon an evaluation of the morality inherent in modern political economy.[3]

Kant recognized that nature, the "merely given," could no longer be regarded as comprising a moral order to which human subjects assented. The basis of moral subjectivity had to be found in this capacity to "give order" itself. Autonomy, the "giving of one's law to oneself," superseded any claims to fitting into a pre-existent natural order. Kant recognized that ethical subjectivity rested on universality and autonomy, on the claim to be an end in itself and not only a means to other ends.

> Everything in creation which he [man] wishes and over which he has power can be used merely as a means; only man, and, with him, every rational creature, is an end in itself. He is the subject of the moral law which is holy, because of the autonomy of his freedom.[4]

This disposition of humanity over nature leaves aside the natural basis of humanity—most clearly in the family, but also the formation of community in pre-reflective tradition and locale—as a virtually pre-ethical state. Such involuntary community is a pre-modern relic which, after the Renaissance assertion of the domination of nature, must appear as a constraint, albeit a necessary one, to be transcended by the ethical subject. As Hegel put it:

> The family, as the immediate substantiality of mind, is specifically characterized by love, which is mind's feeling of its own unity. Hence in a family, one's frame of mind is to have self-consciousness of one's individuality within this unity as the absolute essence of oneself, with the result that one is not in it as an independent person but as a member.[5]

It is Hegel's attempt to synthesize substantial unity, particular happiness, and universal recognition that places him at the culmination of modern ethics.

It is from the fundamental insight of Kant into ethical autonomy that Hegel draws a distinction between civil society and the state, between the sphere of particular needs and goals and the sphere of universal human ends. In civil society we are each means for all others insofar as we work and exchange. There is only a formal universality here, insofar as we are each members, but there is no relation between subjects as ends. Others are merely means to my separate and particular ends.[6] By contrast, in the state or ethico-political life it is the relationship between subjects as ends in themselves that is at issue. This is no mere formal universality, but it is concretely universal insofar as it is the formation of the rational and ethical community as such that is the content of the mutual relationship of subjects.[7]

Whereas Kant was content to discover the principle of modern ethical life in the recognition of human subjects as ends in themselves and to stress its difference from the satisfaction of needs and desires, Hegel claimed that the formal universality of multiple particular wills pass over into the universal will of the state.[8] Thus, for Kant virtue did not provide happiness and could only be regarded as "at least [a] possible" consequence of morality whose connection with it could not be known.[9] By contrast, Hegel claimed that though the state transcended individual happiness, it should nevertheless provide it.[10] While the state transcends political economy, nevertheless political economy is its prerequisite. Modern ethics struggles to differentiate and synthesize these two concepts of the self. One maintains that the mutual use of subjects as means to the satisfaction of particular, separately defined, ends is legitimate. Second, as the condition of this legitimacy, subjects must also be recognized as ends in themselves. The condition for the appearance of this modern ethical problem is the sundering of natural community by the Renaissance domination of nature which enters ethical theory through Kant's concept of autonomy.

The participation of modern subjects in the involuntary immediacy of natural life is seen as an unavoidable constraint to be transcended by the modern mind. The sundering of immediate connection to the here and now, of continuity in place and time, is the condition for the metaphysical telos of reconciliation in which modern ethics seeks to justify and transcend the historical project of dominating nature by reconciling the self with itself and with the other. Once the ethical subject is defined by its autonomy, it projects its identity with itself and its reconciliation with others. This project can be called metaphysical insofar as it attempts to re-establish, though of course in a new form, the identity and community which modern displacement sunders. However, no account is given of the possibility of this telos. It turns out to be a refigured memory of a continuity of belonging transformed from origin to goal. The account of displacement in modern ethics is underwritten by the telos of its cancelling. A radical investigation of displacement shows that the condition under which the goal of identity and reconciliation is formulated blocks its realization.

Displacement in both space and time is the condition for modern ethics. The pain of schism and of cut which defines this displacement survives the attempted metaphysical cure. In order to probe this pain at the root of modern identity, this instituting displacement must be clarified. The modern conception of subjectivity becomes questionable in the works of Marx and Nietzsche. With their aid we can define the fundamental issue which a contemporary investigation must raise. This is the condition under which the distinction between essential and accidental attributes in the self and its relations to others arises.

In continuity with German Idealism and with modern philosophy as a whole, Marx regarded the tendency of capitalism to break down immediate, natural social groups as a salient feature of modernization.[11] The other major feature, the production of wealth, is also a consequence of the domination of nature through political economy. Capitalism replaces organic social groups imbedded in nature with exchange relationships based on the sale of labour power. Only by the separation of individuals from an encompassing, and to the modern mind domineering, community, could the capacity of individuals to labour be regarded as their property, which they can therefore exchange as a commodity on the market. As with Hegel, the separation of individual and labouring capacity, personality and ability—in the terminology of this essay, essence and accident—was co-extensive with exchange relations between individuals in civil society. Marx observed that the sale of labour power divided individuals into two major modern classes, a structural antagonism which had to be resolved before universal autonomy could be attained.

In tracing the origin of exchange, where each is a means for the privately chosen ends of the generalized other, Marx accounted for the historical relationship between natural community and isolated individuals. Exchange began on the edges of communities, in their relations with other communities. Through a long historical process it migrated from the outside to the inside, eventually becoming the central organizing structure of society and of the activities of individuals. The distinction between labour and labour power, between the concrete activity of an individual and the capacity for such activity, arises with the universal exchange society of capitalism in which the creative activity of individuals becomes a commodity.[12] The alienation of the capacity to labour requires that the individual be distinguished from his or her activities. At this point the distinction between the person abstractly considered as a possessor of capacities and the actual exercise of capacities in concrete activities becomes the central structuring principle of society. In short, the subject is seen as essentially a possessor of human powers which are accidentally, under contingent historical conditions, put to determinate uses.

Such a perspective is possible only in abstraction, that is to say, when it is a question of objectifying the projected possibility of acting prior to its execution, as occurs in the wage contract. Concretely, in use, there is no distinction between the individual and the exercise of capacities. A society based on labour power as a commodity enforces an abstract relation of the self to its activities and of the individual to the combined activity of a group. In each case, the total relation is only established externally as a subordination of activities and individuals to the mechanism of co-ordination of the whole. In short, the relation of part and whole is only possible as an absolute sovereignty of the whole over subordinated parts—the abstract totality as essence and the particulars as accidents without effect on the whole. The path to a reconciliation of self and other is blocked by the separation of essence and accident. While Marx shared much of the analysis of civil society with Hegel, he showed that its origin in displacement subverted its transcendence in the concrete universal of the state. The Marxist procedure is to dismantle the social reinforcements of displacement.

In questioning the nature of modern morality, Nietzsche performed a similar regressive, or archeological, move. Both thinkers turned from the metaphysical telos to a beginning understood as a displacement, to a separation at the source that precludes the reconciliation of essence and accident in self-identity. For Nietzsche, the separation of self from its expressions gave rise to the myth of freedom.

> For just as the popular mind separates the lightning from its flash and takes the latter for an *action*, for the operation of a subject called lightning, so popular morality also separates strength from expressions of strength, as if there were a neutral substratum behind the strong man, which was *free* to express strength or not to do so. But there is no such substratum; there is no "being" behind doing, effecting, becoming; "the doer" is merely a fiction added to the deed—the deed is everything. The popular mind in fact doubles the deed; when it sees the lightning flash, it is the deed of a deed; it posits the same event first as cause and then a second time as its effect.[13]

In the nineteenth century, the works of Marx and Nietzsche brought the metaphysical telos of modernity into question by an archeology which refused to write the telos of authentic identity and reconciliation back into an origin. It is not possible to simply step beyond metaphysical closure, since the description of the closure occurs initially in terms still wedded to the metaphysic and risks using terms for new experiences at the price of misunderstanding. With these two thinkers the presuppositions of the modern framework began to be clarified and overcome, a task which can achieve formulations which do not simply repeat the metaphysic, as it proceeds. We will take up this task by following Husserl's investigations in our century in the next section.

By taking the standpoint that they both called history, Marx and

Nietzsche showed that in use, in the concrete experience of self in social relations, the essence/attribute distinction does not arise. There is only production, will to power, which is the originating praxis which constitutes history.[14] This is prior to the separation of self from capacities, ability to act from action, and other from self. It is prior to object and subject, the fecundity of world-origination.

Such a standpoint shows first, that the essence/attribute distinction in modern ethics is a representation which is not present in the ongoing praxis of productive power. Second, it shows that certain social institutions reinforce this representation as a method of understanding and concrete organization. Third, it shows that the distinction only arises in particular historical conditions, that only the displaced define essence and attribute in self and other in order to elaborate a telos in which the distinction is cancelled and preserved. The goal of modern ethics as identity and reconciliation is undercut by the recognition that schism in time and cut in space cannot be reassembled from its incomplete representations. Rather, displacement must be probed in its productive praxis, in the loss of telos and origin, in the ongoing stream of experience. The dismembered body of the world cannot be reassembled, but we may probe wreckage of the enfolding world for the involuntary body of otherness.

The self/other relation is a further doubling of the essence/accident relation established in the self by positing a substratum behind its expressions. The metaphysical telos of reconciliation that oversees modern ethics can no longer be redeemed once the displacement of modernity has been unravelled. In order to think the other outside the metaphysical frame of identity and reconciliation, we must probe displacement. We must probe the sundering in history and geography that defines the pain of schism and cut on which the programme of modernity is elaborated. With the infinite delay of this telos, we must now return to the fundamental experience from which the part/whole doubling of the self and its redoubling in the other proceeds. The post-modern situation requires a return to the most fundamental condition of ethics, the constitution of the other in the immanent experience of the self.

Modes of Otherness

Without a metaphysical principle of reconciliation, modern ethics could not be taken up into a philosophical articulation that completed and justified the domination of nature. This specific predetermined interpretation of the self/other relation defines a central affirmation of modernity. In the present post-modern situation, radical investigation of the constitution of the other within the immanent sphere of ownness is required to renew questioning of the ground and telos of ethics. In the fifth of his *Cartesian Meditations*, Edmund Husserl described the evidential basis for belief in the existence of the other. It is from this primary constitution of the alter ego that higher level cultural unities are built. Our present situation is without a metaphysical guarantee of reconciliation of subjectivities. Thus, it cannot begin from a dialectic which presupposes the other as given in order to assure the telos of mutual recognition. Rather, we must risk the asymmetrical constitution of the other as foundation of an ethics which responds to the post-modern situation.

In order to inquire radically into the origin of one's experience of an other ego it is necessary to begin by setting aside two assumptions that function throughout common daily experience: the belief in an objective world apart from my experience of it; and, the belief that other subjects like myself populate this common objective world. These assumptions are not regarded as false. Rather, it is only if they are dropped that the constitution of the other can be recognized as a genuine and fundamental question. How, in the indubitableness of the ongoing stream of my experience, does the experience of others arise? How, when I can only experience my own consciousness firsthand, do I come to experience and believe in other consciousnesses like my own? Only by setting aside these two assumptions that are necessary to everyday experience and action, can the proper wonder at the most basic facet of the social world be aroused. Such wonder may be unsettling, certainly of a metaphysic of reconciliation, but it is the only starting point for a contemporary philosophy of cultural identity and civilization.

This does not imply that socio-historical life is regarded as ontologically built out of the activities of individual consciousness. Rather, it means that, while ongoing life rests on the ontological assumptions of the socio-historical life-world, for these assumptions to be made known, they must be suspended in order for their structuring accomplishment to be clarified. In short, the epistemological priority of the suspension of assumptions, which is at its apogee in the transcendental reduction, does not imperil the fact that such assumptions do, and continue to, function in life and action. Indeed, it is just this fact that makes them significant for phenomenological analysis. The movements of ontology and epistemology are inverse. No more can scientific knowledge of the life-world be considered a prerequisite for its accomplishment, than the presuppositions of ontology can be regarded as a prior delimitation of epistemological warrants. The full exploration of this polarity would require a rigorous account of phenomenological enlightenment.

Restricted to the stream of immanent experience as it bears the index "belonging to me"—what Husserl calls the sphere of ownness—it immediately appears that one aspect of this experience bears a specific and distinctive characteristic. My own body is a field of perception and source of action that necessarily accompanies the experience of other bodies and, also, reflexively experiences itself.

> Accordingly this peculiar abstractive sense-exclusion of what is alien leaves us a *kind of "world"* still, a Nature reduced to what is included in our ownness and, as having its place in this Nature thanks to the bodily organism, the psychophysical Ego, with "body and soul" and personal Ego—utterly *unique* members of this reduced "world."[15]

This fusion of sensuous nature and psyche is the sense of my embodiment as an animate organism. It is in this *originally given* evidence that the experience of the other is founded. When the body of the other is perceived by me, there is an "analogizing transfer" from my psychophysical unity to the psychophysical unity of the alter ego. While only the body of the other is presented in immediate evidence, the psyche of the other is appresented through the body. Appresentation is a pairing such that, along with an immediately presented datum, a mediately appresented datum is given. In an external perception, for example, the front of a physical thing appresents a back side. This is not a deduction, or an inference of any kind, but a characteristic of perception. In the case of a physical object, it can be viewed subsequently from another aspect such that the back side is directly presented and appresents another unseen side. This phenomenon of turning around is a peculiarity of physical objects. The appresented psyche of the other cannot in principle be presented directly. Moreover, the body of the other is continuously present as itself and also as the vehicle for the other's psyche.[16] Thus, the other is given within my sphere of ownness through an appresentation based on the similarity of the other's body to mine. However, the precise character of this givenness is such that it can never be immediately present to me. The otherness of the other's psyche remains separate from the ownness of my psyche. Thus, similarity or likeness is not an identity or sameness.

The constitution of the other, of a "there" which complements my "here," accomplishes an expansion beyond my sphere of ownness. I am no longer simply at the centre of the world but can be looked at from over there. Similarly, objects can be looked at from various sides simultaneously. Thus, we inhabit an objective world upon which higher levels of cultural meaning are founded. Most important in this context, the other is not given in empty fashion merely as an other. Rather, the other's body *continuously appresents* the contents of the other's ego. In other words, most fundamentally the other is given as "other" but, continuously founded on this, it displays itself as "this" other—now angry, now sad, now responding to my initiative.[17] The higher levels of cultural meaning founded on the appresentation of the other thus encompass specific contents which are appresented to me through a pairing with my own cultural "body."

Founded on the self/other relation, there are three higher levels significant for cultural identity. First, a cultural group requires communication whereby internal relations are established between the members of the group.[18] Thus, "accessibility is not unconditional,"[19] as with objective nature, but depends on the performance of certain communicative acts which define the content of the cultural group. Second, there is the level of intercultural communication and the empathic procedures requisite to understanding another culture.

> Here I and my culture are primordial, over and against every alien culture.
> To me and those who share my culture, an alien culture is accessible only
> by a kind of "experience of someone else," a kind of "empathy," by
> which we project ourselves into the alien cultural community and its culture.[20]

Third, there is the level of universal civilization which, although it must arise from humans in specific cultural unities, actualizes the essential possibilities of humanity as such.

Husserl's description of the constitution of the other begins from the entry of an other into my perceptual sphere and remains geared to perception. However, I encounter the other, also and simultaneously, in the sphere of action, which Husserl considers merely as one possible modification of the Ego's content.[21] In the primordially reduced sphere of ownness, I am an animate organism and the most basic element in this animation is the body's motility. Thus, the "I can" must be added to the "here" as a praxical modification of the perception of the other.[22] We may ask what is the other's modality that corresponds to "I can" as "there" corresponds to "here"? This phenomenon is discussed here as "display."

The practical dimension of the self rests on the ability to define projects and goals, and to design courses of action to bring them about. A project is an organization of the world, both planned and materially inscribed, such that the meaning of things or people within the world derives from their furtherance or hinderance of the goal. Within this context, the encounter with the other presupposes his or her existence and is directed to what Husserl called the content of consciousness, specifically the relation of this content to my goal. Jean-Paul Sartre described this.

> I group the other's look at the very center of my *act* as the solidification
> and alienation of my own possibilities. In fear or in anxious or prudent

116

anticipation, I perceive that these possibilities which I *am* and which are the condition of my transcendence are given also to another, given as about to be transcended in turn by his own possibilities. The other as a look is only that—my transcendence transcended.[23]

The look of the other encloses me as a factor within the organization of the world around a goal that is alien, and possibly unknown, to me. With this, the centre of my world slips from my grasp and is lodged with the other. I am reified by my original conflict with the other, unless, of course, I am able to reify first. For this description is two-sided and can in principle, even if not in historical fact, be reversed. However, it is not reciprocal in the sense of occurring simultaneously from both sides in the same manner, nor does it move toward dialectical resolution by a successive oscillation tending toward synthesis.[24] Thus, the "I can" in the motility of the other may be called a "decentring" of my orientation.

In his early work Sartre did not carry his analysis any further than this original conflict, though later he came to regard it as deriving from the fact that in all societies known thus far, human action operates within a condition of scarcity. Consequently, the other is a threat to my life and that of my cultural group. Social organization in scarcity defines some as expendables, and we all scramble to reserve this designation for the other. In so doing, we become the other ourselves.

> ... *his own activity* turns back against him, and reaches him *as other* through the social milieu. Through socialized matter and through material negation as an inert unity, man is constituted as Other than man. Man exists for everyone as *inhuman man*, as an alien species.[25]

This concept of scarcity is appropriated by Sartre from a Marxist philosophy of history that is imbedded in the modern conception of the domination of nature for a free and equal society described earlier. However, Sartre's formulation escapes this origin and approximates a more general phenomenological description. While the concept of scarcity may seem to be a materialist cause of social conflict due to an objectivistically-defined, perhaps biological, notion of need and satisfaction, in fact, in its perceptual/praxical description there is no basis for an external grounding of this sort. Rather, scarcity has come to mean, in this context, the most general sense of incompleteness—an unfulfilled project of inhabiting the social domain. It refers to the entire complex of contested terrain in social relations, which carries as a moment that the other may see me in ways I do not recognize, incorporate me in projects I neither invent nor share, and construct a world in which I am a stranger.

The four levels of empathic relationship—self/other, cultural unity, in-

117

tercultural communication, universal civilization—are thus constituted both perceptually and praxically. In perception a here/there relation is set up in which there is an appresentation of meaning in a one-way direction from a primordial sphere of ownness to an empathy with the other. In action the motility of the embodied psyche is overlaid on the here/there relation. The there can be transformed into a here (and vice-versa) and the objective, common world which this constitutes is organized around the projects of the actors. As long as the common world exhibits the characteristic of scarcity with respect to these projects, there is resulting conflict over who is to become expendable. In this sense, action reverses the primordiality of the sphere of ownness in perception. The centring of the ''I'' in the body becomes decentred in the field of action of the hostile other. The body becomes ''like'' an object, reified, rather than ''like'' the appresented psyche. The look of the other freezes the body of the self ''in'' space, whereas centred motility is the source of spatial orientation. Thus, we may speak of a ''double non-reciprocity'' essentially constituted in all self/other relations.[26] It is important to note here that there is no metaphysical guarantee of reconciliation in this description. Indeed, the metaphysical character of modern ethics consists in interpreting the doubleness of these two non-reciprocal relations as inherently reversible, as if the two subjects could be assumed as essentially equivalent in their autonomy from concrete determination, so that their relation could be described as a dialectic and synthesized.

It must be noted that the centring/decentring relation between self and other is not equivalent to the perceptual/praxical dimensions of experience. Perception and action are simultaneously present in any consciousness. It would be misleading to regard perception as more primordial than action, which may well be a version of the modern metaphysic of authentic origin. Action involves perception. Perception is essentially constituted by its praxical possibility. The body does not perceive *and then* actualize a modality of movement. Rather, constitution of the perceived world is through a motile openness to the world. This motility is entwined with intersubjective praxis. Praxical decentring and perceptual centring are equi-primordial. While perceptual and praxical emphases serve to introduce and illustrate the self/other relation, the root phenomenon of centring/decentring is present throughout all its dimensions. Husserl recognized the significance of the continuous appresentation of the specific contents of the other's consciousness which I have termed display. However, because he regarded action as merely a modification of perception, he downplayed decentring, that aspect most apparent in action. While we have access to the consciousness of the other, the other does not look back in Sartre's sense. Thus, Husserl's assertion of the priority of the self, as against its empathic transfers to the other, must be modified and clarified.

Decentring by the other is an equi-primordial experience of the self as objectified within a spatio-temporal field. Thus, in such a respect, the self cannot simply be the source of empathic transfers.[27] Only the centred self can be a source, not only in perception but also in action. Rather, there are two senses of source which need clarification here. Husserl's priority of the self must be understood as a priority of access through empathic transfer, but the condition of this access is that the other display itself— externalize its contents of consciousness. This concept of display is the most primordial form of the decentring described in Sartre's "gaze." In order for the gaze to decentre me within the perceptual/praxical field, the contents of the other's consciousness must be displayed to me as an orga- nization of this field, apparent throughout its many parts but centred through the other. In the case described by Sartre, the gaze disguises its projects and objectifies me as an alien within its field. This is only one of several possible modifications, however, not all of which are reifying. The reifying modifications are dependent on the appearance of the es- sence/accident distinction. In this wider sense, the gaze is also apparent in the case of one's sexual "surrender," for example, which is a decentr- ing display of otherness, but is not necessarily reifying. Sartre's analysis of the sexual act in *Being and Nothingness* could be re-written from this point of view. The description of the reifying gaze forgets the empathic non-reciprocity, indeed as social forces may repress it, and therefore de- scribes display incorrectly as if it were necessarily reifying. Once we have fixed on this fundamental phenomenon of *display of otherness*, the modes of its appearance can be clarified. The self/other relation is at bot- tom a double non-reciprocity in which the self is a source of empathic transfer conditional upon displays of otherness. The former is a means of access to cultural unities, while the latter is the condition for the ac- tualization of cultural unities as such.

The encounter of self and other is a non-reciprocal centring/decentring without a telos of reconciliation whose modalities occur both from the side of the self and from the side of the other. For simplicity's sake the following descriptions consider the encounter of the self with an other. In summary, the decentring modifications of this encounter will also be ac- counted for. All descriptions consider both the perceptual and praxical aspects of the encounter and apply to all four levels of experience isolated earlier. Further analysis will be required to develop the specificity of each of these levels. What is here significant is the fundamental modalities which persist due to the foundation of each higher-level constituted mean- ing in the primordial perceptual-praxical encounter with the other in the sphere of ownness, such that the essence/accident distinction is instituted. There are three basic modalities of this encounter: 1) the other is like the self. The other is yet other, which splits into two variations: 2) the other as enemy, and 3) the other as exotic.

1. The "likeness" of the other.

The other is appresented as a human psychophysical unity through the likeness of the other's body to mine. The specific character of continuous appresentations opens the contents of the other's psyche to me. There are two aspects of the presentation of the other's body which affect this transfer through likeness. First, the presentation of my body to me is as a perceptual and praxical origin of a surrounding world. I am at the centre. Thus, I do not see my body as I see the body of another. I cannot see the back of my head, for example. Perception is oriented and shades off, through fringes, to non-perceived areas. Such areas can be *brought into* my perceptual field through actional modifications. Nevertheless, I do not *in principle* perceive my own body as the body of another which is, in this respect, like any physical object in that it can be turned around, seen as an object placed *in* space and time, and so forth. Second, the sense in which I perceive an other's body as like mine requires clarification. There are differences of race, gender, and size in human bodies which must be overlooked, seen as non-essential, for such a likeness to be perceived.[28] Moreover, the other is always an already encultured body which essentially displays itself through clothing, bodily attitudes, and so forth.[29] In order for the other to be seen as *human* "like" me, such apparent differences in humanity must be overlooked. Thus, the first modality of self/other encounter shows that I never perceive the other's body strictly as I do my own. I must overlook important differences, most fundamentally the incompleteness with which I perceive my body as a physical object. Founded on this, to the extent that I view the other as "like" me, I overlook the physical and cultural differences of the other. We see here the basis for the failure to perceive the other as another human psyche. Such differences may overpower the likeness, in which case we have the second modality of encounter, the enemy.

2. The other as enemy.

To the extent that differences are regarded as essential, the other is not appresented as a properly human psyche. Moreover, the contents of the psyche are not available at all. The other is perceived merely as an animate creature whose contents of consciousness, should there be any, are utterly strange to me. Husserl remarked that the "harmonious confirmation of the apperceptive constitution" is often preserved through a normality/abnormality distinction and that the question of animals enters here. "Relative to the brute, man is, constitutionally speaking, the normal case—just as I myself am the primal norm constitutionally for all other men."[30] If differences overwhelm likeness, the other is essentially strange and incomprehensible to me. The enemy is the human reduced to the animal whose projects are essentially antithetical to mine, whose difference is essential, and whose likeness is merely an accidental attribute.

In discussing Marx above it was shown that capitalism is the society in which one's activity as a means for a generalized other comes to pervade and structure the experience of oneself. One regards oneself as an other. Self-identity is established as a reflection of one's use-value for the other. In this sense, capitalism is a subset of the self-other dialectic that reaches its apogee in the nuclear age. Lacking any positive self-determination, one seeks security by escalating the insecurity of the other. Attributes of the self are legitimized to the extent that they threaten the other, and, of course, the other responds in like manner. Through an escalating dialectic fueled by insecurity, the self seeks identity through its enemy. It recoils from the utterly unlike, the inhuman other, and confirms the self in its humanity. This is an utterly unstable dialectic in which one false step can destroy the civilizing task altogether.

Self and other, friend and enemy, are caught in a mutual embrace which is fueled by distrust, strangeness, and the face of the enemy. Strangely enough, it incorporates its own reversal within this dialectic. Mutual antagonism in the nuclear age requires a curious trust of the enemy to act "rationally" to the deterrent, that is to say, in terms the self can understand, that make the other "like."[31] Trust and distrust are not alternatives, they are opposites within a dialectic of escalation. Dialectical negation no longer offers an escape-hatch, but merely opens up a new round of affirmation. In this post-modern situation, in which the self is its own other and creates the enemy in a gamble for identity, the end of rational autonomy is infinitely delayed. The goal of modernity, in the highest level of subjectivity as end-in-itself, is thwarted by the earlier stages of natural insecurity and the self as a means to relieving it.

3. The other as exotic.

If likeness prevails over difference, as pointed out in the first modality, differences are non-essential, but they may be recognized as attaching contingently to this essentially similar other. Thus, one perceives an

121

"essential humanity" with characteristics that do not serve to attach content to it. The assimilation of races, genders, classes, and cultures to a "universal" human culture that does not question itself, reflects this modality. Also, when ethnic characteristics are regarded as commodities which are available to all, rather than as expressing a definite content of humanity. Often, differences regarded in such a way are attractive, since they are unlike but not threatening. Thus, the exotic other is a source of romantic attraction, a decorative attribute without effect. The consumer society thrives on such exotica. Purchase of non-essential tokens of otherness releases a pleasurable sensation of self. Ephemeral, due to the non-essentiality from which it is derived, such pleasures decay into the cynicism of indifference to otherness. They are only revived by the tinsel of the latest token.

These three modalities of the self/other encounter exhaust the possibilities within the essence/accident distinction. With regard to the otherness of the other, the persisting differences, there are three responses: 1) overlooking and ignoring; 2) reducing to an animal or an enemy requiring incarceration or extermination; and 3) preserving as an exotic. Due to the two-sided character of the self/other relation, each of these can be reversed. The above descriptions were from the viewpoint of a centred self. If the self expires, is decentred by the other, each of these modalities can occur in reverse image: 1) ignoring the self, or experiencing oneself as non-essential and marginal; 2) hating the self, exterminating the self; and 3) exotically preserving one's differences as if they were differences of "just anyone." These modalities also permeate the self/other relationship at the interpersonal, cultural, intercultural, and civilizational levels.

Identity and Plurality

The end of modern ethics consists in the infinite delay of autonomy and reconciliation since this very project redoubles the essence/attribute distinction from which it arises. It requires an archeology of the most primordial constitution of otherness within the immanent sphere of ownness. From such an archeology we can discern the origin of the three modes of otherness in post-modern culture and clear the way for a post-modern ethics that institutes cultural identities through "belonging."

The metaphysical telos of reconciliation attempted to leap over modern displacement, to write over the experience of displacement the historical project of its cancelling. Thus, the framework of cancelling, or redeeming, displacement was inserted into the experience itself. It seems the individualized fear that instituted modernity could only be described in a language that promised its redemption. The framework for curing displacement has been deployed into two dimensions. Origin/telos, from which modernity elaborates the project of the recapture of self-identity, or authenticity is the first. Identity/difference, from which it projects reconciliation with the other, is the second. Post-modern culture, however, initiates an infinite delay of the telos of reconciliation. Reconsidering the two dimensions of displacement as schism and cut opens a new encounter with the constitution of cultural identities.

Post-modern culture is a process of dissolution and recombination of three modes of identity and difference in the self/other relation. The modern telos is not cancelled, but infinitely delayed, so that it becomes a mechanism of recombination and escalation. To the extent that the other is "like" the self, differences are ignored and modern homogenization is extended. The other, like the self, is in *uniform*. To the extent that the other is different, two sub-modes arise. The enemy, the essentially hostile other whose overt acts *disguise* the inner motives, turns even benevolent appearances into sinister tricks. Third, in exotic preservation of the other as staged difference, the *mask* gives a face while hiding an assumption of essential similarity. Clearly, these are not simply options, but are *modes* in which the other appears. Thus, ethical reconciliation requires a uniform to cover difference to enable essentially human autonomy to appear. Such an essential humanity may well be masked in an accidental appearance. These modes interplay on the condition that difference is accidental. If difference should become essential, the enemy appears in disguise. The repetitive cycle of indifference, hostility, and attraction to otherness testifies that what is at issue here is not the objects, but the mode of constitution of the boundary. It is the continual shuffling of this stacked deck that is the site of cultural identity today—authenticity and reconciliation as the modern fuel of a post-modern delay. So our question becomes: Where are our *costumes* for carnival?

These three modes of otherness constitute an infinite delay for the telos of reconciliation. Such a delay cannot, of course, in itself cancel a telos, but it has been shown that the telos and its delay are co-constituted within modernity. Here is a motive for an archeology which shows the condition for the telos. Understanding modernity as a closed system that cannot satisfy the projects it generates, is an entry into a questioning that exceeds modernity. In one sense, post-modern culture is the completion of modernity in its only possible mode—infinite delay. In another sense, it is an entry, not to a programme, but to a question: Where may we found modes of belonging?

The historical condition for the essence/accident distinction which underlies contemporary modes of otherness is displacement. Schism and cut, displacement in time and space, reveal an individualized pain and fear. In Sartre's sense, scarcity grounds the struggle not to be one of the expendables, but "scarcity" itself needs reformulation. The displacement that reveals individualized pain, simultaneously constitutes a world in which the individual cannot belong. There can never be enough wealth to compensate such pain. Production multiplies in all directions. Identities and differences are staged to simulate authenticity and reconciliation. Without cure, pain simply stimulates another round, there cannot be "wealth," and displacement is repeated.[32]

The primordial constitution of self/other relations reveals two aspects which indicate an escape-hatch from this post-modern repetition. First, the incompleteness of the likeness of the other's body to my own, is such that I am a *source* of empathic transfer while the other may decentre me as an occupant *in* space and time. Second, the "conditional access" to cultural groups, is such that participation is founded on the performance of specific acts which define the *content* of the cultural consciousness in question. These two characteristics are revealed only by escaping the metaphysical telos of reconciliation and risking the asymmetrical constitution of the other within the sphere of ownness. From this, two correlative aspects of self/other relations emerge. First, the self, or the cultural identity in question, is the source of empathic understanding of *both* one's own and other identities. Second, *display* of the contents of the other's identity is essential to the actual performance of empathic transfers. Thus, while access is conditional on display, it can only be actualized through a recovery of the self as source. This asymmetrical relation is the primordial phenomenon from which an ethics responding to the post-modern situation must be developed.

Neither of these characteristics of "empathy" and "display" nor both in tandem, should be understood as determinants from which social practice could be derived, as if they were external factors that could be opposed to social practice. Rather, they are constituents of social practice itself. In order to give the most universal expression of this asymmetrical phenomenon, it will be termed expiration/inspiration.[33] The double-sidedness of this phenomenon is often apparent due to the self/other separations and relations that set up social practices. Nevertheless, if we focus on the phenomenon itself, on the primordial encounter which allows of subsequent separations, it must be called spiration—the moment between breathing in and out, the silence of worlded awareness. Spiration is the unity of the meeting-place in the meeting, but also the non-reciprocal relations which are constituted by the modes of this meeting. As breath passes from one pair of lungs to another, aspiration is the invisibility which inheres in the alterities of visibility.

Such a formulation should be free from the misinterpretation that social ontology is being derived from individual consciousness here. By contrast, the procedure has been to effect a phenomenological reduction to the stream of consciousness in the midst of socio-historical life in order to clarify the constitutive acts that are operative in communicative inter-subjectivity. These communications can be focussed on at four levels of abstraction—interpersonal, cultural groups, intercultural, and universal civilization. In each case, spiration devolves upon an expiration/inspiration nexus which is the asymmetrical constitution of differences and relations.

A central theme in modern versus post-modern ethics can be derived from consideration of alternative ways of understanding the border, or boundary, inserted in spiration that constitutes the relation between self and other. The individualized pain of displacement has motivated the modern view of the border as an ending of the self, as an encircling wall with aliens outside the gates. Thus, the essence/accident distinction arises to leap over the wall and proclaim the telos of reconciliation. To the extent that this experience remains within the post-modern condition, the telos of modern ethics is not simply abandoned. When self-identity is threatened by otherness, autonomy is its first line of defence. Such situations will continue to arise and the essence/attribute distinction will retain applicability in such cases. These situations, however, must be comprehended on the wider uncharted ground of spirations of otherness, on which autonomy can neither be grounded nor finally accomplished. Modern ethics is now a circumscribed project, a moment of balance within the infolding asymmetry of post-modern ethics.

For post-modernity, a border is also that which lets one's own territory appear. The display of the other is essential to one's own identity. A border is where the othering of the self begins.[34] Thus, one's own culture is a manifestation of essential humanity which needs the other to appear, and suggests an "active curiosity" with respect to otherness, which does not thereby become a possession, as a condition for self-awareness.[35] Post-modern ethics centres on belonging within the horizon of localized displays animated by an active love of diversity. Otherness, in this sense, is within the gates. As in the New World, ethnicity no longer connotes primarily an origin but a condition among others. When all become ethnics, internal otherness facilitates the empathic entry into one's own identity.

When spiration disburses into expiration and inspiration by instituting a boundary, this asymmetry indicates an involuntary moment inherent in one's location. In history and geography one is located, in the first place, by a schism from origin, and in the second by a cut from the other whose difference is displayed. This no longer founds a project of recovery. In post-modern culture, thought must move beyond, outside, the metaphysical frame. It must probe the schism and the cut to clarify our displacement. One can no longer flee this pain into a metaphysical cure. There

125

may be no cure, but neither can one find cynical solace in a certainty that there can be no healing. Risk is still alive. For thought without guarantees, the probing of schism and cut is a discovery of the pain that displacement has etched on our bodies. One must explore these wounds with one's own fingers, plunge into the suffering that has made us, and disturb the unhealing scab to feel the free running of red blood. Only with this blood can the exile connect with civilization. Not in "return," nor yet in "arrival," but only on a thin wager to find meaning in the wandering.

Acceptance of the involuntary, of what we are *made* by our bodies and their response to others, motivates an empathic eagerness for displays of otherness. The central issues for post-modern ethics concern non-reciprocal relations, such as race, gender, and class. Ethnicity, another non-reciprocity, brings to the fore the centrality of cultural identity to all of these. The modern focus on authenticity and reconciliation cannot formulate these relations properly since it will always tend to reduce the asymmetry of the double non-reciprocity to a self-certainty and autonomy. By focussing on the schism and cut whereby spiration constitutes modes of otherness, the foundations of a post-modern ethics can be elaborated. It is precisely what is not shared, that is now the central theme of ethics. Only from this starting point can possibilities of belonging be instituted which recognize difference, our separation from origin, and yet sustain possibilities of identity.

Displays, like history and geography, can never be cancelled, but only covered, as uniforms conceal diversity. Displays can be disguised, to conceal the essence of the enemy. They can be staged, transformed into masks which conceal one's own essence, and can be worn by anyone. But displays may also be costumed, celebrating the appeal of otherness, painting oneself in the colours of carnival.

Notes

1. The opening of intrapersonal communication, the interior space of modernity, is instituted by the self becoming other to itself, as discussed below briefly with respect to Marx. This requires careful comparison to Plato's interior dialogue to place the present inquiry into post-modern ethics in relation to ancient ethics. That task is not attempted here.
2. See my "Reflections on Technology and Humanism," *Queen's Quarterly* 90, no. 4 (Winter 1983).
3. The work of C. B. Macpherson is central in this respect. See, in particular, the contradiction he discerns between self-development and utility in liberalism. I have discussed Macpherson's work in relation to these two strains of modern ethics in "On

Macpherson's Developmental Liberalism" *Canadian Journal of Political Science* XV, no. 1 (1982).

4. Immanuel Kant, *Critique of Practical Reason*, Lewis White Beck, trans. (Indianapolis: Bobbs-Merrill, 1956), 90.

5. G. W. F. Hegel, *The Philosophy of Right*, T. M. Knox, trans (Oxford: Oxford University Press, 1952), 110, par. 158.

6. *Ibid.*, 122, par. 182.

7. *Ibid.*, 160ff., par. 260.

8. *Ibid.* Thus, the concept of *Aufhebung* is the central discovery of Hegel since it unites the domination of nature and ethical autonomy through historical synthesis.

9. Kant, *Practical Reason*, 123.

10. Hegel, *Philosophy of Right*, 281, addendum 158 to par. 265.

11. See, for example, Marx's paean to the revolutionary spirit of capitalism in the first section of *The Communist Manifesto* in *The Marx-Engels Reader*, Robert C. Tucker, ed. (New York: W. W. Norton, 1978), 473-8.

12. See *Capital*, vol. 1, ch. 6, "The Sale and Purchase of Labour-Power." This distinction of a subject as the owner of capacities has been traced in early liberal political economy by C. B. Macpherson in *The Political Theory of Possessive Individualism: Hobbes to Locke* (Oxford: Oxford University Press, 1962). Marx's work is discussed here solely as a diagnosis of capitalism and modernity. However, one can see in this formulation the source of the failure of his solution. Once the self is fully alienated as other, there is no basis from which it can rebound to become the subject of history. Only the assumption of an essence of self can provide the basis for a rebound from alienation to subjectivity.

13. Friedrich Nietzsche, *On the Genealogy of Morals*, Walter Kaufmann and R. J. Hollingdale, trans. (New York: Random House, 1969), 45, first essay, sec. 13.

14. Reiner Schurmann, "Anti-Humanism: Reflections on the Turn Towards the Post-Modern Epoch," *Man and World*, xii, no. 2 (1979).

15. Edmund Husserl, *Cartesian Meditations*, Dorion Cairns, trans. (The Hague: Martinus Nijhoff, 1969), 98. Emphasis in original.

16. *Ibid.*, 112f. It can be noted here that Husserl overlooks the entire range of complex questions concerning media of communication and, specifically, the role of the body as such a medium. Consequently, a prejudice in favour of face-to-face communication in the living present is introduced without justification into phenomenological descriptions. For a clear example of this, see Alfred Schutz, "Symbol, Reality and Society," *Collected Papers*, I (The Hague: Martinus Nijhoff, 1971), 318. This requires detailed investigations which I reserve for future study.

17. *Cartesian Meditations*, 119.

18. Rene Toulemont, "The Specific Character of the Social According to Husserl," *Apriori and World*, W. McKenna, R. M. Harlan and L. E. Winters, ed. and trans. (The Hague: Martinus Nijhoff, 1981), 228. Toulemont is summarizing Husserl's published and unpublished investigations.

19. *Cartesian Meditations*, 132.

20. *Ibid.*, 134f. Husserl concludes the quoted section with the observation that "[t]his empathy also calls for intentional investigations." The present essay is intended as such a contribution.

21. Compare *Cartesian Meditations*, 110, 119.

22. Ludwig Landgrebe, "The Phenomenology of Corporeality and the Problem of Matter," *The Phenomenology of Edmund Husserl*, Donn Welton, ed. (Ithaca: Cornell University Press, 1981), 263.

23. Jean-Paul Sartre, *Being and Nothingness*, Hazel E. Barnes, trans. (New York: Philosophical Library, 1956), 263.
24. *Ibid.*, 364. Sartre would, of course, call this a dialectic and proceed to differentiate it from Hegel's. However, it is unclear in what sense there can be dialectic without reconciliation. Since a critical history of dialectical thought is hardly possible here, the term double non-reciprocity is used to signify this fundamental difference.
25. Jean-Paul Sartre, *Critique of Dialectical Reason*, Alan Sheridan-Smith, trans. (London: Verso, 1982), 130.
26. Alfred Schutz criticizes Sartre for taking over Hegel's optimism regarding the interchangeability of self and other. "Sartre's Theory of the Alter Ego," *Collected Papers*, I, 197ff. The present analysis focusses on the description of decentring, which is a valid phenomenological datum. However, the extent to which this implies dialectic was indeed overestimated by Sartre. See note 24.
27. I am excluding from present consideration phenomena such as mirrors and reflections of all sorts, partly because of the considerations mentioned in note 16. More fundamentally, such phenomena involve the recognition of myself as seen by an other and, in this sense, are founded on the phenomenon now under consideration.
28. The case of gender was pointed out by Eugen Fink in the discussion of Alfred Schutz's "The Problem of Transcendental Intersubjectivity in Husserl," *Collected Papers*, (The Hague: Martinus Nijhoff, 1970), vol. 3, 84. Such considerations have not yet been systematically introduced into phenomenological descriptions.
29. See my paper, "The Phenomenology of Material Culture," presented to the Husserl Circle Annual Meeting at the University of Ottawa, July 1985.
30. *Cartesian Meditations*, 125ff.
31. David McReynolds, "Star Wars: An Analysis," War Resister's League Pamphlet (September 1985). This is the motive for Star Wars, another level of dialectical escalation that attempts to remove the assumption of the rationality of the enemy.
32. This, in short, is why the Marxist programme fails. There is a burgeoning literature on need in Marx as both "historically defined" and "capable of being overcome" in a generally wealthy society, a contradiction which is founded on this analysis of displacement. See, for example, William Leiss, *The Limits to Satisfaction* (Toronto: University of Toronto Press, 1976), 75-8.
33. I have developed this description, in part, from Emmanuel Levinas' use of inspiration in *Otherwise Than Being, or Beyond Essence*, Alphonso Lingis, trans. (The Hague: Martinus Nijhoff, 1981), 111, 140ff, 180ff.
34. The question of a different understanding of boundary is broached in Martin Heidegger, "Building Dwelling Thinking," *Poetry, Language, Thought*, Albert Hofstadter, trans. (New York: Harper and Row 1975), 154. There, he says a boundary is "that from which something *begins* its presencing." This understanding has been made possible by Husserl's concept of horizon, and it requires further detailed description to rescue it from Heidegger's ontological framework. The theme here has been primarily the presencing of the other itself, not from where it begins. This beginning would be comparable to the notion of spiration in the present account. A comparison would be too far afield here.
35. Of course, the self is not lacking anything necessary to essential humanity in this need for otherness. What is at issue in this new formulation is a reconception of the relation of part and whole, especially as it affects the understanding of the self and of culture. See Richard Zaner, *The Context of Self* (Athens, Ohio: Ohio University Press, 1981) and Clifford Geertz, "The Impact of the Concept of Culture on the Concept of Man," *The Interpretation of Cultures* (New York: Basic, 1973).

Dušan Pokorný

Homelessness and Justice

The two presentations we have heard may be said to be two responses to the condition of displacement. In both of them, the contemporary man (whether we call him modern or post-modern) is seen as having lost the place where he could feel at home, although the deprivation is the result of actions whose true import has remained hidden to him. The ensuing homelessness is responded to in different ways. Angus seems to be accepting it as another fall of man and invites us to make do with what is left, while Kontos harkens back to Ithaca and, at least in a part of his being, still searches for means of regaining it. Even if not absolute, the difference is fundamental, and my response to the two arguments will bring out its meaning in as wide a context as the generality of the formulations requires, even if they themselves might have been originally intended to cover a narrower ground.

I

Angus treats the post-modern condition as radically different from the modern, because the telos of mutual recognition, while not abandoned, must now be indefinitely postponed. The end of modernity signals also the demise of the ethics of Kant and Hegel. Hence there is the necessity of a post-modern ethics based on Husserl and on Sartre.

In this chain of reasoning, "end of modernity" suggests the cessation of a state of affairs. "Necessity of post-modern ethics" appears then as the result of a reflection on that change of historical circumstances. Now, even though both the formation of social reality and the reflection on it are historical processes, they are not one and the same process. Therefore, it is still possible, and necessary, to observe that, if the ethics of Kant and Hegel are said to have been rendered invalid by the end of modernity, then the new ethics will have to be measured by, or judged in terms of, its adequacy vis-à-vis the state of affairs that has come to be called post-modernity.

In the presentation under review, the focus is on reflection and its conclusions. However, Angus has also something to say about the underlying circumstances. Under the heading of "Modes of Otherness," he sees the exotic other against the background of the consumer society's obsession with non-essential tokens and the other as enemy is expressly situated in the nuclear age. This is, I believe, an indication that for him—as for several other proponents of post-modernity—the delay of the telos of mutual recognition is closely associated with the emergence of cultural identities centred on consumer choices and with the presence of weapons of mass destruction.

I agree that the duality in the social meaning of contemporary technology—the appearance of more choice in respect of "things," and the fact of less choice in matters of "destiny"—is a significant discontinuity in the history of man. I also agree that, in an important sense, the promise of modern ethics has remained unfulfilled, but my understanding of the relationship between the elements of the picture is different from that presented in Angus' contribution. That difference is reflected also in my approach to the search for solutions.

To begin, we have to note that the appearance of the *individual's choice* in the sphere of consumption tends to conceal the real necessity of *social* determination of genuine *needs*. For the present debate,[1] two such instances are, I believe, of crucial importance. Even within the countries which now have, taken as a whole, access to modern technology, there exist groups that have been shunted to a side-track with no exit: the chronically unemployed; many members of racial and ethnic minorities; the youth with no education and no (socially induced) yearning for one; the ill, the disabled, or otherwise disadvantaged; a large part of the elderly. It is true that, in these countries, "poverty" is sometimes a social status, rather than immediate physiological deprivation, and that it is also gilded by trappings such as television screens. For the most part, however, the "box" signifies only a choice of more or less immersion in stereotyped and commercialized entertainment which yields a picture of the world that is delusory from the point of view of both those who "have made it," and those who have not. The effect on the latter is particularly

130

damaging because their innate striving for an internally consistent life-world makes them adopt sense-giving schemata that are essentially alien to them. Decision making based on the instrumental rationality of the market is manifestly unable to deal with this problem of poverty amid plenty. The only hope is the restoration, and indeed expansion, of the sphere of political decisions guided by the ethical principle of equity.

Serious as it is, the plight of the poor and underprivileged in North America and in Western Europe is merely a miniature of the problem as it exists on the world scale. At present, the "high" technology based on "high" science also widens the gap between the have-nations and the have-not-nations. It is true that, just as the initial industrialization, in what are now the economically developed countries of the world, opened the possibility of gains for the poor and desolate within those societies, so the present technological revolution contains in itself the potentiality of material improvement for today's distressed and underprivileged at the level of nations. However, the former possibility started to be realized only after several generations had elapsed. In the present case there may not be that much time. In the political sphere, the Europeanization of the world which began with the voyages of discovery and robbery in the fifteenth century is, especially since World War II, being followed by a rather rapid de-Europeanization. In its substance, this development has to be seen as a part of the restoration of the "natural face of the earth." In due course, it is bound to bring about fundamental changes in our position in the world.

All this is also to be considered when we turn to technology and war. Although the Soviet Union is an imperialist power bent on expansion, it is unlikely to launch a military attack in Europe, or directly on the United States, unless (i) the Great-Russian chauvinists gain complete control in the Kremlin, or (ii) the societies of Western Europe and/or the North-American subcontinent are gravely weakened by internal social conflicts. (The Bomb would play a key role in case (i), but not in (ii).) Since World War II, all wars have been fought in the economically underdeveloped countries. If there were to be another world conflagration, this is where the fuse would most likely be ignited. The reasons are plain. On the one hand, for the overwhelming majority of the people living in those areas, the prospect of an atomic war is remote. It cannot compete with the urgency of hunger, with immediately experienced oppression or with local wars using weapons of much more down-to-earth technology. On the other hand, the prevalence of poverty as a material condition (not just a symbolically mediated social status) makes it much easier to present even arbitrary goals as justified by the "reason of history" and to make a case for ends legitimizing any means whatsoever.[2]

If we are to speak of post-modernity, then we have to see both sides of

131

this new moon: the "consumed identities" of a small, "choosing" minority of the world population *and* the needs of the underprivileged majority. These needs cannot be met within the limits of choice-making as we understand it. The fact that they are not satisfied threatens the identity (whether modern or pre-modern) of the people concerned. To be sure, this is not to say that the moral questions put before the former are the same as those confronting the latter, or that the interrelation between the two human conditions is immediately visible. The argument is merely that no reflection is adequate, and no self-reflection reasonably complete, unless we see "our" identity as conditioned by "theirs." Nor is this just a matter of abstract speculation, since at issue is a sizable redistribution of wealth.

A few examples will suffice to illustrate the point. To the extent that the current national debt in the economically developed countries has not been brought about by armament, its most important cause has been the governments' tendency to provide benefits that would be *seen* as redistributing income, without imposing the taxes that would *actually* redistribute it. At the international level, it is fairly obvious that the enormous debts accumulated by the developing countries—some 900 billions in U. S. dollars—will have to be written off, or new loans will have to be granted to make possible a gradual repayment of the old ones. Either way, a redistribution of assets will occur. Even more important, at least in the long run, is the fact that the present relation between the prices of the primary goods exported by the underdeveloped nations and the prices of the primary goods sold to them by the economically developed countries is biased against the former. This state of affairs can hardly continue indefinitely. Other things remaining equal, the cost to the industrialized countries of a movement toward equity in the over-all "terms of trade" will be high.

All in all, when we take a closer look at the factors that short-circuit mutual recognition, it may turn out that the transformation of the "other" into a potential enemy threatening "us" with death, is less important than the emergence of the "other" as a potential claimant for a share in "our" standard of living. In any case, injustices are now *perceived* to be injustices—or rather, they are at present understood as *systemic*, not merely random—to an extent that has hardly existed before. However the established order of things stands in the way of meaningful remedies. Ultimately, it is more in this sense than in any other that we are living beyond our means.

All this is also a commentary on modern ethics. In it, the distinction between "choice" and "need" was made in the context of that between "contingent" and "necessary," "partial" and "universal." The second formulation made explicit that the legitimacy of needs was grounded in a perception of the whole. However, the notion of the whole, and therefore the understanding of the necessary, varied from one thinker to another. In Kant, the kingdom of ends was the realm of private ends only to the extent that they were compatible with universal law. Universally valid meant *whatever* will pass the criterion of the categorical imperative.[3] Hegel rightly criticized this notion of practical reason as formal, or empty, and endeavoured to replace it by ethics that would be both objective and concrete, that is, contentful. The individual's pursuit of happiness as well as the society-wide system of satisfying particularized needs were to be subject to the sovereignty of truly universal "needs-and-chosen-wants," that is, those expressing the unity of objective and subjective freedom.[4] However, one could hardly overlook the feudal remnants in the visible structure of the state in which this unity—or substantive practical reason—was to reside. Neither at the level of the individual state, nor at that of the world mind, do we find a convincing account of how to proceed from the individually chosen to the socially needed-wanted. (These observations will no doubt call to mind Marx's critique of Hegel, but Marx failed to realize that he was dealing with a problem of ethics.[5] That proved to be a fundamental limitation of his argument.)

In conclusion, if post-modernity demonstrates the failure of modern ethics, it does so because the conflict between choices and needs is now coming to a head. This is, then, also the touchstone of post-modern ethics. Is it better equipped for dealing with *this* problem?

II

Angus proposes basing the ethics of post-modernity on (i) the self as the source of empathic transfers and (ii) the display of the content of the other's identity. The two sides are said to be mutually implicative, but essentially non-reciprocal and thus non-totalizable. Put another way, they are intended to assist in forming a whole, but the whole is not to be founded on reconciliation, or on mutual recognition. Rather, (i) and (ii), taken together, yield double non-reciprocity. The question, then, is whether the whole here envisaged is such that it can resolve the conflict between choices and needs in the above sense of the terms. At this stage, of course, statements (i) and (ii) are still too bald to permit an answer. Before going any further, we have to find out more about their meaning, which requires an inquiry into the argument underlying them.

1. Angus starts from the proposition that we cannot "presuppose the other as given in order to assure the telos of mutual recognition." This opening statement is meant to reject Hegel and to prepare the ground for the adoption of Husserl and Sartre. So the first thing to do is to restate

Hegel's position. For the present purpose, it may be done as follows:

(a) Both "this" self-consciousness and "that" self-consciousness are *given* to each other as "reflection out of *bare* being." In this form, each has the other "before itself" immediately. In this context, "history" may be said to be seen as a moment, a cross-section of a flow.

(b) The "being there," being "as an object," means being "for another." Therefore, one *is* to the extent that one is *recognized* by the other.[6] The two are thus engaged in a process of mutual identity formation. This process clearly occurs in history as a *movement* (the flow whose cross-section we spoke of above).

(c) Individual acts of recognition are never without "presuppositions" in the form of the present, ordinary-language transmitted, inter-subjectively shared, sense-giving "shapes" and "patterns" of (self-) consciousness.[7]

(d) The shapes are "objective" in the sense of "non-arbitrary" because they have been developed in the course of previous history. At each stage of the formative process, they are both valid *and* subject to reflection—"thought" being directed "against" the forms already "familiar to our minds"—as to their adequacy in relation to the purpose of the whole movement of history (e). This critique, however, is again a historical process. Hence it has both validity and limitations.[8] No individual can ever become aware of all the presuppositions underlying his life-world and free himself from them; nor can a society, or even mankind, except

(e) at the Summit of all the movement, when comprehended History becomes one with Absolute Spirit.[9]

From this complex position, then, what precisely is rejected? Or, more generally, how has it been responded to?

2. Since some of the distinctions made in paragraph 1 are not present in Angus' discussion, his answer will be reconstrued from what he does say, or from the sources he has used.

(α) These days one does not have to be a proponent of post-modernity to reject the notion of (e) as a state attained, or attainable, in a historical sense, or even as a point toward which world history necessarily moves, albeit in an asymptotic manner (that is, coming closer and closer, without ever reaching it). One may still wish to retain (e) as a source of criteria for the understanding and assessment of actual historical situations. For example, one may say that the relations which form a society are consciously entered into, and the "product," society as a network of intelligible relations, can and ought to be transparent. However, Angus rejects (e) even in this sense, as indeed he must, for a new ethics must install its new criteria of comprehension and judgment.

(β) In Hegel, whatever precedes (e) is a "promise" not yet fully realized. Starting with the master-slave relation, involving a recognition that is only "one sided and unequal,"[10] we go through numerous "forms" or "schemes" which are still inadequate, that is, still on their way to (e) but not yet there. As a consequence, the acts of recognition (c) will not exhaust all the possibilities of the "bare being's" (a) unfoldment into an identity (b) as rich as possible. A part of the inadequacy is the persistence of other forms of the domination-subjugation relation which, even if less constraining than slavery itself, continue to make the recognition less than fully mutual and less than completely equal. One by one, they are subjected to critical reflection (d) from the point of view of the standard (e). In Husserl, too, there are master-servant relations that are said to bring about unity, although they are not "reciprocal."[11] Indeed, the condition of subservience is said to become a part of the person's universal habitude, making, for instance, a slave who revolted, but lost, "acknowledge... his duty [Sollen] retroactively [nachträglich] for the time during which he violated it."[12] The duty appears here as given and "static." The legitimacy of the obligation is not seen as conditional, as in due course inevitably challenged by critical questioning (d). Needless to say, this is not a reflection on Husserl's attitude to slavery. The argument merely shows that the difference between Hegel and Husserl cannot be adequately expressed in terms of "mutual recognition" versus "lack of reciprocity." Ultimately at issue is the meaning of history.

(γ) When Husserl started his phenomenological revolution, the transcendental ego was outside history altogether. In retrospect, he wrote that the "I" had been for him a *solus ipse*, and "all constitutional components," or the hole phenomenon "world," were "merely contents of this one ego."[13] In a later fundamental investigation which Angus takes as his point of departure, Husserl allowed for the existence of other "monads" and for intersubjectivity at their level.[14] He still held that the phenomenal reality was accessible only to an inquiry that, although no doubt historically situated in the psychophysical world, must be "absolutely free from... the universal 'prejudice' of world experience,"[15] including the experience of being in society and in history. So it was still also true that the construction of the environing world is *without* the sphere of "already-given actualities or concepts of actualities"[16] and that "everything existing for me must derive its existential sense exclusively from me... "[17] Clearly, "the intersubjective [remained] an extension of the subjective" and "the social and historical [was still] subsequent to the individual."[18] In this respect, then, the difference between the two phenomenologies may be summed up. In Hegel, if we "bracketed" the Absolute, we would still have genuine human history, albeit seen as the process of formation, and replacement, of "forms of life." In Husserl, if we excluded the transcendental ego, we would be left with nothing, that is, with nothing that is *real*, nothing insofar as phenomenology is concerned.

(δ) It is a part of the position outlined in (γ) that (δ α) it is "in me [that the other] becomes constituted"[19] and that (δ β) the "I," the "I-pole" of the phenomenological attitude, is originally given in the sense of an "immanent time flow of experiences [Erlebnisse]."[20] Against this background, we should read also the other founding block of Angus' argument, the passage from Sartre quoted in Angus' note 23. For the words "I grasp... ," "I perceive... ," reflect the basic position taken earlier in Sartre's chain of reasoning: (δ α) "The man is defined by his relation to the world and myself."[21] At the same time, (δ β) "these possibilities that I am" are at the moment fixed, being "given also to the other," and the acts of transcending them are still seen as occurring without overt acts of one on the other. The "transcendence transcended" from which we start has nothing to do with the dialectics of mutual identity formation (b) and excludes any relations of moral nature. The other is still only a look, and he acts on me "by the pure upsurge of his being."[22] Later, of course, Sartre did move to the sphere of overt acts, and Angus follows him there to the point of accepting the contention that all societies known thus far have been living under "conditions of scarcity." However, that claim is now widely recognized to be false. There is anthropological evidence to show that it is not scarcity that "creates" society, but that (as Aristotle pointed out) it is society that "creates" scarcity. It is only a particular, rather late type of culture, that makes man believe that his needs and wants are naturally boundless.[23] From this point of view, the problem of ethics starts, not with attempts to determine who is to be dispensable, but with the question: *Why* is there scarcity at all?

(ε) When Husserl started to think about intersubjectivity, he realized that he would have to consider the problems of ethics. In substance, his answer was to invoke a "community of love" [Liebesgemeinschaft].[24] In doing so, he neither broke new ground nor established a clear relation between his phenomenology and this fragmentary discussion of ethics. However, in 1935 he said that "[t]he European nations are sick" and proposed as a cure the "synthesis of theoretical universality [a feature of scientific knowledge] and practical outlook with universal interests," an outlook which appeared first as the mythical-religious attitude.[25] In this reasoning Husserl not only came as close as *he* could to a truly historical discourse, he also addressed, albeit not in moral terms, an ethical problem of momentous proportions. Sartre, having finished *Being and Nothingness*, wrote several hundred pages of a book on ethics.[26] In part, he wanted to explain in it that he had changed his mind about the nature of freedom. While writing *Being and Nothingness*, he still believed, "like the old Stoics [that] one was always free." (Stoics, said Hegel, never went beyond this: "In thinking I am free because I am not in the other . . . ")[27] Around 1943 that ceased to be true for Sartre. He came to understand that "there are situations in which one cannot be free" and that "[t]hese circumstances arose out of the freedom of the others."[28] We do not know how he would have tried to resolve the problem. He never finished the book on ethics, but he did say that he had "explained his thoughts on the subject in *The Devil and the Good Lord*"[29] and made it clear that, to attain freedom, it is necessary to "bring about a different relation between man on the one hand and history and the world on the other."[30] Thus both Husserl and Sartre tried to return the self-exiled "I" to history when confronted with a major social crisis—anticipated (Husserl in 1935), or actual (Sartre in 1943), or imaginary (Sartre writing in 1951 about a civil war in Germany four centuries before)—although neither of them quite made it. Yet the moral of the story could not be more obvious. If one wants to start with Husserl and Sartre, and if one does so in the face of another historical crisis (be it of the kind Angus has in mind, or the one I have in mind), then it goes against the grain to use the two thinkers' initial, radically ego-oriented teachings.

Keeping in mind these antecedents, let us now return to the consequents: Angus' points (i) and (ii) and their interrelation.

3. In the conclusion of his argument, both (i) the self, the potentiality of "empathic transfers" and (ii) the displayer, or performer, of otherness are designated as "cultural identities." They are no longer the "primordial ego" or "my own concrete being," and the "pure other."[31] They have a specific content, provided by their association with cultural groups. However, these groups themselves are the result—a level—of the constitution of the objective world (in "the existence sense") out of "my primordial 'world'."[32] To use one of Sartre's examples, I *first* see a man as a pure, culture-less entity whose only background is a park, a lawn, a few benches.[33] This is related (existentially, not socially or morally) only to myself, as another entity stripped of all cultural determinations. *Then* I may use the mediation of intentionality[34] (that is, that property of *mental* acts which takes them out of the sphere of truth or *reality*) to build up the communities or cultural groups that "I" share, or do not share, with "him." At this stage, of course, I do not act, yet. I am only engaged in the construction of the world within which I will act, but I have already taken one crucial step that will determine the meaning, for me, of the whole sphere of morality. I have started with, and have thus retained the freedom of a retreat to, the perception of others, as well as of myself, as entities whose "purity" not only permits, but also demands, the absence of any sense of ethical relations.

Intrinsically, "I" owe nothing to "you," and vice versa. Indeed, we mutually "decentre" each other, we "disintegrate" each other's universe.[35] Subsequently, "you" appear as enclosed in your group, denying "me" access to it, demonstrating your otherness as my insufficiency, my failing and "I" reach out to "you" to complete "myself," to "feel myself into you,"[36] so that "you" can figure in the "immanent experience of myself." We are thus linked only by "implication." There is no mutuality, no commitment to the other in his own right and thus no effect of such a commitment on the formation of my own identity. Hence there is "double non-reciprocity." No act can, even in principle, evoke another, for there is no standard of "adequacy" and no basis for ethical judgments. Which brings us back to Hegel.

In essence, Husserl's *epoché* and the related techniques are attempts to make the ego step out and shed all vestiges of the "forms of life" (c). In fact, however, we can never do that. No matter how far away from the "naive" acceptance of the surrounding world Sartre wanted to get, he still had to use the ordinary, "naive," historically developed language to get there. He could step out of French into German, but there is no way of transcending all languages, of moving to a metalanguage that is no language at all, and accomplishing thus the equivalent of stepping out of all history. Closer to home, we do not just "see" a man between two benches of a nameless park. We see him, say—to use another of Sartre's images, except from a later period—as one of the "old men [from] poorhouses who have been labourers or have followed very humble trades [and] have no future left anymore," men whose "life moves toward death with no future other than that of a moment immediately following the present."[37] That is, we see "the man" always already culturally situated, and therefore related to us in a moral context. Since we are what we are, we feel he should not be what he is. For we see him within a "framework" that is not ethically neutral, but rather within a "scheme" of "world interpretation *and* interaction."[38]

This is crucial, but not sufficient. Yet the remedy is not in going back to an *epoché* that does away, even if perhaps unwittingly, with ethicality as an original, ever-present, intrinsic aspect of human life. On the contrary, the nature of the crisis confronting us seems to call, not for an attempt to eliminate the "schemata," but for a critical inquiry into them, in the hope of bringing the acts of recognition closer to full reciprocity. These acts are always be based on the "forms of life" (c) so we cannot afford to banish the very thought of the latter. We have to examine their adequacy. A crucial part of this endeavour is to go beyond Hegel in the sphere of "needs." Since "norms regulate the legitimate chances for the satisfaction of needs,"[39] it is necessary to see to it that the norms are not only "ideally valid"—"deserving of assent by all those affected"—but also "de facto established" by an actual recognition of those concerned.[40] That still leaves us with many questions, mainly about the meaning of consensus, but that would be a theme for another occasion. Now, let me just say that, if a new ethics for the present is to emerge, it is most likely to be in the process of coming to grips with the momentous question of which individual wants should be chosen for the status of the fundamental, socially recognized needs.

III

Kontos' Odysseus may appear first as a hero demonstrating the duality of the pre-modern "involuntary belonging." The king is still *always* half-immersed in the community (wherein his legitimacy as ruler is founded) and the king is already *always* half-away from it because it is abroad that his *areté* will be most visibly demonstrated (and his legitimacy confirmed). So it seems as if the Odyssey—his departure from Ithaca, the tribulations of his journeys, the twists of his homecoming—were a kind of dramatic "reflection" on the original type of "belonging," indeed perhaps the only true, radical "reflection" available to him. At close quarters, however, it will be found that the duality is grounded in the "immersion" itself, in that it can never be complete, never totally unreflective.

In this respect, again, we may learn from the distinction between Husserl and Hegel. In the former, the "naively direct living immersed in the world" is a "fundamental *historical* mode of existence,"[41] that is, a situation, a *state of affairs*, that at some time in the past actually existed. There is a sharp break between this period and the following age of science and true philosophy. Hegel, too, spoke of "natural consciousness," but he immediately added the words: "which presses toward true knowledge." To stress that it is *within* the natural, naive consciousness itself that the "motor" of movement is to be found, he separated, beyond any doubt, the superficial attitude of scepticism ("shilly-shallying about this or that presumed truth") from the historical process of the "Soul['s] journey through its own configurations as though they were stations appointed by its own nature." In the same vein, he went out of his way to emphasize that is it *always* "the universal that is the true [content] of sense-certainty" and that it is "as a universal that we utter" that content. Thus the "immediate" is always already mediated by the "reflection" contained in the historical development of the ordinary language. From this point of view, then, if we were to try and identify immersion pure and simple, we would again be travelling along a curve that comes closer and closer to "it," without ever attaining "it." That is also how to start to understand the meaning of "self." "The simple 'I'," too, is a "simple universal."[42]

139

This is, I believe, the source of Kontos' insistence, throughout his presentation, on Ithaca not being a "place." Rather, it is "the metaphor for the topography of the formation of the self" (Kontos note 3). For in this sense, Ithaca is a part of the *symbolic* mediations underlying the conception of the "self," a thesis which we are bound to depart from and deny, but always *within* the range of the possibilities that *it* unfolded (opened) and determined (closed) for us. Ithaca is thus the "locus" where the struggle between selfness and otherness takes place, where recognition from others is experienced, or is felt to be absent. At this level, the problem of exile is that of realizing—much more keenly than the "homegrown" Hegel does—that the *lack* of recognition is also a part of one's identity formation. For Ithaca posits for us the standards according to which we measure the performance of others vis-à-vis us, although there is, in fact, no reason to expect that they will be bound by those standards, rather than theirs. There is, therefore, a sufficiently wide, but still meaningful sense of "can," which allows one to say that those who *can* return, *will*, and those who *cannot*, are always *self*-exiled. It is their Ithaca as the *home* (the meaning of the place) that makes them reject Ithaca as the *place* (in which to be at home).

It might perhaps be objected that none of this is true of Odysseus, the ruler who leaves voluntarily, always wants to return, and indeed does return. However, there are still good reasons for thinking of him as symbolizing the loss of Ithaca (Kontos note 3), and in more ways than one might initially suspect. As Kontos notes, Odysseus' very return is ambiguous. He first denies his identity. Although this is, at one level, an understandable ruse, at another level it poses the question of the relation between the man who departed and the man who returned. The question persists even after he had made himself known to all and sundry, for Homer wisely refrained from saying much about Odysseus' life after he resumed his rightful place in the palace. Kazantzakis may well have been right when he made Odysseus choose exile again (Kontos note 3), but the moral of the story depends ultimately on the meaning of Odysseus' departure and of the journey as a whole. In this respect, it seems to me, Kontos has allowed himself to be somewhat led astray by Horkheimer and Adorno who construe the Odyssey as "a palimpsest upon which the premonitions of the bourgeois existence will be inscribed."

A palimpsest is a parchment which has been written upon twice, and the meaning of the analogy depends on the relation between the original inscription and that superseding it. It is true that the Greeks did not sail for Troy to retrieve Helen. Rather, they embarked on a war raid intended to secure metals, mainly iron.[1] It is also true that Achilles' *areté* was courage, while Odysseus described himself to the Phayaks as the man known all over the world for his cunning. Yet neither the avidity, nor the mendacity were of the bourgeois kind. The *oikos* of the time was intended to be self-sufficient. The main exceptions were metals for tools, weapons, and articles of treasure, but the latter were not traded, in the market sense of the word. They instead were given away as gifts or were destined to be lost in wars. That is not to say that they were given away for nothing, only that the response to them was measured, not in terms of value, but in terms of adequacy and appropriateness, as laid down by ethical norms.[44] Somewhat similarly, cleverness was *areté*, but *areté* was not cleverness ("cunning" was prowess in thought, in argument, in devising stratagems). In a word, the difference is between Odysseus finding himself at the limit of reason as substantively defined custom and the man of a market-based society beginning to experience the limits of reason as calculativeness pure and simple.[45]

Where Odysseus is most removed from the exile of today is in the sphere of language. There was only one language in his world, and even the Cyclops spoke it. Moreover, while the use of it may be deceptive, language itself is not. It is still thought to be the source of truth about the world. Now, one may leave his or her country because the language there has become unbearably distorted, confirming, time and again, day after day, the rottenness of "the state of Denmark," and at the same time testifying time and again, day after day, to the helplessness of people in the face of the big lie. Of course, in coming from "there" to "here," many will again experience an alienation from language; yet there is a saving grace. It comes from the possibility of saying in the acquired language what could not have been said in one's own. That possibility exists not only because of the change in social and political conditions. The fact is that the "other" language inevitably diminishes or suppresses some sensibilities and develops, even generates, others. More precisely, it imposes on us "reflection" where by rights there should be "immediacy."

To return to where I started, to the two responses to displacement, I will sum up Kontos' response as one which realizes that belonging cannot be entirely voluntary. For him it is still true that "I belong to history before I belong to myself."[46] By contrast, Angus appears to lay much more stress on volition. Even if he realizes some of its limitations, he still believes that displacement will find its solution *within* itself, as a (some) displacement of the displacement. For my part, I agree with Claude Lévi-Strauss that personality is the individual's new totem and has to be understood against the background of the ancient ones.[47] Using my words, rather than his, I would say that there are no "free-flying bodies" whose meaning could be determined solely by interaction with other such allegedly "free-flying bodies." The identity formation of all depends vitally on the nature of the "forms of life" within which they in fact meet. It is within this sphere of "forms" or "frameworks," that the question of "belonging" is ultimately decided.

Notes

1. In a different context, and speaking of industrially developed countries, where the level of material well-being is sufficiently high, one might add the reluctance of men (including those favoured by the present distribution of wealth) to approve measures aimed at ensuring equality for women in terms of job opportunities (often presupposing publicly funded child day-care), salaries and wages, pensions, and rights in joint property.
2. We must also keep in mind that, over the last several decades, even within most of the developing countries, the tendency has been for the rich to become richer and for the poor to become poorer.
3. I. Kant, *Groundwork of the Metaphysic of Morals*, H. J. Paton, trans. (New York: Harper and Row, 1964), 82-4, 100-2 [Berlin Academy edition, 415-17, 533-4].
4. See mainly *The Philosophy of Right*, para. 123, 135, 189, 352.
5. Explaining why "scientific socialism dates from the discovery" of the theory of surplus value, Engels wrote that "From a scientific point of view, an appeal to morality and justice does not help us an inch further." *Anti-Dühring* (Moscow: Progress Publishers, 1969), 180, 243. I have shown elsewhere that, on the contrary, the theory of surplus value—as well as its basis, the theory of value—can be legitimately construed only as ethical statements. See "Marx's Philosophy of Surplus Value," *The Philosophical Forum*, XVI, no. 4 (Summer 1985): 274-92.
6. Hegel, *Phenomenology of Spirit*, A. V. Miller, trans. (Oxford: Clarendon, 1977), 104-5, 111.
7. *Ibid.*, 17, 49, 56, 104, 120. See also the "forms of life" (Charles Taylor, *Hegel* (Cambridge: Cambridge University Press, 1977), 216t, and "schemata of world interpretation and interaction," Jürgen Habermas, *Knowledge and Human Interests* (Boston: Beacon Press, 1971), 192.
8. Hegel, *Phenomenology of Spirit*, 18, 50, 492.
9. *Ibid.*, chapter VIII.
10. *Ibid.*, 116.
11. Edmund Husserl, *Zur Phänomenologie der Intersubjektivität*, Gesammelte Werke, vol. XIV (Den Haag: Martinus Nijhoff, 1973), 169-70, 269. (The quotations are from notes written in 1921-2.) I owe the first reference to George Alkalay's dissertation, "Toward a Recovery of the Philosophical Foundations of the Phenomenology of Social Totality," 1986, part III, 32.
12. Husserl, *Zur Phänomenologie*, 182.
13. Edmund Husserl, *Cartesian Meditations*, Dorion Cairns, trans. (The Hague: Martinus Nijhoff, 1977), 150.
14. *Ibid.*, 89. Angus mentions also Husserl's *Crisis*, but not in connection with ethics. See also (ε) below.
15. *Ibid.*, 35.
16. *Ibid.*, 154.

17. *Ibid.*, 150.
18. Introduction by Quentin Lauer to his translation of Husserl's *Phenomenology and the Crisis of Philosophy* (New York: Harper and Row, 1965), 56.
19. E. Husserl, *Cartesian Meditations*, 149; see also 128.
20. Husserl, *Zur Phänomenologie*, 272, also 296.
21. Jean-Paul Sartre, *Being and Nothingness*, H. E. Barnes, trans. (New York: Philosophical Library, 1956), 257. For the meaning of "world," see para. 3.
22. *Ibid.*, 263.
23. Aristotle, *Politics*, 1257-8. George Dalton, ed., *Primitive, Archaic and Modern Economies: Essays of Karl Polanyi* (Garden City: Doubleday, 1968), 98-9. Cyril S. Belshaw, *Traditional Exchange and Modern Markets* (Englewood Cliffs, N.J.: Prentice-Hall), 110. As for Sartre's own position, I believe that his understanding and use of scarcity cannot be adequately represented by juxtaposing pure subsistence and a "more general sense of 'incompleteness'." First, scarcity is a concept characteristic of modern economics, rather than of classical political economy. Marx defines commodity as the unity of value in use and value in exchange, while a typical contemporary textbook of economics speaks of goods that have prices because they are useful and scarce. The replacement of value in exchange by scarcity amounts to the replacement of an institutional characteristic (only the market system produces commodities) by one which is deemed to be culturally invariant (on the grounds that "to live in the conditions of scarcity" is considered to be an intrinsic part of the condition of being man). It is on this basis, then, that the general equilibrium analysis removes the subsistence wage floor and, at least in principle, allows for wages that are equal to zero or even negative. Second, Sartre himself distinguishes between (a) scarcity as a "relation of man to nature" and (b) "this particular scarcity" (260) which appears to be associated with one man's position relative to other men, whether they are as yet without any historical or institutional determination (members of a queue (260-1)) or are already seen at least against a background (however vague) of a place in history and a set of institutions (two classes; 794). Scarcity in the sense of (a) is a "material condition" (113) and, as such, is "the context of the whole investigation"; in other words, it is, like scarcity in modern economics, presented as an anthropological datum. Scarcity in the sense of (b) is also a "material exigency," except that it need not, although it may, be "directly experienced [as] scarcity" (260, 739). This seems to be what Angus calls "incompleteness." This, however, is not just an aspect of social life *as distinct* from a physical constraint. Rather, it is a material parameter that has *taken the particular, mediated form* of a limit situated in the "social domain". The alleged materiality of the parameter cannot be ignored if we want to understand what Sartre means by "dispensability." After all, he speaks of scarcity as a "mortal danger" (735). All references are to Sartre's *Critique of Dialectical Reason*, A. Sheridan-Smith, trans. (London: Verso/NLB, 1982).
24. Husserl, *Zur Phänomenologie*, 175.
25. Husserl, *Phenomenology*, 150, 168-9.
26. Simone de Beauvoir, *Adieux: A Farewell to Sartre*, P. O'Brian, trans. (Penguin 1981). The references are to Sartre's replies to questions by S. de B. See p. 180.
27. Hegel, *Phenomenology*, 120.
28. S. de Beauvoir, *Adieux*, 358.
29. "Heinrich, the priest," says Sartre about one of the leading characters in the play, "is a man who has never been free, because he is a man of the Church and because at the same time he has a relation with people which is absolutely unconnected with his ecclesiastical education. People and Church contradict each other. He himself is the place in which these forces come into conflict and he can never be free." *Ibid.*

30. *Ibid.*, 261.
31. Husserl, *Cartesian Meditations*, 107.
32. *Ibid.*, 106.
33. Sartre, *Being and Nothingness*, 254.
34. Husserl, *Cartesian Meditations*, 109.
35. Sartre, *Being and Nothingness*, 255.
36. In German, empathy is rendered as Einfühlung.
37. S. de Beauvoir, *Adieux*, 426.
38. See note 7.
39. Thomas McCarthy, *The Critical Theory of Jürgen Habermas* (Cambridge: MIT Press, 1978), 313.
40. Jürgen Habermass, *The Theory of Communicative Action* (Boston: Beacon Press, 1984), vol. I, 88-9.
41. Husserl, *Phenomenology and Crisis*, 166.
42. Hegel, *Phenomenology of Spirit*, 49, 60, 109.
43. M. I. Finley, "Wealth and Labour [Archaic Greece]," in G. Dalton, ed., *Tribal and Peasant Economies* (Garden City, N. Y.: The Natural History Press, 1967), 407-9.
44. *Ibid.*, 409-11. Horkheimer and Adorno miss this point completely when they write that "the exchange of gifts stands for *equivalence*" and speak of "equivalent *value*" instead of "adequacy" in an ethical sense. *Dialectic of Enlightenment* (New York: Herder and Herder: 1972), 49 [emphasis mine].
45. Horkheimer and Adorno overstated their point when they wrote that "[i]n words, Odysseus discovers what is called 'formalism' in fully developed society" (*Dialectic of Enlightenment*, 60). For traditional customs are formulated substantively and mythical names, although they may be used deceitfully, still cannot be validly compared with, say, the "contracting parties" of bourgeois laws.
46. Paul Ricoeur, "Ethics and Culture: Habermas and Gadamer in Dialogue," *Philosophy Today* (1973); quoted in McCarthy, *Critical Theory of Habermas*, 180.
47. *The Savage Mind* (London: Weidenfeld and Nicolson, 1976), 214.

144

Discussion

Silence

Alkis Kontos: I would like very much to strip ethnic background from the individual, totally, everything except the self and Ithaca, and start again. This is a hypothesis, of course, because this cannot be done. It is as if ethnic groups started on the wrong foot. That is why I start with Ulysses, but really Ulysses is a temporary metaphor. Ithaca is solid, though it is also plastic because one sees it differently. Ten years ago I was thinking of Ithaca somewhat differently, much as one thinks of one's childhood. One begins to change. Childhood was Paradise, now it is Hell. It is a cumulative effect of the give and take and I would like to end, as I did with El Greco, as a metaphor for a single Greek in a totally different environment without the community. He was married to a Spanish person. He went through the Inquisition as if he were Spanish. He responded in the same way, but there was in his mannerism something that was Greek. He was named the Greek, though he had a name. Language in and of itself is not the issue. That is why I identify with him in a silent moment at sunset. There is something very important that he must have had pre-linguistically, something of what he was. That something, and this is a tension I experience in the symposium, is something we must blindly celebrate, constructively appropriate or renounce. I think it can be renounced publicly or privately, but constructively.

Dušan Pokorný: What do you mean by "pre-linguistic experience"?

Alkis Kontos: In the sense that before he spoke, he ate. El Greco is an extraordinary fusion of Sartre's tension. Existence precedes essence but essence is in existence. That is the problem. He is El Greco, whatever that may mean, but it is being defined. It is the same with blacks and women, in some fundamental sense. They have a sense of what they are, but there is a constant redefinition from outside that can be immensely destructive if one appropriates it and believes it. Unveiling Ulysses, one comes to a naked leg, where the scar is, which is the scar he had before. That is his continuity, but at the same time, he has new scars that only he can see.

Myth and Metaphor

Patricia Mills: It seems to me the return to Ithaca requires that there be women there who recognize him. Ulysses reveals himself to the father.

Alkis Kontos: Had this been an essay exclusively on Homer, the first objection I would have is to the facility with which Homer domesticates Ulysses upon his return. I think it is inconceivable that a human being who went through twenty years of those experiences could resume so easily where he left off. That is the first problem, but if one forgets that and starts the process, he is first instinctively recognized by his dog. The dog dies, therefore it is a silent recognition. It is only between them. Then the servant recognizes him. She keeps saying, "But you look like my master. You look like my master." He denies it, so it is important. They know now who he is. He discloses who he is to his son. The only person he does not intend to disclose it to then and there is the father. He cannot sustain the pretense when the father cries about the lost son. The person who sustains ignorance the longest is Penelope. Penelope is not tied to him by blood.

Patricia Mills: Her recognition is not based on the scar, but on the bed. In this journey, the women all stay home. The point is, that there is somebody there waiting who can recognize him. This relates to Kostash's paper in that it is the women. If you adopt this civilizing myth, it is the women who stay home.

Alkis Kontos: Yes, but the metaphor itself can be appropriated in infinite ways. The only point I want to suggest is that Ulysses fundamentally is clinging to one thing. It is not persons per se; it is Ithaca. That is the metaphor. Imagine that five years before he returns, he gets a message that Penelope remarried and has children. Would he ever return to Ithaca? Would Ithaca be the same? When he is at his lowest he does not say, "I wish I could see my son and my wife." He says, "I will see a last glimpse of Ithaca and then I die."

Patricia Mills: When he goes down to ask about them in Hades, he asks about his father, his son, and then his wife at the very end. Yet it is the women who have always been there—Hegel does this brilliantly—in order to maintain a sense of the home and homecoming and to relieve that alienation of the journey out as an exile. It is always the woman who has to be there to reconcile. So I ask: Can you use the journey of Ulysses to say anything about women? I mean, can you use him to say that women can make this journey in the same way? Can you use Ulysses to say that?

Alkis Kontos: Yes. The answer is very simple. If Penelope did it, the person with whom Penelope would be incapable of sustaining the pretence would be with her mother. That is exactly what I am saying. Homer is adamant that it is natural, the predicament. The point is that if you can take the metaphor literally, then it is no longer a metaphor. The complexity, or the freedom, within the metaphor is precisely that he lives with a specific purpose. He is trapped in a long exile. Homer tells us he returns and is reintegrated totally. There is the immigrant who thinks he does the same and then cannot return, meaning that he does not fit anywhere. There is the immigrant who leaves and says he does not want to return. In the fundamental sense the common denominator is not that Ulysses returns or he does not. Rather, it is Ithaca.

Patricia Mills: But Ithaca is represented by certain people.

Alkis Kontos: It is not. Ithaca is the metaphor for ethnicity. That is what you are resisting now. You want to concretize it, but by concretizing Ithaca, you quickly are telling me that Sekyi-Otu's background in Ghana is different from mine, therefore we are different. What makes it Ithaca? The origin or departure is constantly different except that since it is always an origin, it must be measured as a journey of exile. That no two exiles cry over the same origin is the fate of exile. It cannot be the same. Two people cry about the death of my father. We are not crying about the same father, but we are crying about the death of our father. To insist that their fathers are the same is grotesque. Nobody is suggesting that. It is the loss. It is the loss of Ithaca. Ithaca could be China for me. Ithaca could be something else. I said in the paper that I would almost willingly destroy the metaphor purposely to reconstitute it. It is simply this: in *Citizen Kane*, the movie, Ithaca for him, in this sense, is Rosebud.

Patricia Mills: I would not want to say you can simply take this and use it to explain women's position. In women's position in the family, which Kostash points out and Antigonne represents, there is an oppression within that homeland which is unique. The memory, which may be the memory of exile and is painful for that reason, has a pain, another kind of pain, in the home.

Alkis Kontos: It is a natural metaphor he is giving us. It is more complex. Do not read it strictly politically. I think your warning to me is more than welcome. You are telling me not to read it apolitically, but the political cannot take over the whole thing.

Dušan Pokorný: When Kontos says that what he sees really is Ithaca, then the objection to that might be that that is a place full of people and that the people come in a distinct form into the picture of Ithaca. However, I can very well imagine a situation in which I would want to return somewhere, want to see that my mother is there, but still would not face her because I had left her. That is where one performs the transition from the older person to the mythological structure. I want that mythological structure but I cannot bear the thought of encounter with the people who in reality formed that structure.

Ato Sekyi-Otu: In this debate between Kontos and Mills, I think she is saying that metaphors are not innocent. They are not socially innocent. There is a novel on which I have written a short paper called "The Grammar of Revolutionary Homecoming," which is about how one depicts the point of origin. How does one depict that original home? How does one depict the itinerary of homecoming? Who are the pathfinders? Is it one here, one patriarch going and returning, or is it the whole community? The book is called *Two Thousand Seasons*, the African equivalent to the *Iliad*, really, which is very bourgeois. It is not one hero, it is the whole community which has their community violated. The metaphoric equivalent of Ithaca becomes Anoa, the name of a woman, who in fact was the original prophet who predicted the suffering of this people, the need to change their ways and to return. Eleven boys and eleven girls are sold into slavery. They revolt in the slave ship and decide what to do. Should they go back symbolically, or literally, to Anoa? Should they stay in some new home? Should they found a new community? There is nothing to which they can go back. Should they go back to the tribal chiefs who sold them into slavery in the first place? Throughout this protracted journey, the founding figure is a woman, the mother, but they are not just mothers, they are women. The very structure of the novel is a revolutionary communitarianism. Even more importantly, the group that decides on the revolutionary option decides not so much to go back to Anoa, but to chart a path toward Anoa. With that change in prepositions, both the origin and the destiny become somewhat indeterminate, something to be negotiated. Soon, this archetype of origin, homecoming, is inseparable from the role that women play in it, in this political novel, and the absence of one central character.

New World

Myrna Kostash: In the New World there are totally different problems. We are talking about something that has very little human history.

Ian Angus: I think it is important to the Ithaca story that the Greeks imagined themselves as autochthonous. They imagined that they came from and belonged to this soil. We tend to produce the same kind of narrative, but there is a problem with taking narratives of this sort and talking about them in the New World. We know, and we cannot help but know, that we came here. We inscribed our narratives, our grids, on a full space, with sacred places and meaningful configurations. We said we did not care about that, about the native people. We did not encounter a tabula rasa. We did not have a clean slate. We wiped the slate clean. If there is a mythical narrative for us now in the New World, it must deal with bringing to thought what was going on and what we thought we were doing when we were wiping the slate clean.

Roman Onufrijchuk: Here is where I would part with the word "we." I cannot say what my particularity did on the prairies, but I do know that when they wiped that slate clean, they broke their backs. They cut the furrows and they farmed the land. They put their own dead into that soil to become fertilizer for the grasses that grew on it. Pardon me for talking like this, but that is part of that particularity's experience. For within this particularity to speak about being autochthonous is perfectly acceptable because it is the bones and the blood and the breath of the ancestors in the soil that makes it possible.

Myrna Kostash: There is an extraordinary moment in the novel by Rudy Wiebe, *The Temptations of Big Bear*, which totally changed my perception of ethnic history. That was the point of view represented by Big Bear and his companions at the rise of the hill on their horses when they are watching the first railway track come in. The whole heroic saga of the laying of the railway by immigrants is suddenly totally put into question. It is ambiguous to say the least. Suddenly I saw that this railway track is going to bring my ancestors in this total rupture, and that the immigrant saga is no longer heroic. It is deeply, deeply ambiguous.

Secondly, where are women in all this? Not only is Odysseus an exile, he is an adventurer. Where is the mythology of female adventure? We do not have adventures. We make settlements. We are in homes. This happened again on the prairies. Robert Kroetsch talks about the contrast between the house and the horse. Women are always confined to the home, and again it is ambiguous, because the home is also the settlement and the beginnings of human life, the hearth. Even in the New World we are not allowed to get on a horse and wander off into the horizon as the transcendental ego or anything else. [Laughter] We do go into exile but it is internal. We go mad, become Cassandras or we have nobody to marry, but we never get out. I do not understand why Kontos insists that this myth has to be universal. Why?

Alkis Kontos: It is universal only in the sense of no place and the place. For you it might be different. I think, after listening to your paper, that your Ithaca is your home revised. It is not in Australia. It is not in Sweden. You will not find a home there. It is the question of roots. One is rooted in some place. That is the point.

Roman Onufrijchuk: With respect to the horse and the hearth, for my particularity, it was not a question of the horse and the hearth. It was a question of the hearth and then in the winters the forests to cut wood so that they could afford to buy a plough. It was working as the "white nigger" on the rail lines. It was not some kind of adventure, some kind of great big fling in the forest.

Exile's Return

Leslie Armour: There is something which puzzles me about this in relation to our general topic of ethnicity. Ulysses was not an emigrant or immigrant. He always intended to return. The person in the ethnic community in Canada not only does not intend to return but in many cases return is inconceivable. The Ukrainian Canadian, by and large, would regard it as inconceivable that he should return to Ukraine. The Chinese students who come to my Oriental Philosophy class are very torn because it is incredible to them that they should ever go back to China. They do not have an Ithaca in that sense. It has become something quite different. It is no longer a place, and so they are very puzzled and worried about what it is they are trying to hang onto. Ulysses' problem is simple, especially if he has the wife, the kids, and the dog at home waiting for him. The member of the ethnic community has nothing waiting for him, and indeed if he went back to Ukraine he might in fact be in a state of shock, or if he went back to China he would find that he did not belong there. There is nobody waiting for him.

150

Roman Onufrijchuk: Of the Ukrainians who emigrated to Canada, there are a great many who came here with no intention of ever going back. I am talking about the first wave, 200,000 or so people between 1896 and 1910. There was, however, a proportion of those people who not only planned to go back but in fact did go back. They then started their lives there anew based on the money that they had made here. In all three migrations, the sense of what Kontos calls Ithaca, what they called Ukrainia, was very, very real. Even today there are second- and third-generation people who have never, ever seen Ukraine. They go and yes, it is a state of shock. There are not people in costumes dancing in the streets. It is not a show. They meet somebody with the same name, in a village, whence their grandparents emigrated, and these people offer some salt and bread. Suddenly all the structures collapse. All that is left is you and these people. You say to one another, "we are kin," because it is from this place that they came. There is weeping, and there are torn emotions, and people are just drained. They have never seen these people before. They will never ever see them again. Yet there is this immense emotional experience of having been to the place whence the family came, two generations ago, to settle this land and to be part of this reality in Canada. There is that other dimension where that Ithaca is very real. I know many people who have been through this experience who are second- and third-generation people.

Leslie Armour: I think we need to distinguish between three things. There is the traditional wanderer like Ulysses, who was involved in all kinds of interesting mythical relationships, and who has his counterparts today also. There is the exile like me, who went to Cleveland to avoid the battles over Canadian philosophy. There is also the immigrant who, though he is pulled and torn, made a deliberate decision which he frequently thinks of as a positive decision. He decided to go there because it was a good thing to do. He tries to hold onto that positive aspect as much as he can. It may be eroded by the reality which it meets, but they are three different conditions.

Roman Onufrijchuk: They are indeed, except that I would argue that within some ethnicities, at least within the particularity I know, all three of those things exist. There are people who are exiles. There are people who are immigrants. There are people who are just fundamentally wanderers.

Ato Sekyi-Otu: I would endorse what Onufrijchuk is saying in response to Armour. That inability to go back, even the knowledge that going back might be lethal, does not obliterate the equivocation. There is still some fantasy of ultimately either going or wanting to go. I know this of many people. Then you try to... Now that Ghana is completely screwed up, the whole of Africa is my Ithaca. Yet I am involved with the craziness of buying a new house. I doubt if my kids would ever survive in any part of Africa right now. It remains some kind of irrational fantasy, certainly for those of my generation.

The Philosophical Turn

Ian Angus: There is a basic issue which is central to the discussions here. On the one hand, there are various modes of social belonging for which language is the most common metaphor now—a claiming of belonging or social ontology. A lot of people think that one can only be a social actor and be concerned with justice if one begins by assuming the social as given. Is it only possible to talk about justice and history, if you are unwilling to risk raising the question of how this ontology is constituted in experience? Obviously, I do not take this position. On the other hand, there is the question of the constitution of the social. This question is very similar to what Kontos means when he says, "let us begin again." That is what I think I am doing. I do not think in beginning again in that sense that I am making up history. I reflect from my standpoint here and now where I stand with the questions I think are important. I begin again to think, to reconstruct, to look at how it came to be that way and how it might come to be in some other way. That is probably the main motive in my work. That beginning again is the philosophical turn away from the world in order to build it up again in imagination. You must reconstruct the world in which you live, otherwise it lives through you. This tension is in fact what we must deal with here, because when one starts to reconstruct things like community and social ontology and language, the very real possibility arises that one will look around and say, "I do not want to go back in, and I live in my utopia now." That is the utopian moment of thought. This is indeed a risk, but it seems to me not an avoidable risk because the only way out of that is to say, "I live the ontology which comes down to me as it came down to me." All of the talk here about project and future, what ethnicity may mean now, not just what it has meant, can only be talked about seriously if one takes that risk. That is the risk of saying, do not try and undo the displacement. Take that, even embrace it. The epistemological question, the turning away, is not properly understood as the continuous separation of living in utopia. It is a moment that is inescapable when one is thinking and reconstructing, because everything we do here is a work of the imagination in which we try to reinsert and reinscribe ourselves back into the social ontology. I say let us do that, but let us not pretend that we simply carry forward. Let us make a little space, in Hannah Arendt's phrase, between past and future. There is always a between, and let us take seriously that between which is also the boundary between the self and the other as well as between the past and the future. There is the moment at which one is not located, if one takes seriously the experience of thought.

Leslie Armour: Lupul has posed here the question of what to say to people who regard trying to preserve Ukrainian culture as an unproductive, backward sort of thing. Whether it is depends very largely on which way you pose the questions that you are now posing. If the problem is that there exists a shared social reality out of which one must individuate oneself with a great deal of effort and struggle, then of course, what Lupul is trying to do is extremely vital. He is preserving the materials to individuate oneself. If, on the other hand, one begins with individual experience and must create the social reality from it, then it will be unproductive to try to create the Ukrainian past out of one's own inner life. If the social reality comes first, then one becomes individuated because one is first a Ukrainian and that gives a framework. If that social reality which has come down to us through the years is the very material that we have to use to individuate ourselves, then all those things Lupul is doing are extremely vital. I think the whole question of whether one wants to preserve the humanities in general depends on that question. There are all sorts of questions, for example, "how do you do sociology?" If we are already ready-made individuals and must construct a society, then it is a problem essentially of logical quasi-mathematical construction. If on the other hand we must digest the social realities first, then of course we need to preserve the openness of sociology to all this past. It is very vital to decide which way to approach the matter.

Ian Angus: There is more than one "first" here. If the question is, "do you think because you are in history or are you in history because you think?" then the only answer is, "I think starting from where I am now on the basis of everything that has come down to me, everything which I have learned, which of course is from other people, and all inscribed in language in a hundred different ways."

Leslie Armour: You have a ready-made subject in this sense. The ready-made subject always turns out to be empty, even Husserl's transcendental ego.

Ian Angus: It is not a ready-made subject. The transcendental ego is not the main point here, but the transcendental ego is not a subject. It is not anything other than ordinary experience looked at transcendentally, that is to say, from the viewpoint of how it is constituted. The main question here is the relationship between epistemology and ontology. The question is the relationship between how you were inscribed socially and historically and how you come to know. I am committed both to the prospect of changing things and knowing in some way. You can try to avoid that. At least in some interpretations Marx tried to avoid that, but he did not really because he thought he could in a Hegelian fashion derive consciousness from history. It seems to me, at least for me now, since we are discussing Ulysses, that "History is a nightmare from which I am trying to awake," as Stephen Daedalus says. There is no logic in history unless it is a logic of destruction, in my opinion. Unless you lay your bets that there is something out there in the social ontology that is going in the right direction, so that one can try to avoid the radical separation between ontology and epistemology.

Ato Sekyi-Oto: Not necessarily.

Ian Angus: If there is nothing necessarily, then one has to say, "where is the source for saying that it can go here, rather than there, or just anywhere?" At that point one is in between. In between, the received social ontology will not provide a direction.

Ato Sekyi-Otu: What history represses gives us clues.

4. COMMUNITY AND PLURALITY

Leslie Armour

History, Community, Ethnicity, and the Thrust of Technology in Canada

Ethnicity implies historical continuity. An ethnic group is not like a political party or a new variant of the Orange Lodge or an association to clean up violence in Lacrosse. It cannot be created. It must be found and it must be general. Ethnicity does not derive from a specialized social institution like a trade union or an Irish folk-dancing society. Rather it is something which permeates all aspects of one's life, whether strongly or weakly. It is a way of looking at things in relation to the past.

I do not mean, of course, that it is unchanging. To be of Ukrainian or Chinese origin in Canada toward the end of the 1980s, is to be subject to a quite different situation from that which faced one's predecessors in the 1930s. One emphasizes one's Ukrainian or one's Chinese origins now, by and large, because it is something which helps to orient one and because it offers relief from rootlessness or meaninglessness. In 1936, one might have accepted one's origins because one had no choice, but one cannot invent an ethnic background. It may change even through being known, but it must be there in the first place. Obviously, therefore, its preservation requires, minimally, the ability to maintain in prominence some past experience which is capable of giving structure to the present.

The possibility of maintaining one's ethnic identity and the *need* to maintain it in Canada are both related to the fact that Canadian society has its roots in communities which escaped the full thrust of Enlightenment individualism. Our social organization is much shaped by that fact. It must be possible, however, if ethnicity is meaningful, to maintain the sense of the past in a way which is relevant to one's present experience. I shall suggest specific notions—representation, for instance—which might facilitate this process

Communities achieve their continuity, as a rule, by the establishment of institutions which derive their legitimacy from past experience and their relevance from their ability to organize present experience. Institutions, in this sense, are essentially devices for facilitating, channelling, and directing behaviour as well as devices for settling disputes and determining the acceptability of behaviour. Any society has a great array of political, legal, economic, religious, educational, linguistic, and cultural institutions. Insofar as these institutions are regarded as legitimate, there is always some community in relation to which they *are* legitimate. A society may, evidently (as ours is), be made up of a number of communities.

There is an interesting—I think dialectical—relationship between communities and institutions. A community is whatever it is that is capable of legitimizing one or more institutions. A community which issued in *no* institutions could not be identified. The community really maintains its existence and identity in and through various institutions. The first problem about ethnic communities, therefore, is that they exist among *other* communities. The issues and even the name would not arise in societies (if there are any) which consisted of only a single community. No pluralistic society could work unless all or nearly all of the communities regarded at least some of the institutions as legitimate. In Canada, even those who disapprove of money accept, I think, as legitimate the institutions created by the legislation governing legal tender, but a community which regarded as legitimate *all and only* those institutions regarded as legitimate by other communities would lose its identity. In that case, its past would become irrelevant. Relevance thus implies that this experience makes it desirable to legitimize at least some distinct institutions. Nonetheless there are difficulties which these simple facts pose for ethnic communities.

The legitimization of distinct institutions is difficult for many reasons, not least because of what Harold Innis called "the bias of communication."[1] I will indicate some of the much more complex issues which Innis had in mind, but the simplest notion of bias in communication is the obvious one that messages travel more easily in some directions than in others. The Ukrainian in Canada can write to the Prime Minister, but many filters stand between him and his leader. The Prime Minister, by contrast, can reach the Ukrainian directly. It is easier for the Ukrainian to learn about the culture around him than to transmit his own culture. He will learn English or French from his neighbours. They will not learn Ukrainian. Cultures are propagated, after all, by natural forces. They are, like other natural forces, propagated from centres of concentration. It is a curious fact that, given enough concentration and a simple enough cultural element, distance from the centre may, nowadays, make little difference. For complex or subtle elements, distance from the centre is still very important. Clearly, the simple elements of the blue jeans and rock music culture flourish in Moscow as well as in Peoria, Illinois. If you want to keep up with the latest trends in literary criticism or philosophy, however, you had better visit Paris now and then. The force of simple cultural elements depends in large part on the ability of the propagators to fill the environment with attractive objects.

Thus technology has swamped the environment in Canada with artifacts (from furniture to newspapers) which represent elements of a general culture dominated either by affluent and influential consumers or by those who can, or think they can, influence such consumers. Their simplest aim, of course, is to create a situation in which mass production can be matched by mass consumption, a culture in which for the most part everyone wants the same things.

This popular culture is complex and by no means may be dismissed out of hand, but some of its elements may give us pause for thought. The atmosphere we live in is rich in sexual symbolism. It is not just that "sex sells," but that it is convenient to stimulate desires which are almost universal and, to an important degree, independent of culture, education, and intelligence. It is an interest, furthermore, which the manipulators hope can be made dominant so that, once aroused, it can be used to sell any kind of product and to blot out distractions from competing interests. It is also somewhat curious, I think, that much popular music which pervades public drinking places and fills the airwaves is designed to be played at volumes which blot out all distractions. Thus, for instance, it diminishes the frequency of relaxed conversation of the sort which has traditionally fuelled divergent interests and public criticism of the status quo. Equally curious is the "blue jean" culture (and lesser variants such as the "punker" culture) which provides a kind of uniform for the young (and sometimes the not-so-young). It proclaims submission to a general culture in which Chinese and Polish teenagers, alike, can conveniently advertise their separation from their pasts. Such a culture not only propagates easily through media of mass-communication, it is specifically designed for propagation which cuts across cultural lines. It is sometimes associated with North America though its elements can be found everywhere—in Moscow or Calcutta as well as in Youngstown, Ohio.

In the nature of things, however, the lines of communication are peculiar. The originators of the main stream of communications, if they exist, are very difficult to find. Journalists blame the culture on the advertisers, the advertisers on their clients, the clients on the competitive nature of the world marketplace. No one, except, perhaps, a popular musician here and there, claims to have invented it. Even the popular musicians who claim to be expressing their deepest emotions and their most profound beliefs would be described by most sociologists, I suppose, as people feeding back the culture on which they were nourished. At any rate, it is not as though the originators of the messages were there to receive proposals for a change in the message.

It is easy enough to find the television stations and newspapers through which such messages are passed, but they usually claim to have no control over the process. Recently, the CRTC announced a reduction in the amount of French music which French language radio stations in Canada must play. The station owners who had asked for the change, claimed they were not opposing French music but that they were being forced by circumstances. The CRTC itself pointed to the financial difficulties of the stations.

The creative minds of the advertising industry are generally impervious to ideas beyond a certain degree of complexity. There is no way in which you or I could persuade them to pay professional attention to, say, George Grant on the metaphysics of community. They are not usually to be found reading the back issues of philosophy journals though they may occasionally, I suppose, dip into sociology journals. Technology ensures not only that information passes in a certain direction but that only certain information passes at all.

Those who represent a special culture—a culture aimed at people with a shared past, or a specific education, or a sophisticated taste in music or art—are hard put to it to reply. Ethnicity, in particular, if it is to survive, must find a space in this environment in which to express itself. An ethnic group faces, in addition, the problem of deciding what its message is and what institutions could be created to express it.

The problems of ethnic groups in a country like Canada are compounded by the fact that even the basic shared experience so vital to any continuing culture can be divisive. How many different perspectives can be developed by Polish or Ukrainian immigrants on their homeland? In how many different ways will their children envisage that homeland? Polish and Ukrainian ethnic groups, for instance, are transplanted. The transplantations took place for many reasons. Economic hardship and lack of opportunity at home, political oppression, and the redrawing of old national boundaries have all played their parts. The implication is that *some* part of the past is to be *rejected*. There will be many different views about what that is. As well, large scale mass movements provide ideal cover for quite different sorts of people ranging from those with serious personal problems to war criminals. Ethnic communities are very often deeply divided about how to treat such people.

160

Native groups in Canada found their environments changed around them. They, too, are inevitably divided, as a consequence, about which parts of the past they should retain and at what cost. They, too, have members who have clashed with the new social order. In their case the problems are often superficially more dramatic. When their members take to drink, land in jail, or become in other ways burdens on the social system, the native communities are naturally divided about whether they are to be regarded as wayward or as victims of oppression responding in the only ways they know or which are open to them.

These twin sets of difficulties—a pattern and technology of communication which makes any message hard to get across even to their own members, and a tendency toward internal division—pose serious problems of survival for ethnic communities. Before we decide that the struggle is so unequal as to be uninteresting, we must, however, dig further. It is important to ask what a community is. I have said that a community, essentially, is a group of human beings which has the cohesion and awareness of a common life necessary to render institutions legitimate. Institutions in turn are, at bottom, sets of rules accompanied by some means for their application to some aspect of human behaviour. At one extreme there are institutions which operate through visible bureaucracies. Political institutions (or components of a single political institution) are usually like this. Parliament is kept in being by elections officers, judges, public officials, social workers, and policemen, who see that its members are chosen, its rules recognized, and, within limits, its wishes carried out. Such institutions may precede, bypass, or outlive legitimacy—the acceptance of the community—though the consequences of their so doing are usually serious.

At the opposite extreme are institutionalizations of the culture—language, for instance—which only exceptionally have visible bureaucracies to control them and which survive only poorly once the community ceases to regard them as legitimate devices for communication. In between are economic institutions which may, like language, survive just because they are the accepted way of doing things, or may be maintained by bureaucracies whose sustenance they provide. Such arrangements may be deeply embedded in the culture.

How do we know when an institution is regarded as legitimate and how do we know whether a given community really exists? It is not enough for a community to find itself counted in a statistical table. There are just under 300,000 Canadians of Dutch origin. They do have a place in the statistical tables, but in English Canada, at any rate, they blend so easily in terms of cultural traditions, religions, and general outlook with the traditionally dominant communities, that it would be quite hard for them— even if they so wished—to maintain a genuinely distinct community in

Canada. Modern Dutch art is not easily recognizable like Haida art, and no Dutch social customs arouse the wonder the potlatch does. The personal and social values which members of such a group exhibit are so widely shared that, at least to the eye of the majority of citizens, newspaper writers, and broadcasters, they tend simply to disappear between censuses. It is worth noting that even a distinctly English culture—as opposed to the powerful Scottish culture—has been hard to maintain in Canada for the same reasons. A culture like that of the Swiss becomes mingled with the French, German, and Italian cultures. By contrast, the Doukhobors, though their numbers are dwindling somewhat according to the 1981 census,[2] certainly do form a community. The evidence of it is that a measure of tension and sometimes of open conflict between some of the institutions sanctioned by sub-groups of them and some institutions regarded as legitimate by most other Canadians continues to erupt on a fairly regular schedule.

Sometimes, however, one cannot easily tell whether an institution is regarded as legitimate. Institutions which survive after the communities which rendered them legitimate have disappeared may confuse social and political life. Many people are uncertain, for instance, about the place and function of the monarchy in Canadian life. It came to us as a natural part of the community to which it originally belonged. It drew strength, in the aftermath of the American Revolution and the War of 1812, as part of what distinguished us from the Americans. The test of the monarchy's continued legitimacy, however, is not to be found in a public opinion poll but in its use. It is precisely the kind of institution which would be used only in a crisis. A deeply divided parliament, a government which violated its own constitution and managed to escape action from the courts or a government which in some other way departed from the normal canons of human decency would, in theory, bring it into play. We would then find out if it were regarded as a legitimate institution. A public opinion poll could only turn up something quite different, such as evidence about whether the institution called forth immediate animosity or enthusiasm.

Communities may be submerged under the apparent acceptance of institutions, only to come to life in unexpected ways. The Canadian government's abolition of the potlatch did not destroy the underlying communities of the Haida and the Kwakiutl, but it rendered them ineffective and their people demoralized for two generations. When we study the culture of the Kwakiutl and the Haida, we quickly learn that their attitude to the whole institution of property as well as their notions of personal relations clashes with that of the dominant community. The community is surely kept in being, in part, by its failure to assent to institutions, even though it is greatly weakened by the difficulty of establishing institutions of its own. Yet the Haida community was still capable of creating a crisis over logging rights in the Queen Charlotte Islands which involved the federal and provincial governments.[3] When one looks at situations like this, one cannot doubt that, in Canada, we have many communities.

I have argued elsewhere[4] that Canada is held together by a certain notion of community, one which, though in constant tension with rival views, has tended to emphasise a pre-Enlightenment sense of the common good against post-Enlightenment individualism. The French were here before the Enlightenment. Their reasons for accepting the British and the reason for their willingness to pour hot liquids over the Quebec wall so as to discourage the advancing Americans during the American Revolution had little to do with any love for the British. It had to do with their belief that the British crown might enable them to survive as a community and avoid being swamped by an American culture. That culture was closely related to the new intellectual climate in France—a climate which put an end to the French crown in the name not so much of communitarian democracy as of the individualism of the rationalist Enlightenment. Though the British had deposed the Jesuits and the Recollets in Quebec, they had left the main structure of the church intact and the church represented an institution through which men were responsible to God not one by one but *collectively* and through a visible institution.

The most influential ingredient in the English Canadian mix was Scottish. In fact, at most times there were more Irishmen than Scots in Upper Canada,[5] but a great many of them came from Northern Ireland and brought with them a culture which had remained essentially Scottish through the Irish experience. Later more Scots came with the Highland clearances. They maintained, again, a tightly-knit clannish sense of community. They were by no means disciples of Adam Smith—even the intellectuals among them. Though our universities were dominated by Scottish intellectuals, the philosophers included, among those who left a clear record there seems not to have been a single devotee of David Hume or of the economic theories of the later Adam Smith. They brought first the Scottish philosophy of common sense which had strong ties to the moral sense theories of Frances Hutcheson and the early Adam Smith. Rightly or wrongly they tended to see the famous "Adam Smith problem"[6] as the conflict between the communitarian moral sense theory and the individualist economics of the *Wealth of Nations*.

We talk loosely of English Canada, but Canadians who spoke English came more often from the Celtic fringe, Wales, Ireland, and Scotland, than from England proper. Only British Columbia, perhaps, was strongly influenced by English culture. In 1842, Celtic fringers outnumbered Englishmen (or descendants of Englishmen) about three to one in Upper

Canada. By the 1971 census, the English had caught up. There were about 4,000,000 persons of English descent and almost exactly the same number from the Celtic fringe.

Still later waves of migrants arrived from Europe, not from western Europe, but from eastern Europe where a much stronger sense of community prevailed and where the new notions of individualism had taken little root. Hutterites, Doukhobors, and other groups with an official and organized communitarian doctrine were, to be sure, a tiny minority of the settlers. The others were closer to them in outlook than they were, say, to boulevardiers from Paris or thrustful Cockneys. Family, community, and church were at the centre of their lives. Their entertainments were often collective and their concern for one another ran deep, and indeed still does. There is a great reluctance, even now, to abandon any member of the community, whatever his record.

It is very important, I think, for us to realize that it is this common tendency among communities which did enable us to create a set of unities which have permitted us to live together in a modern state embodying at least two and conceivably more "nations." Though it is this, as well, which makes for a good deal of confusion about the persistence and significance of the sub-communities. Both our strengths and our weaknesses proceed from here. It is because of this pre-enlightenment view that, though we have come close to splitting from time to time, especially along French-English lines, it always seems, in the end, that we have more in common with one another than with anyone else. Whatever divides us, our actions and our speeches usually seem, in the end, to make sense to one another.

It is worth noticing that, though education in Quebec is in many respects very different from that in Ontario, the basic patterns and presuppositions carry over from one to the other. Though Radio Canada has been set free from the CBC in most of the respects which influence content, the pattern of programming is so much the same that a listener from Moose Jaw would, were it not for the language and various local issues, feel absolutely at home with what he found being broadcast in Quebec City or wherever both AM and FM radio are available—opera on Saturday afternoon, hockey at night, newscasts on the hour with the same format and same tone of voice, and chatty attempts to be "radio of the people" while sounding distinctly superior.

The weakness is, I suppose, that the various communities are inward looking. By and large, not one of the communities was, at any time, particularly concerned about the others. There are, I believe, no chairs of Ukrainian studies in Quebec universities. Equally, the Ukrainian community in Winnipeg has shown little interest in mastering the peculiarities of Quebec culture and history. It was not from them that the recent thrust to restore the rights of French speakers in Manitoba came. Indeed, in Manitoba itself, though the French community at an early time tended to defend its Ukrainian co-religionists, it later tended to abandon them on the question of language rights in the schools and, in turn, to be abandoned by them. The doctrine rather has been live and let live.

We have been able to create a network of public services—health care, unemployment insurance, family support schemes, public broadcasting— some of which Americans have lately been citing as unfair subsidies to our industries and our workers. For we share a fondness for the idea of the family and, at bottom, we suppose that we are all at some level responsible for each other, and that life should be lived without the kinds of traumas which the community can obviate. The many thousands of people huddled in shopping centres and cardboard boxes on cold winter nights remind us that we are not very diligent at seeing our ideas actualized, but still, the ideas are there.

Such communities as ours, though held together by a common view, have also tended to be inward looking and very aware of historical continuity. As a result, their different roots and shared experiences have made regionalism and a preference for decentralization natural. Once again the idea of transfer payments—the equalization, to some degree, of wealth across these communities—has become so well established as to have been enshrined as a principle in our new constitution. I think perhaps we are the only country in the world of which this can be said. There was no significant objection to this entrenchment. The present government seems to have some doubts as to what it means, but surely has no intention whatever of removing the principle.

Live and let live, however, works well only under certain circumstances. Originally, there was a certain natural separation between the communities. Quebec, dominantly French, was settled along the St. Lawrence. The dense population of anglophone Upper Canada was around what is now called the Golden Horseshoe, from Toronto to Niagara. Kingston and Ottawa were isolated pockets. Only Montreal was a major centre of interface between the two cultures. Conflicts resulted in minor centres of interface, in the Red River valley, for instance, but they were settled rather brutally though decisively in a way which increased the isolation. Acadians in New Brunswick struggled with a separate culture and were never overcome either by the Quebec culture to the north or the Anglo-Saxon culture to the south. Isolated still further, Nova Scotia, and even parts of New Brunswick, could be so Scottish that the Scottish philosopher A. D. Ritchie[7] used to spend his summer vacations there in order to get a real feeling of what it was to be Scots without the English forever breathing down his neck.

Later, rivals among the ethnic groups tended to concentrate in areas where they formed large enough groups to have an influence on the way in which local institutions took shape. Ukrainians and other Eastern European groups on the prairies never became a dominant group and often suffered embarrassment and even persecution, but they were numerous enough to acquire a measure of political influence and to influence the flavour of their surroundings. Winnipeg was not like Toronto, however much its Anglo-Saxon citizens might have wanted it to be. Germans joined the Pennsylvania Dutch in Kitchener and Waterloo and made it, if not wholly their own, certainly a community quite different from London a few miles away. British Columbia bore the marks of English remittance men, Scandinavian fishermen, and Finnish loggers.

The outlook which this fosters is quite brilliantly expressed in the philosophy of Rupert Lodge. Lodge, a nephew of Sir Oliver (the celebrated British physicist, principal of Birmingham University, and proponent of psychical research), went to teach in Winnipeg in 1920[8] and remained there almost until his death in the early 1950s. He arrived as an idealist in the then popular British tradition. Faced with classes quite different from those he knew in Oxford, his philosophy underwent an abrupt and interesting change. He came to see philosophy itself as representing a triad of quite distinct and irreducible outlooks on life and the world. These outlooks he dubbed pragmatist, realist, and idealist. There was no way, he thought, that the fundamental outlooks of these groups could be reduced to one another or reconciled. Besides having roots in the American philosophical tradition, the pragmatic tradition represented for him, I think, the pragmatic American-influenced culture which had overtaken many of the educated young. The hard-headed realism he mentioned, obviously characterized the groups with roots in Ontario, and especially in Toronto, who largely controlled economics and politics in Manitoba. The idealistic yearning for community in turn characterized many of the immigrants from Eastern Europe who hoped to find a better life in Winnipeg. This last view he thought the right one. He tried to integrate it with the neo-Hegelianism he had learned at Oxford but he insisted that what he thought was right could not *finally* be proved right. Only a culture of toleration would enable it to win out in the end.

Faced with these interlocking cultures, he thought one had to adopt a philosophy of compromise, which is one of the versions of what Dr. Trott and I have characterized as "philosophical federalism."[9] Lodge's version simply accepted the fact that there is an irreducible plurality. Lodge's solution, however, depended on a certain distribution in space and time and, as I have said, on the real ability of different communities to legitimize distinct institutions.

Central to the problem, as it has turned out, has been language. When cultures are thrown together without a dominant controlling culture, the result is apt to be a reversion to a kind of language known as Creole. Derek Bickerton has found these Creoles—all of which, astonishingly, have the same kind of pidgin grammar—in Mauritius, in Hawaii, in Hong Kong, in the Seychelles, on the island of Reunion, and in many other places.[10] Out of these, new languages perhaps will emerge and with them a new unified culture, but this is not what happened in Canada.

What the Quebecois like to call "les allophones" have all, in fact, tended to learn English. Lately legal devices in Quebec have been adopted to try to force those who live there to learn French or, at least, to educate their children in that language. It is too early to say whether permanent progress has been made but even French has been relatively powerless in relation to English. Apart from the native peoples, few ethnic communities, I think, have managed to maintain their language truly intact and effective into a third generation. The Doukhobors, whose feelings of distinctness have usually been quite strong, have maintained a measure of attachment to Russian in the face of great difficulty, but the degree of success is not easy to measure. Many indigenous languages are in peril.

Once you speak English and not Cree or Haida or Ukrainian or Flemish or German, the main thrust of the information reaching you bears the culture of those who speak English. The pragmatic American culture—if that is what it is—will surely flow into Winnipeg. It may be rejected—as perhaps the history of politics in Manitoba shows that it has been rejected by many people in recent years—but this rejection is likely to affect people at a very deep level rather than on the surface. The sense of community, for instance, remains even when many specific surface aspects of an ethnic culture have disappeared. Even that, however, will require for its support a new genuinely Canadian culture. Both the fact that the culture carried most powerfully by the language is non-Canadian and the fact that the various sub-cultures are isolated from one another will militate against it. The creation of a Canadian culture is not an easy matter, and it has had to be helped, under the circumstances, by deliberate action.

This situation seems to force us, in fact, to ponder the question as to whether the best chance for the survival of the basic values involved in all our communitarian cultures is deliberate action tending toward the maintenance of the variety of ethnic communities or deliberate action aimed at forming a single specifically Canadian umbrella culture. The scales are somewhat tipped toward the latter by the fact that the process of community formation may have come to an end in Canada. Earlier in Canadian history, one would have assumed that, if there were an influx of Vietnamese people into Canada, there would be a Vietnamese community as there had been a Chinese community and a Polish community, but it is no longer so clear.

As I said earlier, mass production has surrounded us all with artifacts and fashions which bear mysterious messages. A young Vietnamese girl will almost certainly live in a big city, wear blue jeans, perhaps get a punker haircut, and become a bearer of the messages of the hour even before she has begun to decode them. She will have few means to express the messages of her own culture. She will have to learn English immediately and, in the process of adaptation, she and her fellow immigrants will shed much of what they brought. They may live together in the sense that many of them will live, for a time, in less desirable parts of town, but they will disperse (and be encouraged to disperse) as part of the process of finding their feet.

These new immigrants are much less likely to favour the option of maintaining ethnic communities for the simple reason that they are unlikely to have such a community to save, unlikely, that is, if one looks fifteen or twenty years into the future. This forces us to reconsider our original questions. To begin with, we need to ask what we can do to reinforce ethnicity. The possible strategies might be divided into three groups—constitutional, economic, and cultural. All of them are controversial, and action which would be really successful is regarded by some people as bizarre.

Constitutional support for ethnicity is perhaps least controversial, least costly, and, in fact, most likely to be achieved. Our present methods of representation are simply geographical. We took up the practice of representing people by their place of residence from the British and the Americans. At the time of confederation it seemed reasonable, for the cultural and ethnic communities I have been speaking about were then widely separated in space. They were so widely separated in space that something so basic as their different attitudes to time hardly seemed to be noticed.

Harold Innis pointed out that it is different attitudes to time, reinforced by methods of communication, which most clearly distinguish communities and that the great change came about through the introduction of writing which made the past seem both continuous and distinctly linear.[11] Oral cultures tend to measure time by the passing of seasons and of generations—events which are cyclical in nature as well as repetitive. Written cultures do not distinguish the cycles from each other and may lose, in fact, the comforting sense of repetition. In Canada, we can see this phenomenon in many ways. The cultures of the native peoples were essentially oral, but, equally, many of our "allophone" immigrants did not come from the educated classes and did not arrive with large libraries in their luggage.

The dominant English and French cultures were much more closely tied to their own pasts by a written past—one which continued to grow—in their own languages. We avoided the confusion which must result from mixing such attitudes by accepting the spatial separation of communities. Geographical representation achieved this end. The French community, which had a strong sense of history and a passionate commitment to classical literacy, could elect representatives who embodied central traits of their culture and who understood clearly what their charge was. The English (or rather Scottish and Irish) community in Ontario was almost equally tied to notions of historical continuity. Though they were different in kind and in implication, they too dominated a geographical region.

The greater mixture of influential population groups in the West, together with the opportunities the West presented, pulled part at least of the population away from concentration on the past. It became clear that for many people present economics was more important than past culture. The difference between East and West was great enough to bring about eventual clash. The East saw time as cumulative with the past embodied in the present. The West saw time as discontinuous with the future as the primary reality. One was thus (historically, and relevant to the present) defensive and protective, while the other was prepared to embrace whatever economic success demanded. Our endless battles over free trade are fed partly by the differences between the agrarian economy of the West and the industrial economy of central Canada, but they also exemplify this basic cultural difference. Geographical representation allowed the two sides to maintain their relative strengths for a considerable time and perhaps prevented either side from gaining a decisive advantage.

Gradually, however, demography changes. Populations changed. English Canada became literally more English. Populations also spread and impinged on one another and continued to interact, creating distinct cultural minorities as well as majorities. A French-speaking voter in British Columbia was always effectively disenfranchised in respect of his cultural interests. French voters in Manitoba quickly joined him in disenfranchisement, but French speakers in Ontario came to be represented only precariously. The English minority in Montreal has lately found itself isolated to a degree which it has found painful. The ethnic groups on the prairies rose from conditions of discrimination to a brief period of political influence only, I think, now to be increasingly swamped in a population which has as its culture a rather weakened version of the traditional anglophone Canadian ideology.

One may wonder, then, whether some change is in order. Could we adopt a measure of representation by ethnic group? No one has ever been happy with the Senate. Why should it not be turned into a place where such communities could be represented? There need be nothing racist about such arrangements. Anyone is surely free to decide that he belongs to the Scottish group or the Ukrainian group. Such groups might well find it desirable to make some straightforward requirements for membership—knowledge of an appropriate language, grasp of some crucial elements of the culture or whatever—in cases where it is suspected that one group is simply trying to take over another. Representation would be divided according to the size of the group and recruiting would be an interesting and desirable activity. Such groups might, to be sure, wander far from their original purpose, but a democratic society is always changing.

Such representation would enable the communities to put substantial pressure on the system to achieve the things they want. Ukrainians have fought a so far not very successful battle, for instance, to have schools in which Ukrainian is, at least some of the time, the language of instruction. While the division of powers puts education in the hands of the provinces, it is, in any case, substantially funded through the federal government. A senate of communities could certainly address this problem along with many other problems associated with making multilingualism a reality to be taken seriously.

Economic support for ethnicity is clearly more controversial than constitutional, but there are some possibilities worth thinking about if one cares to explore them. There are actually some new kinds of property in sight and we can, if we wish, invest some or all of these communities with some or all of them. Once upon a time water and air were free for the taking. We are slowly learning better and learning that industrial users, for instance, will have to be charged a fee both to limit waste and to provide funds to clean up the air and the water. The native peoples want control of their environment, and we could give *all* ethnic communities a say in such things, through some elected body, and empower them to collect royalties from those who use and dirty the environment. The royalties could be used both to maintain the quality of life and to strengthen the ethnic communities or promote institutions of their choice. If the environment could be genuinely improved, new wealth would be created and the system would not simply function as another tax.

Cultural strategies, the third heading, of course include such things as support for ethnic languages in the form of grants to ensure that they are studied in universities and colleges, that books in such languages are produced, and that radio and television are available in them. The difficulty here is that it is hard to secure real use for such languages. We have difficulty providing for a general Canadian culture in English and French, and the media with the most punch—television above all—are costly to operate.

If we really wanted a multilingual country, the ideal would be to adopt a standard second language for everyone. It would be something like Esperanto or the Chinook jargon which once served for all the native language groups as well as the traders and missionaries on the west coast.

Gradually, we could try to transact more and more common business in that language so that everyone might live his own life in the language of his choice. Virtually no one, I fear, would support such an idea even as a very long-term strategy. The reasons, of course, are economic. There are such great advantages to doing business in English, especially on the North American continent.

We should realize that the United States is quite quickly becoming a bilingual country, too. Temple University in Philadelphia has recently voted to require all its undergraduates to become proficient in Spanish as well as English and this movement is certain to grow. Perhaps as North America becomes polyglot, a polyglot solution will not seem so bizarre. There is no reason why we should not try to promote some semi-artificial language as a way of making people aware of the pleasure of meeting someone else in a language in which no one has the advantage. The problem is just to find a sufficiently simple language and then to discover an effective way of teaching it. The Chinook jargon, which served as a lingua franca among at least eleven native language groups on the Pacific Coast and which employed English and French words, phrases, and structures as well, was the closest approach to a "Canadian language." Perhaps there is much to be learned from experimenting with it. It would also be a way of restoring some lost dignity to some of our native peoples. I think it would always remain a second language, as it did among the coast Indians. I fear I am almost alone in finding such a suggestion anything other than absurd. A crucial point, however, is that all methods of supporting ethnicity demand rather radical departures from our current ways of doing things. Thus, paradoxically, though they might save the communities, they are not actions which the communities naturally or easily endorse. For such communities tend, because they are historical, to be rather conservative.

Should we then adopt the other strategy and simply strive to preserve some of the values which our plurality has produced and create a genuine all-encompassing Canadian culture? We do need to make a choice. Plurality, in theory at least, provides a better chance of finding a place for everyone. Uniformity is bound to create winners and losers. Now, the native peoples seem to be the big losers, but there are others in prospect. At any rate, we live in what may be the last moment of historical time in which real decisions of this kind might be made. I think Canadians have increasingly found that in a society given to rapid change and in the midst of a technology which tends to undermine personal identity, ethnicity holds out the possibility of continuity and of meaningfulness, but the situation is very confusing. There are new technologies which may help us to maintain diversity if we are determined, but there are technological processes, as well, which undermine ethnicity itself.

171

It is here that we must look again at what is happening to technology and to our views of time. Recall, for a moment, Innis' theory about the way in which an older cyclical time, characteristic of oral cultures (the time which is based on birth and death, on the seasons, on the repeated stresses of family relations produced by intermarriage and by the growth and occasional division of tribal structures) comes under stress when writing is introduced. Writing favours a linear time. Written records also focus attention on the past and call attention rather sharply to the difference between a closed past established by those records and an open future. Indeed, I suppose we might say that in Western civilization there has been a gradual shift toward a society preoccupied with the future, but dependent on the past not only for its information but also for its basic values and dogmas.

It is no accident that this civilization was for a long time dominated by Christianity, an historical religion which looked forward to a final triumphant end to the world. Innis' thinking was much influenced by Charles Cochrane's *Christianity and Classical Culture*.[12] The invention of printing inevitably increased dependence on the past, for no one any longer had any excuse not to know what had happened. Popular education of a kind based on knowledge rooted in the past was greatly facilitated by the ready availability of all the classics in book form. Time itself and existence in time thus become all-important. Innis argued[13] that the philosophies of Bergson and Alexander, and even of Russell, are by-products of this movement. Eternity becomes inaccessible because the powerful emotions associated with concentration on present feelings blot it out.

Curiously, however, since of all moments of time the present is most important, dependence on time tends to become concerned with the present. Hence the nineteenth-century philosophies of Bentham and Mill became powerful. Their values centred on pleasure—par excellence the value of the present. Philosophers like Bradley and McTaggart reacted against them but they did not become popular figures like Bentham, Mill, Bergson, and Russell.

It is hard to know when one talks of cultural trends and technologies just how they are related, but it is certainly true that concern with the present was followed by the development of technologies which focus on the present. Radio introduced what one might call the present at a distance. Formerly, to be present, one had to be there, but on the radio, what one heard was to all intents and purposes present wherever it took place. People wanted to know what was going on now. Marshall McLuhan pointed out that, to a large extent, the medium always structures the message and, he thought, may eventually come to dominate the message.[14] Radio was ephemeral and its messages were limited to the immediate attention span of the listener. Television obviously went a step further. Our culture, as Innis had pointed out, was so bound by attention to visual sensation, that being able to see what was going on was much more effective in creating conviction than being able to hear about it. With television, the thesis that the medium has become the message is, for that reason, much more plausible. What one sees is reality. If it is seen on television it happened; if not it did not.

Less noticeable, perhaps, is something else which has only gradually overtaken us in countries where commercial television is the order of the day. Television has come to be dominated not by the present but by the future. The advertiser wants something to happen in the future—ten minutes, ten days, or a month from now. He wants you to buy something and so he paints your future—surrounded by attractive girls (or muscular young men), admired by all, wealthy, and without care. In the future your piles will be cured, and, if you spin the dial to a religious programme, you may also learn of the certainty of your salvation.

The rest of the television content, of course, has to match this hopefulness. For the most part television drama is eschatological. It deals in the ultimate triumph of the good guys over the bad guys. The scene is still an ultimate future where justice always prevails. It works, of course, by adapting an old religion developed amongst nomadic peoples of the Middle East (people struggling against the opposition of settled civilizations) and transforming it into a modern battle of cops and robbers. For the moment, cowboys and Indians have largely faded from the scene and the struggle has moved to the city. The hero, now a Dirty Harry on some police force, is still a person detached from the official urban civilization. In a way, the past still dominates, but it is the future toward which one is to look.

One of the features of this future is that what I have been calling ethnicity has no place in it. The commercials—American in inspiration if not in actual production—may feature Blacks, Orientals, and Hispanics, but they have all been absorbed into the central successful community. One never hears anyone speak a strange language in this future. The hero of a cops and robbers show is never a Ukrainian whose aim, once he has cleaned up the world, is to re-establish his ethnic community.

The message of the mass media is clear. Ethnicity has no place in the future. The reason is an obvious one. Television has to communicate with everybody. Almost certainly this must be done in a single language and the number of messages must be limited if profitability is to be maximized. There are many channels, but they do not really differ very much. The future, to be sure, may bring about change. Television stations may become specialized—as radio stations have already—but, like radio stations, they will almost certainly be largely confined to the most popular messages.

This may make the situation sound truly hopeless but, less noticed, there has been another technological change under way which promises to bring still further changes. Changes in information storage and reproduction systems have made it possible now to store enormous amounts of information in tiny spaces and to reproduce it cheaply in short runs. The computer, the laser printer, the telephone line, the microfilm, and even the video-cassette make possible the separation of cultures. Ethnic cultures could even be buttressed by a computer data bank available through a cable television channel. Ethnicity does depend on the past even though it is not confined to it. Until recently the vast amount of information needed to sustain a genuine ethnic culture has been available only in the largest libraries and in a form chiefly accessible to scholars. Now every community can possess—without having to possess its own skyscraper library—whatever it needs, and can distribute it in limited quantities to whomever wants it. It may be that translation facilities will eventually make even the multiple language problem far less important.

We need to notice some things about this new technology, however. Most evident is the fact that, though it makes information available, it does not do so in a way which has the impact of television, though the video-cassette can come close to it. The continuous flow of events from the networks through the same little window to many people simultaneously creates a new reality. It is hard to match that. Secondly, it does not create a preferred direction of time. It allows information to be mixed and matched. It mixes retrieval of the past with computer techniques from which one may extrapolate the future. Even to read an eighteenth-century manuscript on microfilm makes one slightly giddy. The past is so obviously mixed with the future. Information about past, present, and future all come to the user through the same channels. Perhaps this will revive the notion of eternity, but perhaps it will only add to our confusion.

Thirdly, we do not have a clear policy about this material. The new technology is not always cheap and not easily available to the poor. Nearly all the money we spend on publishing and on subsidization of the arts goes toward distributors of culture whose investment is in traditional technology. We subsidize orthodox book publishers. We feed the insatiable television networks. We build new libraries to house traditional books. If anyone may gain from the changes which are now possible, it is the ethnic communities. Yet, as I said, they tend to be conservative, to be fearful of the confusion of time which modern technology implies, but surely they can make the jump to time-neutral technologies more easily than they can survive in the uniform future of our television culture. Or is the ability of television (and the ability of all the most powerful visual media), to manufacture reality really too strong to be resisted?

Notes

1. Harold A. Innis, *The Bias of Communication* (Toronto: University of Toronto Press, 1951).
2. There were 6,700 Doukhobors in 1981 against 9,170 in 1971, but the tendency for Doukhobor groups to fragment suggests that it may simply be that the missing people no longer reported their religion in a way which led the census takers to call them Doukhobors.
3. Revealing recent accounts of the Haida culture include Mary Lee Stearns, *Haida Culture in Custody: The Masset Band* (Seattle: University of Washington Press and Vancouver: Douglas and McIntyre, 1981); and Margaret B. Blackman, *During My Time: Florence Edenshaw Davidson, a Haida Woman* (Seattle: University of Washington Press; and Vancouver: Douglas and McIntyre, 1982).
4. Leslie Armour, *The Idea of Canada and the Crisis of Community* (Ottawa: Steel Rail, 1981).
5. See Donald Harman Akenson, *The Irish in Ontario* (Kingston and Montreal: McGill-Queens University Press, 1984).
6. For a discussion of the Adam Smith problem, see Leslie Armour, "Smith, Morality and the Bankers," *Review of Social Economy*, XXXIV, no. 3 (December 1976).
7. Ritchie included two essays on New Brunswick in his *Essays in Philosophy and Other Pieces* (London: Longmans Green, 1948). In one he advises anyone "going to America" to "avoid New York City, Niagara Falls, the Salt Lake of Utah and trash of that sort; let him go to St. Stephen, Calais, or St. Andrews..." (p. 203).
8. For details see Leslie Armour and Elizabeth Trott, *The Faces of Reason: An Essay on Philosophy and Culture in English Canada, 1850-1950* (Waterloo: Wilfrid Laurier University Press, 1981), ch. 12.
9. *Ibid., passim.*
10. Derek Bickerton, *Roots of Language* (Ann Arbor: Karoma Publishers, 1981). For a summary, see *Scientific American* (July 1983): 116-22.
11. Innis, *Bias of Communication*, especially the essay "A Plea for Time," 61-91.
12. Charles Norris Cochrane, *Christianity and Classical Culture* (New York: Oxford University Press, 1957).
13. Innis, *Bias of Communication*, 89.
14. Marshall McLuhan, *The Gutenberg Galaxy* (Toronto: University of Toronto Press, 1962).

Manoly R. Lupul

Ukrainians:
The Fifth Cultural Wheel in Canada

It is now generally agreed that what can be identified today as the multi-cultural movement had its beginnings in those groups and individuals who came forward as Ukrainians to articulate their ethnocultural aspirations before the Royal Commission on Bilingualism and Biculturalism, it-self an offshoot of Quebec's Quiet Revolution in the early 1960s. It is now also generally clear that while the constituency of white-ethnic Uk-rainians[1] is at the base of multiculturalism, it has been joined by four other constituencies in the multicultural movement. The Ukrainian special agenda, retention of culture and language, differs from the preferred agenda of each of the other groups.

The first of these other constituencies—the performing arts—is the largest and its folk-arts agenda emphasizes mainly music, song-and-dance, handicrafts, ethnic food, and festivals such as Heritage Days cele-brations. A second related constituency—contemporary ethnic studies—encompasses a scholarly and intellectual agenda, which includes history, archives and museums, and the literary arts. The next constituency—the native peoples—is the oldest in the country with a territorial agenda whose centrepiece is the settlement of land claims. The fourth constituency—the visible minorities—has a race-relations agenda con-cerned to counter discrimination rooted in colour.

Of the five constituencies, the Anglo-Celts and the francophones, who make up 75 per cent of Canada's population, are most comfortable with the performing arts and ethnic studies as expressions of multiculturalism.

177

This is largely because multiculturalism is commonly understood to be rooted in ethnicity and the French, English, Irish, Scots, and Welsh in Canada generally do not view themselves as ethnics. They can, however, appreciate (and even participate in) the ethnic arts. They can certainly benefit from ethnic studies, especially when Canada's past is probed or when the adjustment process of today's immigrants is bared. Over time, the Anglo-Celts and francophones have passed on their narrow understanding of multiculturalism as essentially folk arts and heritage or history to another 10 per cent of the white-ethnic population: the Scandinavians, Danes, Dutch, Belgians, Germans, and settlers from Normandy and Brittany. The Anglo-Celts, in particular, have always viewed those groups as the most desirable of Canada's "other" immigrants. This is not only because of the parliamentary traditions, education, literacy, hard work, thrift, cleanliness, temperance, and predominantly Protestant religion of such groups, but also because of their willingness, and even eagerness, to give up their European mother tongues for English and, in the process, to cease being ethnics.[2]

Thus in the pursuit of their own agenda, Ukrainians have been able to count on little support from 85 per cent of the Canadian population. Nor have they reached out to the native peoples and visible minorities for assistance. Partly this is because the agendas of both are so controversial and demanding that the retention of culture and language as a concern becomes for them distinctly secondary. There is also the simple reality that ethnic Ukrainians are indistinguishable from other Caucasians, both in their physical appearance and in their weak record of human relations with both the native peoples and visible minorities. One cannot say that Ukrainians have necessarily been more prejudiced than other Caucasians, but neither is it possible to point to any special efforts by them to cultivate friendly relations with either of the two other constituencies.

One could almost say, therefore, that in today's multicultural movement Ukrainians stand practically alone in their support of the retention-of-culture-and-language agenda. That agenda is currently more focused, as it was before World War I, on cultural retention through bilingual education. It is true that in the Prairie provinces that agenda has been assumed by five other ethnocultural communities through the German, Hebrew, Chinese (Mandarin), Polish, and Arabic bilingual programmes in Alberta and the German bilingual classes in Manitoba. However, with enrollments in each of the above programmes in any year seldom above fifty-five,[3] one cannot say that the Ukrainian agenda as a model for others and as an underpinning for multiculturalism will ever be more than a fifth cultural wheel. It is a kind of spare tire alongside the main folk-arts, intellectual, territorial, and racial agendas or wheels which currently furnish the main underpinning for multiculturalism.

178

To understand the circumstances which account for today's difficult (and to the writer, disappointing) status of the Ukrainian agenda, an appreciation of Canada's policies toward immigrant cultures during the last one hundred years is important. It is the anglophone majority which has predominantly set the tone for the host society's orientation toward immigrant cultures. The francophone minority, even though itself often at the mercy of the anglophone orientation, has not been much more understanding of the cultural aspirations of other minorities. It might even be said, given the circumstances of two intolerant linguistic communities, that the Ukrainian agenda was, from the beginning, practically fated to end up as the fifth cultural wheel in Canada.

The mind of the English-speaking majority at the turn of the century has been characterized as one favouring Anglo-conformity. Central to that was belief in the primacy of the English language and the view that "Canadians were British in their historical associations, political ideals, their preference for law and order, and their capacity for self-government."[4] Important also was the belief that the geographic location and climate of northwestern Europe bred certain human qualities which made immigrants from that part of the world very much more desirable than those from southern, central or eastern Europe (or from anywhere else, for that matter). In short, in the racial pecking order which was an integral part of Anglo-conformity, those nationalities or peoples who blended most easily with the Anglo-Celts, especially in the matter of language retention and usage, were the best people and the most valuable immigrants. All others occupied the non-preferred category, a term which became part of the lexicon of Canada's Department of Immigration and Colonization during the interwar period.[5]

As selective as the anglophone Anglo-conformists were, Quebec's francophones were equally sensitive about immigrants. They looked upon most immigration policies as plots to swamp them, especially once it was clear in the 1870s and 1880s that few settlers could be expected from rural France.[6] There is much evidence that the politics of immigration greatly concerned the French Catholic clergy who occupied the key hierarchical positions in western Canada during the period before World War I. In this, they were joined by Quebec nationalists like Henri Bourassa and Armand Lavergne, who were as critical of the immigrants from eastern Europe as was the Liberal editor Frank Oliver in Edmonton or the Conservative lawyer R. B. Bennett in Calgary. In the end, francophones stood by helplessly as the West was won by others, even as ideal potential settlers in Quebec steadily drifted south to New England, to contend there with the American melting pot. The frustration was tremendous, as Bishop Vital Grandin of St. Albert showed in his bitter letter of November 1889 to the hierarchy of Quebec, in which he begged that at least "the crumbs which fall from your tables,'' the New England expatriates, be redirected his way.[7]

Of all this, the Ukrainians who began to settle in the West in April 1892 had, of course, no knowledge.[8] Nor was such knowledge, at first, important. Although their arrival was certainly noticed, Canada, when they arrived, was in the throes of one of the worst economic depressions it has ever experienced, and all newcomers were a welcome sight. More-over, the Anglo-conformists were quite confident that "the cultural patterns already fully imprinted upon western Canada would limit the extent to which immigrants could alter Canadian values and standards."[9] Nor were the Ukrainians in any position to assert their cultural aspirations. Coming mainly from two principalities—Galicia and Bukovyna—within the huge Austro-Hungarian empire, they, unlike the Doukhobors who arrived in 1899, had a serious problem of identification. Between their own inarticulateness and the ignorance of the host society, they found it difficult to convey adequately their denationalized condition. As a result they were given various labels: Galicians, Bukovynians, Austrians, Ruthenians, Russians. With very few leaders and practically no clergy until November 1902, their identity was further confused by Protestant, Roman Catholic, Russo-Orthodox, Greek Catholic, and socialist initiatives to win their support.[10]

In the circumstances, it is significant that the first to articulate their particular cultural agenda was the Roman Catholic Archbishop of St. Boniface, Adélard Langevin, in January 1902, in response to Presbyterian pressure on the government of Manitoba to provide schooling for "Galician" children.[11] The archbishop had had very little contact with Ukrainians and he had primarily Catholic religious goals in mind when he applied to them the French Catholic thesis of an inseparable connection between language and religion. Nonetheless, his intervention gave impetus to the bilingual Ukrainian schools which began to emerge shortly thereafter for cultural (and largely secular) purposes. Manitoba set the model of bilingual schools, staffed mainly by young immigrants conscious of their Ukrainian origins, who had some schooling in the Old Country and teaching certificates from the Ruthenian Training School in Brandon. It was adopted in subsequent years in Saskatchewan and (much more reluctantly) in Alberta. Thus for at least a decade in many prairie school districts the Ukrainian agenda was officially in place. It was there largely because of young men (and a few women) who identified themselves as Ukrainians, were familiar with the sad history of Ukraine's domination by its neighbours, and longed for the day of its independence.[12]

Among the teachers and other leaders, including the Ukrainian press of the time, however, there was no attention paid to the long history of

English-French relations or to earlier clashes over language and culture in the schools. This was true even at the height of opposition to bilingual schools in the Prairie provinces during World War I and their abolition in 1916. The French, on the other hand, were naturally apprehensive about combining their interests with those of the new immigrants. No alliance between them and the Ukrainians (or the German Mennonites and the Poles, who also had bilingual schools) was ever struck, even during the worst days of the controversy over bilingual schools in Manitoba in 1915-16. In 1900 Archbishop Langevin had already explored with his advisers the possibility of joint petitions to Ottawa in the matter of francophone grievances, and it became firm policy that the French would include or help others only after they themselves had obtained justice.[13] This position came down unbreached to our own time.

There is no evidence that Ukrainians recognized that in pursuing their cultural aspirations, they were adding a third wheel to the wobbly, two-wheeled Canadian cultural cart. The Ukrainian position on the relationship of their agenda to the cultural development of Canada that came down to us was articulated by *Ukrainskyi holos*, shortly after the newspaper's inception in 1910. It was formed in Winnipeg with strong support from the bilingual teachers. Loyalty to Canada and respect for Ukrainian traditions, the paper declared, were not mutually exclusive. One could be a good Canadian citizen without ceasing to be Ukrainian. In addition to their own language, Ukrainians wished to learn English, for they had no intention of building their own separate Ukraine in Canada. National unity had to be built on justice for all, not on English unilingualism. If allowed to develop their own culture fully in Canada, Ukrainians would gradually adopt the best aspects of Canadian culture and become Ukrainian Canadians.[14]

Despite the severe setback which their agenda suffered in 1916, Ukrainians were much encouraged during the interwar period by the growing popularity of the view of Canada as a cultural mosaic. The essence of this view Governor-General Lord Tweedsmuir captured in his speech to them at Fraserwood, Manitoba, in September 1936:

> ... You have accepted the duties and loyalties as you have acquired the privileges of Canadian citizens, but I want you also to remember your old Ukrainian traditions—your beautiful handicrafts, your folksongs and dances and your folk legends. I do not believe that any people can be strong unless they remember and keep in touch with all their past. Your traditions are all valuable contributions towards our Canadian culture which cannot be a copy of any one old thing—it must be a new thing created by the contributions of all the elements that make up the nation. ... while we [Scots] mix well with others and gladly accept new loyalties, we never

forget our ancient Scots ways, but always remember the little country from which we sprang. That is true of every race with a strong tradition behind it, and it must be with a people with such a strong tradition as yours. You will all be better Canadians for being also good Ukrainians.[15]

In the concept of the mosaic the most desirable aspects (or elements) of an immigrant group's culture are joined together with those from other groups to form a colourful and, it is hoped, pleasing whole. Among the elements singled out, however, language was usually conspicuously absent, as it was in Tweedsmuir's speech. Since the omission ruled out much good immigrant literature, individuals like John Murray Gibbon, a Canadian Pacific Railway employee fascinated by folk culture, and Watson Kirkconnell, a professor of English and classics at Wesley College (Winnipeg), and McMaster University (Hamilton), until 1948, who appreciated how much of a people's soul could be revealed through literature, developed ambitious projects to make available immigrant literature in translation.[16] In fact, literary translations so impressed Kirkconnell that as late as October 1970 at the Manitoba Mosaic Congress in Winnipeg—the first multicultural conference organized by government in Canada—his banquet address, "Many Voices, One Chorus," recommended a three-tiered literary approach "to create greater inter-ethnic understanding." There would be a collection of "folk tales of all our people" for use in the elementary schools, an "All Nations Reader" for the secondary schools, and an "All Nations Bookshelf" ("comparable to the Everyman's Library's array of foreign authors") for adults. All would be in English translation.[17] From this speech, the numerous Ukrainian Canadians present should have gathered that even good friends could see no place for their agenda in Canada's future. That they failed to do so can be attributed to the circumstances which had brought them to the conference in the first place.

The most important circumstance undoubtedly was the clear realization that since the early 1960s francophones outside Quebec had been articulating a cultural agenda for the schools much like the Ukrainian one. From 1916 to 1950, Ukrainians had been totally unable to affect the schools, even in their own bloc settlements. In Ukrainian curricular content, the schools were practically divorced from the community. Today it is hard to believe that even at the annual school Christmas concerts, often held in *narodni domy*—community halls built and maintained by Ukrainian-speaking parents—Ukrainian Christmas carols were seldom sung. When Ukrainian did return to the public school curriculum in Saskatchewan in 1952, in Alberta in 1959, and in Manitoba in 1962, it did so only as a language of study and only at the secondary school level. This presupposed a knowledge of the spoken language which only the most recent homes of the postwar wave of Ukrainian immigrants could guarantee. What most grandchildren of the first settlers, and others without such homes, needed, however, was the opportunity to acquire the language through the same type of bilingual or even immersion classes being demanded by the francophones.

Not surprisingly, when the Royal Commission on Bilingualism and Biculturalism, established in 1963, gave Ukrainians the opportunity to present their case, they did so eagerly. Statistics were invoked on behalf of a mythical "Third Force"[18] and, in the name of multiculturalism, the commission's very name was challenged. For the first time, Ukrainians even reached out to the francophones. What was termed "a historic agreement on Education rights" was signed at a meeting in Winnipeg in 1965 between a surprised Premier Jean Lesage (then on a speaking tour of the West) and the Ukrainian Canadian Committee (UCC, which had requested the meeting). The UCC accepted French and English as *languages of instruction* in the schools where numbers warranted in exchange for Lesage's recognition of "the languages of ethnic minorities... as curricular *subjects of instruction* from the beginning of the elementary level wherever ethnic groups have large enough communities to warrant it."[19] Not surprisingly, the fourth volume of the commission's report late in 1969 recommended that "the teaching of languages other than English and French, and cultural subjects related to them, be incorporated as options in the public elementary school programme, where there is sufficient demand for such classes."[20] Apart from the vague reference to "cultural subjects," the recommendation essentially took the existing Ukrainian situation at the secondary-school level and extended it to the elementary schools. When compared to the early period of Ukrainian bilingual schooling, the Ukrainians had greatly diluted their agenda.

For this retreat from their traditional agenda, three factors were perhaps most responsible:

1) By 1965 the leadership of the UCC consisted primarily of immigrants who had arrived after World War II and the second generation born in Canada. Both groups were reared close to the organized Ukrainian community. As their children were usually fluent in Ukrainian, its study as a school subject, with cultural subject matter loosely attached, was all that they really needed.[21]

2) One of the members of the royal commission was Professor Jaroslav B. Rudnyckyj, a postwar émigré and teacher of Ukrainian language and literature at the University of Manitoba, who was close to the UCC leadership. He not only would have known about the agreement, but his strategy was to affect the schools through the recognition of Ukrainian as a regional language in certain districts in the Prairie provinces.[22]

3) The fifty-year interval since the abolition of bilingual schools had

taken its toll. Evidence of much language loss was readily available[23] in spite of the Ukrainian community's own considerable efforts to teach Ukrainian. For many the language was gradually acquiring symbolic status. Hence mere recognition of it as a school option was sufficient to validate the status of Ukrainians as a pioneer people in Canada and as legitimate spokesmen for their difficult cultural predicament: Russification within the Soviet empire as a result of Ukraine's political and cultural domination by Moscow and assimilation everywhere else as a result of immigration.[24]

The return to the Ukrainian agenda in education through the first English-Ukrainian bilingual classes in Edmonton in September 1974 caused considerable eyebrow raising in Ottawa. Ukrainian became the language of instruction for 50 per cent of the school day in social studies, fine arts, health and physical education, and Ukrainian language arts.[25] It was the first attempt to implement the comprehensive recommendations on "Retention of Culture and Language" in the first report of the Canadian Consultative Council on Multiculturalism (CCCM, now the Canadian Multiculturalism Council).[26] The Ukrainian initiative was modelled on the francophone agenda, even as the francophones themselves were beginning to move away from bilingual to immersion classes on their difficult road to francophone schools. With the federal government supporting French language education, the writer (then a member of the CCCM executive and president of the Ukrainian Canadian Professional and Business Federation which was a prime mover within the Ukrainian bilingual education movement) approached John Munro, the minister responsible for multiculturalism, for assistance. As a result, the federation received a grant in 1975 to fund the publication of the Ukrainian readers and workbooks (the *Tut i Tam* series) which Alberta's Department of Education had begun to prepare. The grant was unprecedented not only because of its size ($56,000 when the maximum under the "Culture Development Program"[27] was $15,000), but because the minister had still to provide an official reaction to the CCCM's report. Subsequently, in 1978, in response to additional pressure, the project received a supplementary grant of $88,000.

In January 1977, a "Cultural Enrichment Program" had already been introduced by John Munro which ignored most of the recommendations under "Retention of Culture and Language" and officially sanctioned the church-basement approach to cultural retention. Annual formula grants were made available to so-called Saturday schools conducted by ethnocultural communities on weekends and after regular school hours.[28] It was a most bitter defeat for the Ukrainian agenda, but the government's Quebec caucus was unwilling to support more, according to the minister.[29]

Nor was the matter helped much by the constitutional outcome in 1982.

In the submission of the Ukrainian Canadian Committee to the Joint Parliamentary Committee on the Constitution in November 1980,[30] the Ukrainian agenda was clearly spelled out in the following suggested amendment to section 23:

> Citizens of Canada shall have their children receive their primary and secondary school instruction in the language of the majority of the population of the province in which they reside and in any other language(s) in accordance with the expressed desire of parents in any area of the province in which the number of children of such citizens is sufficient to warrant the provision out of the public funds of such minority language educational facilities in that area.

In support of the above, the brief declared:

> ... if the Government of Canada can invade provincial rights in education on behalf of one minority in Quebec and another in the other provinces, we would submit that it can do the same for other ethnocultural minorities whose linguistic and cultural needs are equally pressing. In places like Edmonton, there are classrooms in the public schools in which the languages of instruction, besides English, are Cree, French, German, Hebrew and Ukrainian—classes which are conducted on a bilingual basis. We would submit that if a Canadian constitution is to guarantee minority language rights in provincial educational systems, that guarantee should not be confined to one linguistic combination but embrace all that are viable...

The brief not only supported the primacy of French in Quebec and opposed the right of the English linguistic minority to remain unilingual in a province where 80 per cent of the population was of French origin, but it also argued that descendants of other ethnocultural backgrounds in Quebec had to become trilingual:

> The original clause... carries the unfortunate implication that all other ethnocultural minorities are of little consequence in Quebec. While they must certainly learn French (because of its primacy) and they should certainly know English (because they live on what is essentially an English-speaking continent), they should also have the right to learn their ancestral language and become trilingual (because they live in a multicultural country which values its cultural and linguistic diversity).

What the UCC sought to achieve was "a basic equality of linguistic status (though not of course of linguistic usage)" to ensure both "a viable multicultural society" and "a stronger place for the main bilingual combination—English and French." It was convinced that "English-French bilingualism in most parts of Canada (and almost certainly in all parts west of the Ottawa valley) can only benefit from the presence of other linguistic dualities which have a living demographic base." What was important was to grant "language rights *in education* to all groups who are prepared to take bilingual education seriously and who wish to press for opportunities which are all too often arbitrarily denied."

The brief drew not only on the French as a model. ("French Canada, in its struggle for cultural survival and development, has relied heavily on the educational system. So must all other ethnocultural minorities who are seriously interested in their own survival.") It also addressed the very sensitive question of the one million francophones outside the province of Quebec:

> While most [francophones outside Quebec] are undoubtedly well disposed toward the proposed Constitution, many are equally uncomfortable with the linguistic-education provision in section 23(1). It is exclusive; outside Quebec, only the French are singled out for salvation, as if their survival as a group were alone threatened. In these circumstances, they are concerned (very reasonably) not to harvest the bitter and frequently ugly results of dis-affection which usually accompany privileged minority status. Section 23(1), if proceeded with, will not cool the hot coals of bigotry in western Canada and elsewhere which, it appears to us, are just waiting to be fanned.

The above was based on inconclusive discussions in Edmonton, in which the writer participated earlier in 1980, between the Association Canadienne Française de l'Alberta and the UCC in Alberta to obtain a school clause from the provincial government that would oblige school boards to respond positively to parental requests for school instruction in languages other than English where numbers warranted.

The brief ended on an upbeat note:

> If Canada is to have a new constitution, we want it to be one with which we as Canadians of Ukrainian descent can also identify proudly. A new constitution is like a new house. In it there must be room for the whole family. We are proud of the Canadian family and we have been so for al-most a century. In our new constitutional house there must not only be room for all of us, but we must enter it through the front door together—culturally equal and, at least in the provincial classrooms of the nation, lin-guistically equal as well.

In the end, the Ukrainian agenda did not prevail, even though section 27 did urge that the Canadian Charter of Rights and Freedoms "be interpreted in a manner consistent with the preservation and enhancement of the multicultural heritage of Canadians." To date, the real potential of this section for the Ukrainian agenda is still not clear.

What is clear, however, is that the constitution has finally bared the fact that Canada is really made up of five categories of people: Anglo-Celts, francophones, the native peoples, visible minorities, and a few white ethnics (mainly Ukrainians and Balts who share similar predicaments). Of these, Anglo-Celts are at the top in terms of power and influence. It could even be said that the main purpose of the Quiet Revolution, the Royal Commission, and the great anguish for a generation over language, culture, and French-English relations, was to get the Anglo-Celts to move over and make more room at the top for francophones. In this francophones have largely succeeded, judging by their increased prominence today in Ottawa's civil service,[31] their increased presence in the business life of Quebec,[32] and the constitutional provisions in the Charter for French-language rights at the federal level and in provincial school systems. Certainly the situation of francophones is a long way from the crisis situation depicted in 1965 in the Royal Commission's *Preliminary Report*.[33] Today the sharing of power and opportunity between the two "charter groups" ("founding peoples" being no longer in vogue) is so complete that the *Globe and Mail* (Toronto) can even admit that "there is a distinct power structure in this country, characterized by John Porter in 1965 as *The Vertical Mosaic*, based on who got here second (the native peoples got here first)," before counselling "later arrivals" to consider whether the "much-touted" policy of multiculturalism will aid their "entry into Canada's benevolent Anglo-Franco establishment."[34] The extraordinary admission with its melting-pot connotations would please any earlier Anglo-conformist, except that now there are to be two melting pots instead of one.

However, two groups who are definitely not slated for any melting pot are the native peoples and visible minorities. Of the two, the native peoples today are almost everybody's sentimental favourite. For most, living conditions are so very difficult and their dilemma so utterly complete that the need for special consideration is readily granted. At the heart of their dilemma is the realization that they can no longer really be Indians or Inuit, yet they also cannot really be anything else. They are almost the perfect half-way people in a society which is generally suspicious of bicultural individuals and is without a tradition for dealing with them. To be bicultural is to be hyphenated (according to conventional wisdom) and hyphenated Canadians may be tolerated in the first immigrant generation but thereafter they are very definitely not the preferred Canadians. In the case of native ancestry, however, it is very difficult and perhaps even impossible, even if it were desirable, to escape the past. Apart from distinct colouring and physical features, there is the portrayal of the native way of life in countless school textbooks and movies, and the fact of relative physical isolation both on reserves and in the more natural state which the north country provides. As a result, it is easy to see existence between two worlds as a permanent condition replacing a former way of life that smoulders but no longer appears able to burst into flame. Yet it is much too withdrawn and unique to be reduced to the folk level of immigrant cultures. In the new Charter, section 25 recognizes the special status of the native peoples. Even though largely symbolic, since no new rights are granted, the section nonetheless does acknowledge that the native peoples possess a definite and separate identity, and section 25(b) even holds out the prospect of additional rights being acquired through future land-claim settlements.

The constitutional situation is less clear cut on the visible minorities. The potential of section 15, the "Equal Rights" section, to protect individuals or groups from discrimination has still to be demonstrated in the courts. Nevertheless, the special attention paid to the problem faced by visible minorities in reports such as *Equality Now!*,[35] the special race-relations units established by police forces in large urban centres, the amendments to the Criminal Code and the Human Rights Act contemplated by the federal government to discourage discrimination,[36] and the concern at provincial levels to improve human relations through more emphasis on "tolerance and understanding" in school curricula[37] indicate that the visible minorities now occupy a place of special attention in Canadian society. Although the place is not necessarily an enviable one, bearing in mind the dreadful impact of racism, there is some comfort in knowing that one's aspirations as an individual are not divorced from one's involuntary membership in a particular racial group and that the state is prepared both to recognize a group's special situation and to validate it through various forms of affirmative action.

With Caucasian or white ethnic groups, the state's role is very much less certain, for ethnicity, unlike colour, is not seen as something permanent which public policy must take into account. Even so, ethnicity is not necessarily voluntary. Certainly, for one born into an ethnocultural community, ethnicity is not voluntary. A child raised in Canada as a bicultural individual in an Italian subculture will experience many aspects of life differently from one reared in a subculture that is Ukrainian. This is not to say that all homes in Canada can have or need to have an ethnic subculture at their base but neither should a society's public philosophy deliberately discourage such subcultures without first providing a rationale for such discouragement that goes beyond the usual cliches associated with "Balkanization," "the Tower of Babel," "ghettoization" and "hyphenated Canadian." Although there is no necessary connection between bicultural individuals and multiculturalism, a society that values the latter should appreciate not only that multiculturalism has its origins in bicultural individuals, but that such individuals today are still one of multiculturalism's most important mainstays. There is, then, an onus upon all who would oppose a constitutional amendment that would guarantee ethnocultural communities access to bilingual and bicultural school programmes to explain how the bicultural individuals produced would harm our society or how our society would be better off without them. In short, until the Ukrainian agenda—cultural retention through bilingual education[38]—is legitimized, Ukrainians are doomed to remain the fifth cultural wheel in Canada. Perhaps that is their proper place and all that they can ever hope for, but they are at least entitled to know why this must be so.

Notes

1. The writer has discussed the Ukrainians as white ethnics in "The Tragedy of Canada's White Ethnics: A Constitutional Post-Mortem," *Journal of Ukrainian Studies* 7, no. 1 (Spring 1982): 3-15.
2. For a discussion of the attitude of white ethnics toward ethnicity and multiculturalism, see M.R. Lupul, "Multiculturalism and Canada's White Ethnics," *Canadian Ethnic Studies* 15, no. 1 (1983): 99-107.
3. In 1985-6 the enrollment in grade one in Arabic was forty-eight, Chinese fifty-five, Polish twenty-eight, Hebrew fifty-five, German fifty-five, Yiddish fourteen, compared to 170 in Ukrainian. *Bilingual Education in Alberta* (Edmonton: Alberta Education, 1986), 15-17, an information package prepared for participants in the Colloquium on Bilingual Education in Alberta, 13 April 1986 (mimeo.).
4. C. Berger, *The Sense of Power: Studies in the Ideas of Canadian Imperialism 1867-1914* (Toronto: University of Toronto Press, 1970), 152.
5. R. England, *The Central European Immigrant in Canada* (Toronto: Macmillan, 1929), 25.
6. D. C. Corbett, *Canada's Immigration Policy: A Critique* (Toronto: University of Toronto Press, 1957), 18-20; M. Wade, *The French Canadians 1760-1945* (Toronto: Macmillan, 1956), 546; M. R. Lupul, *The Roman Catholic Church and the North-West School Question: A Study in Church-State Relations in Western Canada 1875-1905* (Toronto: University of Toronto Press, 1974), 8-9, hereinafter *Roman Catholic Church*.
7. Quoted in Lupul, *Roman Catholic Church*, 57.
8. For a comprehensive recent study of Ukrainians in Canada, see M. R. Lupul (ed.), *A Heritage in Transition: Essays in the History of Ukrainians in Canada* (Toronto: McClelland and Stewart, 1982), hereinafter *A Heritage in Transition*.
9. Berger, *The Sense of Power*, 149-50.
10. For the confusion which the problem of identity caused, see O. T. Martynowych,

"Village Radicals and Peasant Immigrants: The Social Roots of Factionalism among Ukrainian Immigrants in Canada 1896-1918" (M. A. thesis, University of Manitoba, 1978).

11. Lupul, *Roman Catholic Church*, 159-60.

12. For a history of Ukrainian bilingual schools, see M.R. Lupul, "Ukrainian-Language Education in Canada's Public Schools," in Lupul, *A Heritage in Transition*, 215-43.

13. Lupul, *Roman Catholic Church*, 156-7.

14. *Ukrainskyi holos*, 25 May 1910; 8 March, 8 November 1911; 24 April 1912; 29 January, 2 July 1913; 28 January, 11 February 1914; 17 November 1915.

15. Quoted in J. M. Gibbon, *Canadian Mosaic: The Making of a Northern Nation* (Toronto: McClelland and Stewart, 1938), 307. The last sentence, particularly, aroused great popular feeling and is still frequently quoted by Ukrainians and others at political meetings and in private discussions on Canada's identity.

16. Kirkconnell was so fascinated by Canadian literature written in languages other than English and French that in 1937 he began a regular section, "New Canadian Letters" in the *University of Toronto Quarterly*, which he continued until 1967. Gibbon, whom the CPR hired in 1928 to organize a series of folk song, folk dance, and handicraft festivals in western Canada, provided translations for many of the folk songs in his book *Canadian Mosaic* (1938). In a paper to the Royal Society of Canada he argued that the national literatures of ethnic groups should be popularized through selective translations. "A Secular Bible for a New Canada," *Transactions of the Royal Society of Canada* 36, 3rd series, sec. ii (1942): 93-100.

17. *Report of the Manitoba Mosaic October 13-17, 1970* (Winnipeg: Queen's Printer, 1970), 21-30.

18. The concept, rooted in Senator Paul Yuzyk's reference to the "Third Element" in his maiden address to the Senate, 3 March 1964, was popularized by E. Wangenheim, "The Ukrainians: A Case Study of the 'Third Force,'" in P. Russell (ed.), *Nationalism in Canada* (Toronto: McGraw Hill, 1966), 72-91, and dismissed by the Royal Commission on Bilingualism and Biculturalism in the fourth volume of its report, *The Cultural Contribution of the Other Ethnic Groups* (Ottawa: Information Canada, 1970), 10.

19. *Edmonton Journal*, 4 October 1965 [emphasis added].

20. Report of the Royal Commission on Bilingualism and Biculturalism, *The Cultural Contribution of the Other Ethnic Groups*, Book IV (Ottawa: Information Canada, 1970), 228.

21. The size of the organized Ukrainian community is small, estimated at 5-10 per cent of the census figure (473,337 in 1961) or between 25,000 and 50,000 in the 1960s. O. Woycenko, "Community Organizations," in Lupul, *A Heritage in Transition*, 192.

22. Based on J. B. Rudnyckyj, "Separate Statement," in Report of the Royal Commission on Bilingualism and Biculturalism, *The Official Languages*, Book I (Ottawa: Queen's Printer, 1967), 155-69.

23. The percentage of Ukrainians who claimed Ukrainian as a mother tongue declined from 79.5 in the 1951 census to 64.5 in 1961 and 48.9 in 1971.

24. The writer has discussed the Ukrainian predicament in "Bilingualism and Multiculturalism: What Do the Ukrainians Want and Why?" *Svoboda*, 20 and 26 November, 4 December 1971.

25. In 1982 the Ukrainian bilingual programme was the subject of a conference in Edmonton, whose proceedings were subsequently published: M. R. Lupul (ed.), *Osvita: Ukrainian Bilingual Education* (Edmonton: Canadian Institute of Ukrainian Studies, 1985).

26. *First Annual Report of the Canadian Consultative Council on Multiculturalism* (Ot-

tawa: Supply and Services Canada, 1975), 4-12. The section was based largely on a draft provided by the writer.

27. One of the four programmes announced in Parliament by Prime Minister Trudeau on 8 October 1971. *Commons Debates*, 1971, col. 8582.

28. "Notes for an address by the Honourable John Munro, Minister Responsible for Multiculturalism, in Response to Recommendations Submitted by the Canadian Consultative Council on Multiculturalism," Edmonton, Alberta, 29 January 1977.

29. In private conversation with the writer.

30. "Brief to the Joint Parliamentary Committee on the Constitution by the Ukrainian Canadian Committee, National Headquarters, Winnipeg," 27 November 1980.

31. Between 1971 and 1984 francophones in the public service increased from 21.5 to 27.8 per cent, and the percentage in the "office categories" practically doubled (from 13.4 to 25.5). Commissioner of Official Languages, *Annual Report 1979* (Ottawa: Supply and Services Canada, 1980), 152, and *Annual Report 1984* (Ottawa: Supply and Services Canada, 1985), 241.

32. *Saturday Night* (June 1985), 21-2.

33. *A Preliminary Report of the Royal Commission on Bilingualism and Biculturalism* (Ottawa: Queen's Printer, 1965).

34. Editorial, "Mr. Murta's Mosaic," *The Globe and Mail*, 15 May 1985.

35. *Equality Now!: Minutes of Proceedings and Evidence of the Special [Commons] Committee on Participation of Visible Minorities in Canadian Society* (Ottawa: Queen's Printer, 1984).

36. *Equality Now!: Progress Report* (Ottawa: Multiculturalism Canada, 1986).

37. See, for example, *Promoting Tolerance, Understanding and Respect for Diversity: A Monograph for Educators* issued by Alberta Education in November 1985 in the wake of numerous recommendations by the Committee on Tolerance and Understanding, established by Alberta's Minister of Education on 27 June 1983. The monograph offers suggestions for teaching tolerance and understanding in each school grade.

38. Today the classrooms are increasingly trilingual as French is introduced in grade four or earlier.

Ato Sekyi-Otu

Three Syntaxes of Particularity

In the aftermath of the post-structuralist destruction of the metaphysics of social identities, one hesitates to explain ethnicity or any figure of otherness in terms of some determinate and coherent foundation in class experience and class project. Whether the organizing principle is ethnicity or race or nationality or gender, these languages of otherness appear to be so general in their social provenance and programmes as to resist reduction to discrete provinces of material condition and class position. Let us by all means avoid economism and class reductionism. Yet I suspect that attitudes to such concrete formations of particularity, abstracted from vital and disturbing questions of their material conditions and social constituencies, are likely to fall into one of the following categories: a wholly innocuous pluralism sanctioning benign tolerance of all that is entertaining and exotic, of all that constitutes an enriching difference from the bland and brand names of the dominant culture; or a resigned historical fatalism according to which idioms of particularity have no place in the repressive universals of the technological future. (There is, of course, the hostility of metaphysical universalists such as Orlando Patterson in *Ethnic Chauvinism: The Reactionary Impulse*.)[1]

In their alternation between the extremes of defensive apologia for the difference ethnicity makes and a historical despair which would consign it to the museum of antiquity, Armour and Lupul seem to me to exemplify an understanding of ethnicity, otherness, and particularity which is abstracted from the compelling context of material conditions and relations in a specific society, adopted country or site of the world-system. Their definition of the "Ukrainian agenda" in Canada, and their hopes and fears concerning its prospects, seems to me to be dependent upon a wholly *culturalist* understanding of the politics of particularity and otherness. It circumvents their social *formation*. Culturalism and despair over the iron law of technology and its inherent contempt for particularity are at bottom kindred attitudes.

Armour's conception of ethnicity and Lupul's representation of the Ukrainian agenda are in fact paradigmatic of a certain syntax of particularity, once it is declassed and separated from concrete material and existential conditions of its designated social subjects, once it is construed as the generalized self-assertion or indeterminate pathos of an undifferentiated "ethnic group". That syntax of particularity contains a tacit epistemology wedded to an implicit temporality adumbrated by Armour's opening words. "Ethnicity", he says, "cannot be created; it must be found, and it must be general. It is a way of looking at things in relation to the past." Similarly, Lupul's Ukrainian agenda has as its principle of orientation "cultural retention". Let us call its informing principle *retentive particularity*.

This is the grammar of particularity in the indicative mood is reportorial, commemorative, celebratory, nostalgic. What is wrong with this understanding of ethnicity as an experience of otherness? Perhaps nothing is. It is the particularism of those for whom a pre-emigrant or pre-exile mode of being, real or symbolic, is normative; of those who summon the past to legislate for the present and the future. What response is this sort of particularist agenda likely to elicit from the hegemonic culture? It may be administered its last rites by historical fatalists who know that the triumph of technology is the end of particularity. It may be disparaged as divisive by nationalist representatives of a dependent national culture waging a desperate battle to salvage its particularity from a far more invasive technology and empire. Such is the attitude of Gad Horowitz for whom the particularistic communitarianism promoted by "the mosaic celebrator" is inimical to the larger integral communitarianism which alone would save a besieged Canada from complete annexation by imperial U.S.A. According to Horowitz: "The whole ideology of the mosaic came into being not so much to justify cultural diversity as to justify the absence of a national community embracing that diversity."[2]

The dominant response to this syntax of particularity within nations and between nations is likely to be neither a tragic sense of its historical obsolescence nor the defensive nationalists' anxiety over the segregation or dissipation of anti-imperial political energies. Retentive particularity is rather more likely to be tolerated and even promoted for its quaint, decorative, and ultimately innocuous aestheticism. This is in fact the raison d'être of multiculturalism—repressive tolerance of combined citizenship, loyal individuation, and compliant pluralism. The national community no less than the world-system subsists on just such a judicious mixed economy of serviceable identity and difference.

It may not be the case that "the cultural and symbolic demands" of particularist movements "are too easily met" by the hegemonic culture, as Orlando Patterson has derisively asserted.[3] Heritage programmes, language rights, and multicultural education may all have to be fought for, sometimes bitterly, but by and large these cultural and symbolic demands, insofar as they are *only* cultural and symbolic demands, can be accommodated. A discourse of particularity that disavows any subversive intentions, a discourse of particularity that renounces itself as a discourse of negativity, would inevitably find a receptive audience and a legitimate place in the hegemonic culture. The characteristic idiom of this discourse is indeed the idiom of *contribution*, contribution of a "particular message," construed as ethnic, national or racial essence, to the national culture. In more cosmic terms, Léopold Sédar Senghor, in his notion of *Négritude rectifié*—Negritude purged precisely of antagonistic particularism—calls it "the civilization of the universal."[4] Particularity conceived as a gratuitous ethnic property seems destined to embrace the proprieties of cultural diplomacy. So it is that, all irony and self-parody apart, Lupul describes the Ukrainian agenda as a contribution to the creation of "a colourful and pleasing whole." Could there be something sinister about this idiom of contribution? Could it be that a strategy of otherness severed from the materiality of ethnic discontent is doomed to the genteel aestheticism of liberal tolerance? Could it be that a truly liberating particularity, no less than a concrete universality, may be nurtured only by a harrowing sense of a particular wrong suffered by a particular community of social subjects by virtue of the peculiarity of their place in the world?

One condition is that this particular sense of a peculiar wrong is not consumed by the dream of rectifying it dictated by an oppressive anxiety over the burden of the past and the accusation of an imminent future. For if an authentic manifestation of particularity is not a joyous carnival, nor even a genteel tea party at which ethnocultural essences are toasted and celebrated, neither can it be a project called forth by *ressentiment*. Such is the impulse of *restitutive particularity*. Contemporary West Indian literature has given us an inimitable dramatization of this syntax of particularity in the shape of the Martiniquan writer Aimé Césaire's *The Tragedy of King Christophe*.[5]

It was Césaire who, in his *Letter to Maurice Thorez*, declared that the movement of collective individuation known as "black particularism" signalled "nothing short of a Copernican revolution" in the structure and distribution of human agency in the world, in the very ways of seeing and acting legislated by European discourse, and in its latest genre, Soviet Marxism's self-serving allegorization of finite and particular provinces of historical experience. A "Copernican revolution" was demanded by

> the peculiarity of "our place in the world", which isn't to be confused with anybody else's. The peculiarity of our problems, which aren't to be reduced to subordinate forms of any other problem. The peculiarity of our history, laced with terrible misfortunes which belong to no other history. The peculiarity of our culture, which we intend to live and to make live in an ever realler [sic] manner.[6]

It was Césaire who had earlier, in *Notebook of a Return to my Native Land*, evoked this project of particularity in volcanic images of revolutionary catastrophism. It was also Césaire who later portrayed the tragic consequences of such a project from the moment it is inspired and dominated by the force of *ressentiment*. *The Tragedy of King Christophe*, based on the life of the nineteenth-century Haitian emperor Henri Christophe, examines the outcome of a post-colonial strategy of black individuation and autonomous national development labouring under an obsessive concern with the censorious eyes of the Other, the white world. The anxiety of recognition and that dream of difference which the *Letter to Maurice Thorez* identified with "the right to a personality of one's own"[7] here combine to spell an obscene repetition of the repressive past. In the name of racing to save the race, of "obliging our people, by force if need be, to be born to itself,"[8] in the name of this historical necessity to forge an identity *ex nihilo*—"Since we can't rescue our names from the past, we'll take them from the future"[9]—Christophe's distorted plan proceeds to fashion out of "the Haitian clay"[10] not "the yet undared form" of being envisioned by the *Notebook*, but rather "a perfect replica in black" of the "finest" ritual forms and ceremonial artifacts "the Old World has to offer."[11] It is cultural individuation through cultural import substitution!

What is the cherished insignia of this replicative programme? It is the borrowed pomp and circumstance of European royalty, courtly titles, and conventions construed with supreme irony as the local emblems of "form," "the matrix of being." Would such a perfervid pursuit of symbolic goods severed—just as the *Notebook* had characterized the colonial idiom of social production from the captive society's "fauna and flora"—this oxymoron of replicative individuation—produce anything other than a caricature of the hegemonic culture? Would the politics of such an extroverted particularism be anything other than the politics of repressive mimesis, patriarchal "recasting" of this inert "human material," and relentless coercion of this "nation of dunces" [Christophe's words][12] to erect monuments carved in the image of the Other and designed to win his recognition? What began as a heroic work of seizing proper names "from the future" ends up as a forced march to catch up with white achievement in phobic captivity to a tyrannizing sense of time. Marx's "poetry from the past" which actuates the particularism of retentive ethnicity is here exchanged for the fetishism of the future. The celebration of freedom is transformed into a plea of necessity. What could be more consonant with such hopes and fears than an invitation by the very guardians of particularity to efficient technocrats from the Other's world to come and manage the construction of difference? They would be oblivious to ends and means that might constitute the *differentia specifica* of national identity. So it is that Christophe appoints a French engineer, Martial Besse, to design and supervise the building of the massive citadel ironically named Sans Souci. In the name of this totemic emblem of a people's self-determination, with "its own patrimony of beauty, of power, of assurance,"[13] Christophe reduces the Haitian people to slave labour. With this surrender of a project of autonomy to alien agencies and heteronomous impulses, the tragic irony of the Christophean enterprise, the tragic irony of restitutive particularity, comes full circle.

Let us sketch, by contrast, another strategy of otherness, another syntax of particularity. I speak of the otherness, the particularity, the ethnic or racial consciousness, of those who are condemned to invent the past and to remember the future because of the suffocation of the present. It is those for whom particularity, in the language of Onufrijchuk, is lived as a "project" because the collective "inheritance" is experienced as a particular suffering in the context of a national community or in the interstices of the world system. These groups include Palestinian Arabs; migrant workers from the Third World and less developed countries of Europe toiling in the factories, hospitals, and homes of metropolitan capitalist societies; unemployed and unemployable children of West Indian immigrants in Thatcher's Britain and, more recently, in the Jane-Finch "corridor" of Toronto; the dispossessed and marginalized indigenous peoples of North America, Australia, and New Zealand; the dispossessed and proletarianized indigenous peoples of South Africa labouring in the infernal mines of Apartheid capitalism—a peculiar institution in which the idolatry of racial difference is at once demanded and deconstructed by the universalist religion of profit and power.

In these instances, particularity, otherness, and ethnicity are lived neither as descriptions of cultural ideals nor as repositories of mystic primordial essences, but rather as palpable existential *situations*. The consciousness and assertion of difference is here the product of the specific confluence of experiences of exclusion, privation, exploitation, and revolt—

197

specific "fault lines of history"[14] and epicentres of discontent—that are not and cannot be named by canonical narratives of domination and liberation. To deplore this "ethnic salience" in the language of injustice and revolt, this ethnic idiom of discontent, in the name of "the remarkable commonality of class qualities" shared by social groups across ethnic lines[15] is to betray bondage to a metaphysical rationalism or idealism pledged to an essentialist reading of the "normal" configurations of social division and conflict, and "normal" prefigurations of collective individuation and autonomy. It is also to conflate the impulse of *situational ethnicity* and the syntax of particularity that informs it, with other forms to which it may bear a family resemblance in the generic rhetoric of difference, but from which it is profoundly distinguishable in its semantic and political intentions. The working poor of second-generation ethnic minorities in the metropolis or the insurgent youths of Soweto in revolt against confining space, exorbitant rents, enforced use of Afrikaans in school and draconian laws, live their particularity in ways radically different from those of the mosaic celebrant. Condemned to otherness, they embrace a particularity that is prompted neither by a maudlin nostalgia, a *recherche du temps perdu*, nor by the cultural diplomat's civil will to make a contribution to the conversation of humanity. Their relation to their otherness is not at all commemorative or celebratory but agonistic. Of the experience of difference thrust upon these others we may say what Edward Said has recently written concerning the dialectical awareness of human "mixing" and national particularity generated by the Palestinian condition: "That awareness is the achieved product of a political process responding to the travail and expense of separation imposed upon—and, to some extent, creating—a national community, the Palestinian Arabs."[16]

"Every human problem," wrote Frantz Fanon, "must be considered from the standpoint of time."[17] Syntaxes of particularity are especially, indeed constitutively, defined and distinguished by their temporality, by the dimension of time which functions as their principle of orientation. We should expect that a signal characteristic of situational particularity is that it is predicated on the primacy of the future, of the future as an open option provoked by an intolerable present. This is due to the nature of what William Boelhower has described as the "internal epistemology"[18] upon which situational ethnicity is parasitic. If the practice of retentive ethnicity is informed by what Frederic James has called "the tradition of *anamnesis*"[19]—the tradition of remembrance as recognition of ancestral essences—and if the demiurgic delusions of restitutive particularity, with its terrible toll and tragic ironies, derive from its pathetic sense of a *tabula rasa,* the subversive and regenerative programme of situational particularity is, by contrast, animated by *anagnorisis*—the harrowing discovery of a shared community engendered in virtue of a particular collectivity's violation by another collectivity.

The being of such a community is thus neither gratuitously found, as Armour says generically of ethnicity, nor founded *ex nihilo* by the demiurgic act of a führer. It is forged out of the vortex of discontent by a "conversation of discovery."[20] Negotiating a critical and common understanding of a shared violation *is* the occasion of community, the formation of particularity signalled by a "prefigurative politics"[21] of internal autonomy, collective agency and the participatory invention of identity. In its relation to the existing social hierarchy—national or international—the impulse of situational ethnicity is necessarily subversive. For what its protagonists seek is not unhindered access to the retention or replication or exchange of symbolic powers and products such as they are, their own or their masters', but a radical re-ordering of the conditions and ends of identity-formations. They are thus less likely to travel the route notoriously traversed by protagonists of preservative and restitutive ethnicity—the passage from a mystical and even truculent assertion of particularity to an accommodating pluralism or technocratic nihilism, easily appeased, contained, and integrated.

Yet precisely because the strategy of situational ethnicity is not pledged to faith in some primordial essence of the folk, its protagonists are perhaps more likely to work with other constituencies of particularity to forge larger, albeit finite, solidarities. Thus is the possibility of a situational ethics of revolutionary solidarity granted to the syntax of situational ethnicity. The most intransigent narrative of racial particularity in recent African literature concludes its searing evocation of history's terrors with the proposition that in the coming insurrection of violated humanity against their oppressors, "each people of the way will find every other people of the way."[22] This vision of human particularity and universality as cognate projects to which we are summoned by shared experiences of injustice and revolt, is what distinguishes the new particularism from the old.

The standpoint of the old particularism is distributive justice in the reproduction, display and exchange of symbolic messages by cultural communities that assent to the given circumstances of their existence. The standpoint of the new particularism is the prefiguration, by nascent insurrectionary communities, of refashioned conditions wherein the auspicious rivalry of the unique and the universal is viscerally lived and creatively manifested.

Notes

1. Orlando Patterson, *Ethnic Chauvinism: The Reactionary Impulse* (New York: Stein and Day, 1977).
2. Gad Horowitz, "Mosaics and Identity" in H. D. Forbes (ed.), *Canadian Political Thought* (Toronto: Oxford University Press, 1985), 359-64.
3. Patterson, *Ethnic Chauvinism*, 174-6.
4. Léopold Sédar Senghor, *Pierre Teilhard de Chardin et la politique Africaine*, No. 3 (Paris: Cahiers Pierre Teilhard de Chardin, 1962). The notion that each race possesses a "particular message" was central to the thought of W. E. B. Du Bois. See Anthony Appiah, "The Uncompleted Argument: Du Bois and the Illusion of Race," *Critical Inquiry* 12 (Autumn 1985): 21-37.
5. Aimé Césaire, *The Tragedy of King Christophe*, trans. Ralph Manheim (New York: Grove Press, 1969).
6. Aimé Césaire, *Letter to Maurice Thorez* (Paris: Présence Africaine, 1956), 12, 6.
7. *Ibid.*, 12.
8. Césaire, *King Christophe*, 13.
9. *Ibid.*, 25.
10. *Ibid.*, 22.
11. Césaire, *King Christophe*, 21.
12. *Ibid.*, 37, 59.
13. *Ibid.*, 44.
14. Ronald Aronson, "Historical Materialism, Answer to Marxism's Crisis," *New Left Review* 152 (July/August 1985): 91.
15. As does Orlando Patterson in *Ethnic Chauvinism*, 182-5.
16. Edward Said, "An Ideology of Difference," *Critical Inquiry* 12 (Autumn 1985): 43.
17. Frantz Fanon, *Black Skin, White Masks*, trans. Charles Lam Markmann (New York: Grove Press, 1969), 14-15.
18. William Boelhower, *Through a Glass Darkly: Ethnic Semiosis in American Literature* (Venice: Edizioni Helvetia, 1984), 86.
19. Frederic James, *Marxism and Form* (Princeton: Princeton University Press, 1971), 130.
20. Ayi Kwei Armah, *Two Thousand Seasons* (London: Heinemann, 1979), 148.
21. I borrow the notion of "prefigurative politics" from Sheila Rowbotham, Lynne Segal and Hilary Wainwright, *Beyond the Fragments: Feminism and the Making of Socialism* (London: Merlin Press, 1979).
22. Armah, *Two Thousand Seasons*, 205.

Discussion

A Decent Shot at the Transcendental

Leslie Armour: All fundamental ideas—humanity, justice, truth, the old transcendentals—only make sense, as Plato would have said, ultimately when the forms inform the chaos. They have to be particularized, and when they are particularized, they always lose something. No instance in the real world of alleged justice or truth is a perfect instance of its divine exemplar. I might put my whole case for ethnic multiplicity in those terms. If you live in a society in which there is only one culture, what that really means is that truth, justice, and humanity have only one instantiation and we must lose. The whole issue of freedom is involved in this. What is going on in South Africa, in Soweto, is that the legitimacy of the only forms of these transcendentals that are meaningful to the black population is being denied by the population which controls them. It is only in a society which is willing to recognize the legitimacy of what that population can find as intelligible that you are going to have any real freedom. Otherwise you have pseudo-freedom. Everybody has the right, even in Washington, to read aloud Presidential Proclamations in public places. If one's freedom only consists of being able to do what is rewarded as legitimate by the dominant culture, one does not really have any freedom.

Secondly, not every human being will fit into any possible niche. There must always be a chance of making a choice of what kind of community you want. Toleration is therefore a very great virtue and does come out of mosaic multiculturalism, to some degree, because of the mere fact that we do accept the legitimacy of a variety of cultures. After all, culture is a way of putting meaning on human behaviour. There is more than one culture when more than one meaning is given to the same behaviour. In a multicultural society, if one really exists, the fact that I do something that *can* be given an outrageous meaning by you does not automatically entail that it *will* be given an outrageous meaning. It means you will say, "perhaps this is the kind of thing that is, after all, done in some communities." Even if what I am doing does not fit into any of the established patterns, I have a better chance of being tolerated because the society does tolerate a plurality. We have been trying to do this in Canada, however badly, and it has made a society in which a great variety of forms of behaviour are indeed tolerated, in which there is a great opportunity to find one's place. The question is whether we are in the process of obliterating this by means of technology, or whether there are new technologies which we could exploit to open up this space. Ethnicity is not just an aesthetic, ornamental preference for cultural relics of the past. I really do not care much for Ukrainian folk dancing, but on the other hand, when Lupul speaks of strategies to maintain the Ukrainian language, that is different. There are things that can be said in a language and there is a natural underlying logic to it. When I write in French it does not come out the same way as it does in English. That is extremely interesting. Preserving those things is preserving a decent shot at the transcendentals, if you like. Call me a Platonist and in that sense I would be guilty. [Laughter]

Commemoration and Subversion

Manoly Lupul: It is not difficult for me to admit that my approach to the whole ethnic cultural movement and multiculturalism is primarily commemorative and replicative rather than subversive. I am a great believer in the art of the possible. I was very concerned to get greater opportunities for my people. I was in a position to do this. If you want to get something for your people, you must carry your people with you. You have to start there. You have to start with the people where they are, which is largely at the commemorative and replicative stage. One cannot start by immediately advocating sharing power and authority. It is not possible to do that. They would not follow. I wanted to create opportunities for them and then in a sense it is open ended. I do not know what in fact will be the cultural content in Ukrainian bilingual classrooms that have come into being. That really is not my responsibility, nor is the quality of the language taught. There are people who are better qualified than I to provide this. If we do not have them, then we really are in trouble, and if the wider society is not prepared to help then the whole thing is an exercise in futility. I believed that in time it would be possible to fill in this content with something more than just the commemorative and replicative. That has been the nature of the evolution.

I focussed on our agenda because that is our special, unique agenda. We do not have any land claims. That is a fact. We are also very interested, not so much in race relations, but in discrimination which has been a very big item on our agenda. However, here again, our people, generally speaking, now do not feel that they are discriminated against as they once were. I must confess it is fashionable for people of my class and background to say, "I have never felt much discrimination." In fact, they may even go so far as to say, "I have never felt any at all." This is supposed to be a very good thing to say. That means we really have arrived. Nobody would dare touch you, so to speak. Personally, I can become quite excited about discrimination, since I am a small "l" liberal, but the fact of the matter is that visible minorities are not much interested in the whole concept of language and cultural retention and development, in reacquiring a sense of community.

Ato Sekyi-Otu: African immigrants, until quite recently, came here just to study and go. It is only within the past decade or so that a whole new influx of people who could not live in Africa went to Europe. When they could not make it there, they came here. In the past some people finished a degree and in the next week were on the plane back. The other black people, West Indians, of course do not have any distinct written language, only the Jamaican patois. Increasingly, however, as more and more Africans are here to stay, they begin to start language schools—the Nigerians a year or so ago, now the Ghanaians. Some of them can take very regressive forms. Instead of having one Ghanaian community and organizing some cultural programmes, they are breaking up into tribes. It is incredible that the problems from home are being brought here.

Manoly Lupul: It is precisely because of this that I have not encouraged visible minorities to take much of an interest in language and culture. You run into the horrible multiplicity argument. The Anglo-Celt says, "If we give it to you, then everybody is going to want it. Do you know all the various tribes that exist?" As a political academic, one must be mindful of the fact that all things are not possible. The same thing applies to native people, of course. With native people, our agenda is a given. Land is so much more important than language and culture, that the latter is just taken for granted.

Roman Onufrijchuk: I have two things to say. The first is just a narrative, a story, while the other is a comment about retention. The scene was Edmonton, Alberta, in 1978 or 1979. I was in the Army and Navy Store, a discount department store affectionately known as Antoine's Boutique. I was there looking through the shirt section. There were two Ukrainian women standing in the middle of the aisle carrying on. It was a real performance. They were directly in my way but I was not going to elbow them. I moved around them. The woman who was working at Antoine's, obviously an East Indian, approached them and said, "You are blocking the aisle." The older one of the two said, "You don't tell me where to stand. You some kind of immigrant, going to push me around?" I thought to myself, how quickly we forget. Then back in Ukrainian to one another, "Who does she think she is? Where does she come from?"

The other point is about the agenda which Lupul articulates as retention and development of culture, including language. When it is fought out over the issue of schools and education, I think it does necessarily have to become the third strategy, the strategy of the project. The struggle for education has always been a struggle for progress and for liberation. If there is no place where language is real and alive, if there is no dynamic, it cannot develop. If there is a linguistic base or an educational base where those things can become issues in classrooms, it stands much more of a chance. This is not just to defend retention, but it is to argue that when retention becomes at least a partial ground for a struggle that is fought over what people will be taught in schools, then it also opens to the possibility of development, at least that particular agenda. That is not saying necessarily that that is the agenda in Soweto, but in this particular instance I think the educational issue is a key issue.

Leslie Armour: Is it not true, though, that that agenda failed us, as Lupul said, for lack of a means to bring together the various ethnic communities in a way that would create political power? That is why the agenda ought to capitalize on such things as the continuous demand for Senate reform. There is a lot of potential political force there, but the system does not allow it to be organized and be brought to bear. The other option which is in Soweto is not feasible in Canada. In Soweto you can set fire to the place, but the Ukrainian community has too much to lose to set fire to the place. Hence one needs to have a constitutional move to make a political reality. That possibility exists because everybody hates the present Senate. Francophones are interested in that very possibility because it is a way of giving voice to the francophones outside Quebec. If the ethnic communities make common cause with francophones on that question, it could be done. Then it would be pretty easy to carry on our educational agenda because the Senate has a lot of power to interfere with legislation if it does not get what it wants. Some coherent strategy like that is needed. They would want to take that agenda seriously if the Senate were made up of representation by cultural communities. Then that would be exactly the job of the Senate and it would be in the interest of the whole Senate. That agenda would become the number one priority.

Myrna Kostash: Sekyi-Otu, I want to turn back this question to you. You asked me yesterday, rhetorically I suppose because your paper was an answer to it, "can ethnicity be subversive?" I was speechless and did not respond at the time. I was very surprised by my own reaction because I simply assumed that everything I had written and said up to this point about the possibilities of ethnic consciousness shows that it is indeed subversive. It is subversive to Anglo-American cultural hegemony. However, when you put it to me so directly I did not have an answer, because in fact I am not sure. In your examples you do not really give examples of ethnic subversiveness. Instead you describe racial and class subversiveness from conditions of gross exploitation and oppression. That is not my situation as a middle-class, second-generation ethnic in Canada. What I am mindful of then, and what you picked up in your remarks about those aspects of ethnoculture which are in fact antidotes to Anglo-American culture, is perhaps what I am describing as alternative culture or maybe counter-culture. Then, of course, I am mindful of what happened in the sixties, and also what has happened in a certain section of the women's movement. There is this conceit that if one celebrates the phases of the moon and revives the old goddess religion, then somehow this is revolutionary or subversive. In fact these things are parallel cultures. I am going to ask you the same question: Can ethnoculture be subversive?

Ato Sekyi-Otu: In the position of the opposition there has to be some "ethno" to articulate. However disgusted you are by the established Left of the sixties, the feminist movement, and so on, there has to be some attempt to articulate the particular discontents of the. . . . One Ukrainian left wing movement alone cannot possibly have any subversive influence on society. At the very least one needs the alliances of other ethnic groups, and beyond that, of other active centres of discontent. I think we now have the means to analyze why those movements were ignored. Those movements were, in a sense, right-wing movements. Sheila Rowbotham has this wonderful phrase, "the movements themselves have to be prefigurative of the future." You cannot have a fascist organization entertaining the cause of socialism, to put it bluntly. I am thinking of Stokely Carmichael's notorious statement that the place of woman in the Civil Rights movement was prone. We now have the means of explaining how these movements were themselves composite. Having such an understanding through hermeneutic analysis, we need not embrace some new separatism. Ethnicity can become subversive when it is articulated with *other*. When one ethnic is content, when it is understood merely as cul-

205

tural persuasion, the cultural is dead. There is something of its material context eliminated.

Culturalism

Ian Angus: The charge of culturalism applies not only to the two papers here, but to the whole symposium. It raises a very important issue. The charge of culturalism makes an assumption of connection to material conditions. Everybody's favourite theory for understanding material conditions is Marxism. It seems to me, at least at this point, that it is possible to see certain serious problems with that way of posing the question. It is as if there were such things as material realities which are not articulated through individuals and social groups. That is the constitutive question. The other one is in terms of social change. It is as if oppression in itself, and I mean nothing disrespectful to Soweto in this, breeds rebellion. I believe that it does not. Rebellion requires vision to spread and vision is articulated in culture. So I am willing to be convicted on the culturalist question, at least in that understanding of it. The important thing that we lack now in this country is vision. There is a discourse about ethnicity through multiculturalism in which some things were opened up which official culture did not intend to open. Maybe that could happen some more. One does after all have to think about where to come in. The present tendency of cultural alternatives is towards fractionation. That is partly what I was trying to say with the concept of "staged difference." Kostash called it "parallel cultures." It is called "fragmented audiences" in communication theory. We buy whatever we want now. It does not matter if you worship the sun, the moon, or an automobile. It really does not matter. So, the question is how cultural identity is formed because only through people with some sense of identity, through vision or imagination, can it change.

Manoly Lupul: This leads to an area which is a sore spot with me. The multicultural movement definitely lacks vision, but academics, our intellectuals and historians particularly, are the area from which vision might come. They, like Careless, speak of "limited identities" and admit that we are a group-oriented, community-oriented society. It is a mosaic with all that that implies, whether they be Berger, Careless, Martin or Ramsey Cook. However, they then take it nowhere. That is the problem. They do not give it any intellectual attention. What could this country therefore be? We get no leadership from them at all. This is the reason I wanted this symposium so badly. I wanted some new minds, other minds from the academic setting, who were not necessarily part of the multicultural movement, who were at least distant from it. They might help because the historians and social scientists—who talk, by the way, much more simply than most of you do—simply do not articulate what this country could be. The only exception is that now they have agreed it is going to be bilingual and bicultural. What that might really mean in terms of the size of the country and the people who make it up, receives no attention at all. They know that some place out there there are some Ukrainians, that in British Columbia there are some Chinese, and, of course, that Toronto is full of Italians. They will not address what that really does mean.

Leslie Armour: Culturalism was offered as a charge of neglect. The problem about material conditions now is that we are living in a major transition from one kind of industrial economy to another. The old steel and coal economies of the world are in a state of collapse everywhere. Their offspring are being propped up by governments and gradually let go, while a new kind of industrial world is filtering in. Precisely what controls this now is the shallowness of our historical vision. We do not know where that industrial process came from. Our failure to be able to see through into the future is largely because the world-view that we use in everyday life and the world-view that is appropriate to understanding the process of technological change do not mesh. It is a serious problem in economic theory and everywhere. Cultural questions are paramount in that it is the failure of the culture that prevents us from getting a clear view of the material conditions. Therefore the point of attack is in our cultural vision and in our historical vision.

Dušan Pokorný: When Harold Innis was asked what the sources for Confederation were, he answered in economic terms. He said this was a country which needed enormous investments in fixed capital. These investments could not be, on principle, of a kind which could be financed by private capital alone. Therefore, capital must be provided by the government. If Lower Canada and Upper Canada separately asked for loans from Britain, they would each get a certain amount. If the two provinces taken together asked for loans, they would get more than the sum of these two. That is the simple arithmetic of the origin of Confederation. Confederation, he said, was put together as a financial instrument. From that it follows that the special position of the state in Canada has much to do with the fact that it is a country thinly populated with a weak market internally. It would have been immediately swallowed up by the people south of the border who have an immense market. Therefore, the initial financing of the fundamental transportation system by private enterprise collapsed and the government took it over. Now we are entering an era in which these fundamental structural features, depending on the role of the state in the economy, are vitally endangered a) by the presence of the Conservative government in Ottawa, b) by the co-presence of a conservative government in the United States, and c) by an effort on the part of both these governments to make certain irreversible changes in these economic and social structures. That is what the present free trade negotiations are about. Therefore, we cannot separate the material side of the picture from the cultural side. Indeed, at present it is the material side which must be understood to have the upper hand.

The degree of tension between the material on the one hand and the cultural on the other, comes to a head when we talk about language and the real relationships, as it were. The counter-position of the cultural and the material has to be taken very gingerly. There is a distinction between the nation, on the one hand, within which the fundamental structural features of the country are discussed, and the other, where we want to preserve something more than just the fundamental structures. Therefore we should be aware that the people who came here and who are not fully assimilated, or who did not allow themselves to be assimilated, will always be torn between these two aspects. There is the aspect of the citizen who is concerned, if I may simplify, with the question of the redistribution of income and there are the facets of the person who belongs to a particular group where the concerns are of a different kind. It is not possible to solve this internal conflict in such a way that one will be replaced by the other because on the one side you have an assimilation and on the other you have a fragmentation of the country.

Manoly Lupul: At least some of us are conscious of the material dimension of our existence. In fact a group of us are trying to put together a document which might be called, "The sons of the sons of the soil." We are trying to lay a material base to our articulation for the need to survive. What is the material base? We cleared so many acres of land and we built railways. When we first began it was, "we are taxpayers, too." That was the first thing that came up, but now we are going a little farther. We are not just taxpayers, we are also builders. We are not just immigrant people, we are settlement people. We dare not use the word "founding." We might yet. We will see. It is not finished yet but there is a paradox in this thing. If you are that well-established, if you have done all this for so long and are a well-established group, then you must also have done well —not just a lot, but well. So people in government ask why we are even bothering them. If you want it so much, then simply do it, they say.

List of Contributors

IAN H. ANGUS was born in London, England, in 1949 and received his Ph.D. from the Graduate Programme in Social and Political Thought at York University. He is the author of *Technique and Enlightenment: Limits of Instrumental Reason* (1984), co-editor (with Sut Jhally) of *Cultural Politics in Contemporary America* (forthcoming), and has written several articles on philosophy, technology, communication, and ethics. Currently he is teaching in the Department of Communication at the University of Massachusetts at Amherst.

LESLIE ARMOUR is a professor of Philosophy at the University of Ottawa. Born in New Westminster, British Columbia, he received his Ph.D. from the University of London. His books include *The Idea of Canada and the Crisis of Community, The Rational and the Real, The Concept of Truth, Logic and Reality, The Faces of Reason* (a history of philosophy in English Canada, written with Elizabeth Trott), and *The Conceptualization of the Inner Life* (a study in the philosophy of mind, written with Edward Bartlett).

JOSE HUERTAS-JOURDA teaches in the Department of Philosophy at Wilfrid Laurier University. He is the author of *The Existentialism of Miguel de Unamuno* and is engaged in an ongoing research programme on the phenomenology of the living present. Part of this is presented in "Structures of the Living Present: Husserl and Proust" in *The Study of Time*, edited by J. T. Fraser and Nathaniel Lawrence. He has also published surrealist and concrete poetry in French and English.

209

ALKIS KONTOS teaches Political Philosophy in the Department of Political Science at the University of Toronto. He is the editor of *Domination and Power, Possessions and Freedom: Essays in Honour of C. B. Macpherson*.

MYRNA KOSTASH was born in Edmonton. Educated at the Universities of Alberta, Washington and Toronto, she was awarded an M.A. in Slavic Languages and Literatures in 1968. Since the early seventies she has worked full-time as a professional writer, first in Toronto and now in Edmonton. She is the author of three books, notably *All of Baba's Children*, an investigation into ethnicity and its discontents among the Ukrainian Canadians of western Alberta.

MANOLY R. LUPUL is a professor of Canadian Educational History in the Department of Educational Foundations, University of Alberta. His special research interests are the education of minorities in western Canada, the relationship between multiculturalism and education, and the history of Ukrainians in Canada. Among his scholarly works are *The Roman Catholic Church and the North-West School Question: A Study in Church State Relations in Western Canada, 1875-1905* (1974), several contributions in academic textbooks, and numerous articles in scholarly journals. He has edited four books, including *A Heritage in Transition: Essays in the History of Ukrainians in Canada* (1982). Between 1976 and 1986 he was director of the Canadian Institute of Ukrainian Studies, University of Alberta.

PATRICIA JAGENTOWICZ MILLS is a feminist philosopher-at-large currently teaching in the Department of Philosophy at the University of Toronto. Her most recent works include "Hegel's Antigone" in *The Owl of Minerva* (Spring 1986), a critical review-essay of *Marxism and Domination* entitled "Man-Made Motherhood and Other Sleights of Hand" published in *Phenomenology + Pedagogy* (vol. 3, no. 3, 1985), and *Woman, Nature and Psyche* (Yale University Press, forthcoming).

JOHN O'NEILL is Distinguished Research Professor of Sociology at York University and a Fellow of the Royal Society of Canada. He is the author of several books, the latest of which is *Five Bodies: The Human Shape of Modern Society* (1985), and many articles in philosophy, sociology, and literary criticism. He is also co-editor of the international quarterly, *Philosophy of the Social Sciences*.

ROMAN ONUFRIJCHUK was born in Winnipeg and raised on the prairies. He has worked as a journalist and executive producer in various media. He is currently a Ph.D. candidate in the Department of Communication, Simon Fraser University and Programme Director in Fine Art and Design, School for Liberal and Professional Studies, Simon Fraser University.

DUŠAN POKORNÝ is Professor Emeritus at the University of Toronto, where he taught economics, political science, and the theory of science since 1968. Educated in Czechoslovakia, he was an Associate of the Institute of Philosophy, Prague, and a researcher in the Economic Institute, Bratislava. He has written on philosophy and economics in the work of Karl Marx and Adam Smith and on the economics of traditional communities. He is currently working on a book entitled *Personality and Rationality*.

ATO SEKYI-OTU was born at Saltpond, Ghana, 22 March 1941. Educated at Harvard (A.B. in Government, 1966) and at the University of Toronto (M.A. 1969, Ph.D. 1977 in Political Theory), he is presently Associate Professor in the Graduate Programme in Social and Political Thought, York University. His special interests are modern social and political theory, political discourse and the Marxian tradition, contemporary African literature, and literary theory and social thought. He has completed *The Broken Ring of Meaning: Ayi Kwei Armah and the Aesthetics of Remembrance*, a book on the Ghanaian novelist.